Infinitely beautiful

Kulturstiftung DessauWörlitz (Ed.)

Infinitely beautiful

The Garden Realm of Dessau-Wörlitz

nicolai

Contents

"... (Anhalt-Dessau), rightly called the Garden of Germany by strangers from all regions of the cultivated world, yes, even those who had circumnavigated the globe, ... you as yet unborn, when you read this, look back in reverence on the century that produced such a prince."

Friedrich von Matthisson, 1806

PROLOGUE

Infinitely beautiful

"Here it is infinitely beautiful now. Yesterday evening, as we slipped through the lakes, canals and woodlands, I was greatly moved to see how the gods have permitted this prince to spin a dream around himself. When one passes through like this, it is as if one is being told a fairy-tale, one enjoys in full the character of the Elysian Fields in its most tender variety, one thing flows [into] another, no height draws the eye nor one's desires to a single point, one goes about without asking whence one came and whither one is going. The bushes are in their most beauteous youth, and the entire effect is of the purest loveliness."

Johann W. von Goethe to Charlotte von Stein, Wörlitz, Thursday, 14 May, 1778.

How should we approach the Garden Realm of Dessau-Wörlitz? There has never been firm guidance about how to do this, either today or at the time it was created in the sec-

ond half of the 18th century. At that time, people travelled on relatively bad roads, mainly by coach, to the principality of Anhalt-Dessau, and then, on arrival, put themselves in the hands of an expert guide. *Giannozzo*, the air-shipper, a character from an 1801 novel by Jean Paul, approached his destination in a most unusual way. In Jean Paul's "Seebuch", the hero floated through the air in a Montgolfière balloon: "Onward, onward, the south-east is flying right over Wörlitz. With the sun I sank down there into the changing garden, whose views are again gardens. There it seemed to me as though the sun were just rising; all the temples shone as if in the light of dawn – refreshing dew spilled over the earth and the larks' morning songs resounded."

Today's visitors usually approach the Wörlitz region on the Elbe by car, on the A9. Even some way off they are aware of unusually luxuriant vegetation to the right and left of the carriageway. It is scarcely possible to sense the wealth of European cultural history that lies beyond it.

In the year 2000, UNESCO put the Dessau-Wörlitz Gartenreich (Garden Realm) on the World Heritage list. This was not just because individual buildings in this cultural landscape were so significant, or because of the variety of gardens, but because of the ideas behind them: the existing features of the landscape are linked with a far-reaching philosophical-ethical and educational reform programme of extraordinary, universal value.

Anyone wanting to explore this charming landscape in Central Germany, which since reunification has been part of Saxony-Anhalt, should follow in the footsteps of the 18th century travellers and take their time, as they did. The fact is that the originally intended aesthetic experience only reveals itself to today's visitors if they progress slowly; ideally on

The Mittelhölzer guard-house. Dikes offer protection from the Elbe when it floods and, whilst walking, offer expansive views of the surrounding meadows.

foot, on a bicycle, or a little more comfortably, in a horse-drawn carriage.

Carl August Boettiger was probably the first person to use the words "Garden Realm" in his 1797 diary of a *Journey to Wörlitz* for these artfully arranged landscape images, this unique way of beautifying nature in Europe. At this time, it included almost all the territory of the Principality of Anhalt-Dessau, about 700 square kilometres. Now it is largely perceived to be the area between the former royal seat of Dessau and the town of Wörlitz, first mentioned in documents in the year 1004 – still an imposing area of 142 square kilometres. In this conservation area, extending from the Kühnauer Heide in the west to the Wörlitzer Winkel in the east, running along the left bank of the Elbe for almost 30 kilometres, more intensively designed sections alternate with the Elbe water meadows, which have been left almost in their natural state. For about 250 years these open landscapes, sprinkled with arable meadows, orchards and solitary plantations, have borne strange-sounding names like Lobenbreite, Beckerbruch, Streitwerder or Speckinge, Braunsche Lache and Rosenwiesche.

The great house and park ensembles of Mosigkau, Grosskühnau, Georgengarten, Luisium, Oranienbaum and Wörlitz fit in harmoniously between them – staged highlights, arranged like a string of pearls. Ever since it came into being, the Wörlitz Park, in particular, has not just been a place of pilgrimage for lovers of the English-style landscape garden, it is also perceived as being the secret birthplace of the Enlightenment in Germany. Johann Friedrich Abegg referred to Wörlitz and the "garden land" as a large "garden for people" as early as 1798. He wanted his wife, his brother, relatives and friends to join him, because here one could enjoy "the happiest moments of one's life". And like this Heidelberg professor over two hundred years ago, today's visitors to Wörlitz still sense the irresistible magic inherent in this place.

From natural to cultural landscape ‣ This landscape, formed over 10,000 years ago during the Saale cold stage, is shaped by the tributaries of the Elbe, the meanders of the Mulde and the rivers' dead arms, filled by the floods that occur every spring, yet constantly silting up. After every flood, the Elbe made itself a new river-bed, whose slight drop of an average

Infrared photograph of the landscape between Vockerode and Wörlitz, with flood channels that have now silted up. The Drehberg, the former princely burial-place on a hill, ringed with trees, can be made out to the south of the so-called Krägen, an arm of the Elbe, which appears in the picture as dark band.

of 17 centimetres per kilometre meant that, a few centuries ago, the river could have been up to 20 kilometres wide.

A predominantly natural, wooded, cultural landscape has survived here until today, between old flood channels and their silted-up zones, as an ecological refuge for rare plant and animal species. Essentially it forms part of the "Central Elbe" biosphere reserve. This is the largest coherent complex of river-valley, wood and meadowland in Europe, and here, among oaks, hornbeams and ulmus effusa, hoary alder and silver willow, red dogwood, spindleberry and cornelian cherry, the beaver builds his lodge, the black stork hatches her brood and the white stork stalks over the mown Elbe water-meadows. And regularly in autumn, there is an impressive natural display, when thousands of Arctic white geese on their way to the warmer south look for food and rest in the fields between Griesen and Oranienbaum.

Nature herself provided the scale and the design quality for what man has made. It was not just inside the Dessau-Wörlitz landscape gardens that every curve in the path was calculated as precisely as possible, the greatest possible attention was also paid to the connecting roads in between. There are some places in the Garden Realm where the historical roads have survived: with a made-up road and unpaved summer path, fringed by a variety of fruit-trees. Alternating with the useful fruit-trees, the Italian Lombardy poplar plays a literally outstanding role alongside the native oak. First seen in Lombardy in the second half of the 18th century, it was to help the Garden Realm's creators to complete their memories of Italy. The poplars' slender, tall tops, reminiscent of cypresses, are striking landmarks, but they have nothing alien about them, nothing suggesting that they were brought in from the outside. The trees are set in pairs on both sides of the road, as the start or the finish of an artificially and artistically shaped natural landscape. Or they frame the sight lines, often stretching for some kilometres, which according to Jean Paul are "long perspectives, drunk with the sun," running "like shining race-tracks of youth, like heavenly paths of hope".

In an essay on the topography of the Leipzig-Berlin railway, published 40 years after *Luftschiffer Giannozzo*, we find the poetic sentence: "As soon as we arrived in the Duchy of Anhalt-Dessau, the realm of Sylvan opened to our view." The unknown author continues no less enthusiastically: "The whole area is a pleasant meadowland bordered by woods,

lying before our eyes like a great green carpet; here we see pictures like those of Horace or Virgil, those great painters of nature as she really is; here the bull wades through the verdant meadow, here we see the young horse, unbridled in his youthful strength, here we see the countryman's diligence, and the most beauteous wheat field sits among meadows, shimmering with a thousand spring blossoms."

Even in classical antiquity, the Greek doctor Hippocrates was aware that powerful forces emanate from a landscape and its climate, affecting its inhabitants and their creative powers. It was left to the men of the Enlightenment to realize that the historically mature landscape expressed the culture of the time in which it came into being, and was not a paradise garden which they had been granted. Evidence of practical interventions in nature, like dikes and drainage ditches in the "earthly paradise" of the Dessau-Wörlitz Garden Realm, probably goes back over 1000 years. But in the early 18th century, during the reign of Leopold I of Anhalt-Dessau, the legendary Old Dessauer, these measures for improvement were pursued considerably more intensively. Outlying farms and villages were established behind the embankments along the Elbe, like for example Naundorf, Dellnau and Ziebigk near Dessau. "Hear descendants a voice warning you/careful diligence created these hills and these bushes to protect the field-preserving dikes from the destructive ice /Do everything to maintain them." This is the warning to future generations chiselled into a memorial tablet at the behest of Prince Franz, the grandson of the Old Dessauer, in 1795. Now, over 200 years later, his plea for careful treatment of what had been created reminds us of our social responsibility towards this extensive cultural landscape, which, apart from the gardens, which always make an impact on the public, threatens to be forgotten from time to time. The floods in August 2002 have since gone down in history as the "floods of the century". They made it terrifyingly clear how defenceless we are in the face of violent natural forces and how much appropriate protective measures will be needed in the future as well.

Despite the construction of the autobahn (motorway) and the Elbe Bridge in 1938, and the resulting division of the Garden Realm into two halves, key design elements have survived to the present day in remarkable density and complexity. A short time ago, it was still possible to record 85 historic pathways, as well as 53 avenues, 31 ditches, 37 dikes, 111

small architectural items or individual buildings outside the park, and also 118 bridges, 55 borderstones, milestones and signposts, and finally, 25 dike openings for paths. So even this short list shows, on the one hand, how in this landscape the whole is worth nothing without the individual parts. And, on the other hand, it shows how the parts cannot have an effect if they lose their relationship of scale with their mature environment.

The princely patron ‣ "The impression of a great landscape picture is enhanced for the thinking man if he is able to combine it with a story." This quotation from Ferdinand Gregorovius can be applied equally well to a cultural landscape that has matured over the centuries, and whose historical background is familiar. In the case of the Dessau-Wörlitz Garden Realm, this means getting to know to its creator, Prince Leopold III Friedrich Franz of Anhalt-Dessau. According to tradition, and appropriately to his role as future ruler of the little principality, a glittering career in the Prussian army was in store for the heir to the throne, born on 10 August, 1740. His grandfather gave him a Prussian grenadier's uniform when he was only three, and he walked around in it in the fortresses of Magdeburg and Küstrin. Two years later, he underwent military training in the Halle garrison. He lost his father and mother at the age of eleven. He continued his career with his Uncle Dietrich as guardian. A few days after his sixteenth birthday, Franz became a "Volontaire" under his uncle, Moritz of Anhalt, field marshal to King Friedrich II of Prussia. During the 1756 campaign against Saxony, Franz was forced to see how his uncle, Prince Moritz, took prisoner his other uncle, Prince Eugen, who

served as field marshal in the Saxon army, and held him in the fortress of Königstein, near Dresden. Oberhofmeister von Guericke, who accompanied Franz and always gave orders to his uncle, Prince Dietrich, reported that Franz was staggered by this event.

The portrait of the young prince by the Dessau court painter Christian Friedrich Reinhold Lisiewsky must date from about this time: the prince in a distinguished and distanced pose, with an expression that is elegiac rather than spirited, but appropriately prestigious in Prussian uniform and cuirass, and with the customary insignia of a future ruler. Time and the outside world seem to have been removed from this snapshot. A contemporary viewer, aware of biographical details, must conjecture whether the subject seemed too superior at the time to swap his armour, a symbol of prestigious courtly culture, for the garments of an English aristocrat.

After the battle of Prague, the seventeen-year-old finally broke with his family's military tradition in the service of the Hohenzollerns and asked his guardian to release him from the Prussian army. As the protagonist of a fundamentally changing society he was granted an honourable discharge in October 1757, whereupon the Principality of Anhalt-Dessau, concerned with sovereignty and neutrality, was driven almost to the brink of ruin by the end of the Seven Years War, as a result of contributions enforced by Frederick the Great. This war left great loss in its wake, in Anhalt-Dessau as well; there were many dead, villages were burned down, cultivated fields laid waste and cattle stocks reduced.

The moment of his dismissal from Prussian military service was not the only time the young Franz showed himself to be a personality of particular calibre. *Omne tulit punctum, qui miscuit utile dulci* (he who mixes the useful with the beautiful will gain every applause) is the 343rd line of the Roman poet Horace's *Ars poetica*. The ruler's subsequent career was accompanied by this insight. It was not to be marauding warfare in the manner of an absolute potentate, in the style of Frederick, that was to bring prosperity and progress. On the contrary, Franz von Anhalt-Dessau's desire for modernization brought his people peaceful, lasting and blessed prosperity. Equipped with a particular sense of what was practical and endowed with diplomatic skills, after coming to power in 1758, he immediately set about rebuilding his principality, which "you can cover with your finger on a

"Wanderer, choose your path with reason," a programmatic inscription on the stone plaque decorating a narrow passage through rocks in the labyrinth in Neumark's garden in the Wörlitz Park. People passing

through are reminded of their responsibilities to themselves and to the world around them.

Christian Friedrich Reinhold Lisiewsky (1725-1794), the heir to the
throne, Prince Leopold III Friedrich Franz of Anhalt-Dessau (1740-1817,
reigned from 1758), 1756.

map" (G.F. Rebmann), resolutely and single-mindedly. But noble intentions alone cannot constitute an educational ideal; this was able to develop only within an interplay of intellectual and political forces. Against the background of his many connections with proponents of European Enlightenment, Prince Franz became a personality who was esteemed all over Europe. He was driven by the impetus of debates with like-minded colleagues about the perfectibility of the world, and moulded by encyclopaedic thinking on the unity of knowledge, politics and morals, even in technical matters. Down to the last detail that was to form the basis of a functioning society, he used skilful tactics and acted with considerable political acumen. Looking for ideas to help his planned reform activities, directed practically and experimentally, Prince Franz undertook many journeys around Europe. The first took him through Germany in 1763/64, to Holland and finally to England. His visits to these countries made it easier for him establish his membership of a European ruling class that was typical of the 18th century, closely linked in many ways despite numerous large and small wars. The ruling houses in particular felt bound to each other through marriage, journeys and correspondence. Even small countries like Anhalt-Dessau were tied into this "European concert", not least by their marriage policies.

So, the twenty-three-year-old Prince Franz made his way first of all to the British Isles, that model of early industrialization, rather than setting off on the obligatory educational tour of Italy, as so many contemporary representatives of the aristocracy did. This can be interpreted as a remarkable form of "raison d'État", based on a marked sense of responsibility for his subjects, about 30,000 of them. The impressions and experiences the young prince gained in England in particular became guiding lights for his future life and stimulated him to give the future Garden Realm its own distinctive form.

Prince Franz was accompanied on his journey by his kindred spirit, the universally educated Saxon Baron Friedrich Wilhelm von Erdmannsdorff, one of the men who prepared the way for German classicism. The "Princely Anhalt-Dessau Country House" (A. Rode) in Wörlitz, which he designed between 1769 and 1773, is a particularly good example of his buildings: still the radiant centrepiece of the Wörlitz Park today. This country seat represented the spirit of Palladian villas in England with its form, reticent and very lucidly articulated for its day. This building especially showed Erd-

mannsdorff's determination to find an architectural language appropriate to his princely client's enlightened political style.

But this "villa suburbana" meant far more to its architects than a modern summer retreat in the country. Both in antiquity and in Palladio's Veneto, it referred to the whole agrarian setting, in which the manor house functioned as the administrative centre. It was only life in the country that made it possible, on the basis of agriculture and as an opposite pole to prestigious courtly culture in town, for body and spirit to recuperate and perfect themselves through leisure and intellectual pleasures. So Prince Franz and his architect called upon ancient tradition and its continuation in the Renaissance. They may have hoped that it would be resurrected in the Garden Realm if they paraphrased the past's creations stylistically. Not least to complete their subjective vision of an enlightened society.

In art and science, the reorganization of administration, finance and legislation, and in the establishment of modest manufactories, the Principality of Anhalt-Dessau had become a model state in Europe, thanks to the intelligent and moderate rule of Prince Franz. Throughout his life, the prince strove for constant improvement of the human condition through true, precise knowledge and its practical application. The ruler's farsightedness in promoting agriculture and care of the countryside, his concern for his subjects and his tolerance in matters of religion was something in the nature of a revolution from above. As a modern pathway for authority, this also led to impressive reforms in the field of education and social affairs. So Franz von Anhalt-Dessau created institutions for the poor (the first one in Dessau in 1764) and improved public health from the moment government was transferred to him at the age of eighteen by his guardian, Prince Dietrich. And it did not even need such impressive, super-denominational educational establishments such as the Philanthropinum, founded by Johann Bernhard Basedow in 1774, to revolutionize schooling throughout Europe, for Wilhelm Ludwig Wekhrlin to be able to pronounce enthusiastically: "Nowhere can one find the centre-point of the simple and the sublime to so great an extent; never have philosophy and arts come together in a smaller space. Perhaps there is no place on the cultivated earth that so deserves to be looked at by the thinking and sensitive traveller; that busies the imagination more and contains so many objects of wonderment."

Genius loci ▸ This cultural landscape was and still is rightly called a "Garden Realm" – even though large parts of this legacy of the Enlightenment can be experienced only to a limited extent, due to over 200 years of history, two world wars and decades of inadequate socialist economic management. But it has remained extraordinarily authentic: a cultural treasure that is very much alive, and thus not just historical proof that human endeavour towards functional and design unity of architecture and garden art once led to a universal work of art. The Garden Realm can still be seen as a successful fusion of natural landscape and artistically remoulded landscape. At the same time, it symbolizes a very personally shaped, enlightened, late 18th century world picture, directed at the future of man and his world. At the time, the poet Friedrich von Matthisson thought he could recognize "the finger of the genius of humanity everywhere" here. This still applies in a different form.

In the early 20th century, the art historian Wilhelm van Kempen saw a "European, world matter" in it. He said that here was "in a unique way, in a small space, everything that inspired the last years of the 18th century. Nowhere in Germany – not even in Weimar – does the pulse of that time beat so clearly as it does in Wörlitz, the whole picture of the culture of a century, no, of a change in the world, infinitely many-sided, manifold, coming together from the most extreme disharmony to achieve a wondrous, full accord, and spreading out here in Wörlitz, seamless and vibrant with colour."

Despite constant change, from season to season, from historic epoch to historic epoch, we in our world are more closely connected than ever with this phase of history. Mankind's memory is bound to places like the Wörlitz-Dessau Garden Realm. Even though the symbols and allegories of architectural and landscape-design quotations and references were more accessible to educated 18th century visitors than to many of today's viewers, we can still comfort ourselves by stating that the origins of these extraordinary gardens revealed themselves even to contemporary witnesses only after they had lingered here for a long time. It needs time, attention, and perception with all the senses for this designed landscape to unfold its secrets to people. Its appearance, its fragrance and its magic have, for many generations, met man's longing for an earthly paradise. This is particularly true today: especially in the early morning, or on misty evenings, the "garden-land" by the Elbe and the Mulde draws visitors under its spell. You have a chance to allow yourself an incomparable stimulus, to use the influence of this nature-culture space to reflect on your own existence.

It seems scarcely possible today to answer the question: what is nature? Nature transforms itself, and by doing so, our perception of it. This process, which occurs almost imperceptibly, naturally also provokes the question of the extent to which we ought actually to stop presenting nature to ourselves in modern industrialized countries as an opposite pole to civilization. Nature, as it surrounds us today, is not wilderness. It has been shaped for thousands of years, as shown by the example of the Dessau-Wörlitz Garden Realm. So we have to ask ourselves about the role played by an inhabited cultural landscape of the rank and scale of the Dessau-Wörlitz Garden Realm in contemporary society. For, faced with the increasing size and density of cities and transport routes, intellectual attention to the development of landscape under sustainable conditions is needed more than ever before. Thousands of people every day like to seek out gardens and parks as places of recreation. The future will show to what extent these examples of landscape art can transcend material reality and, through their spiritual potential, provide possible approaches to better ways of coping with urgent contemporary questions. Even though maintaining the cultural heritage is enshrined in human rights, we will only be able to do so if acknowledging its dignity, incomparability and inability to be replaced becomes common property.

"Much of the world's splendour has come to nought in war and conflict; he who protects and sustains has drawn the finest lot," wrote Goethe. "Nothing flourishes untended; and the most excellent things lose their value through inappropriate treatment," as the royal Prussian garden director, Peter Joseph Lenné, put it, in less poetic words. In the Garden Realm of Dessau-Wörlitz, the Enlightenment has become a picture, and is omnipresent. Discovering the refreshing and forward-looking powers of these, possibly Central Europe's earliest landscape cultivation measures, and above all exploring the energy inherent in the genius loci productively for the common good, remains the individual challenge to each of us in future.

Most High and Serene Prince
Most Gracious Uncle

I hereby cannot withhold from Your Serene
Highness how, in the present confused and
wretched circumstances, I find myself compelled
to apply most humbly to His Royal Majesty that
I be discharged. I therefore most humbly petition
Your Serene Highness graciously to allow me so
to proceed.   As soon as your permission is
granted, I will complete the letter to the King
and send it off immediately following this
occurrence.   I remain for my lifetime, with the
greatest respect,
        Your Serene Highness's

Dessau   most humble servant
6 October,   and nephew
1757   LffrantzPzAnhalt

Prince Franz's plea for discharge to his Uncle Dietrich.

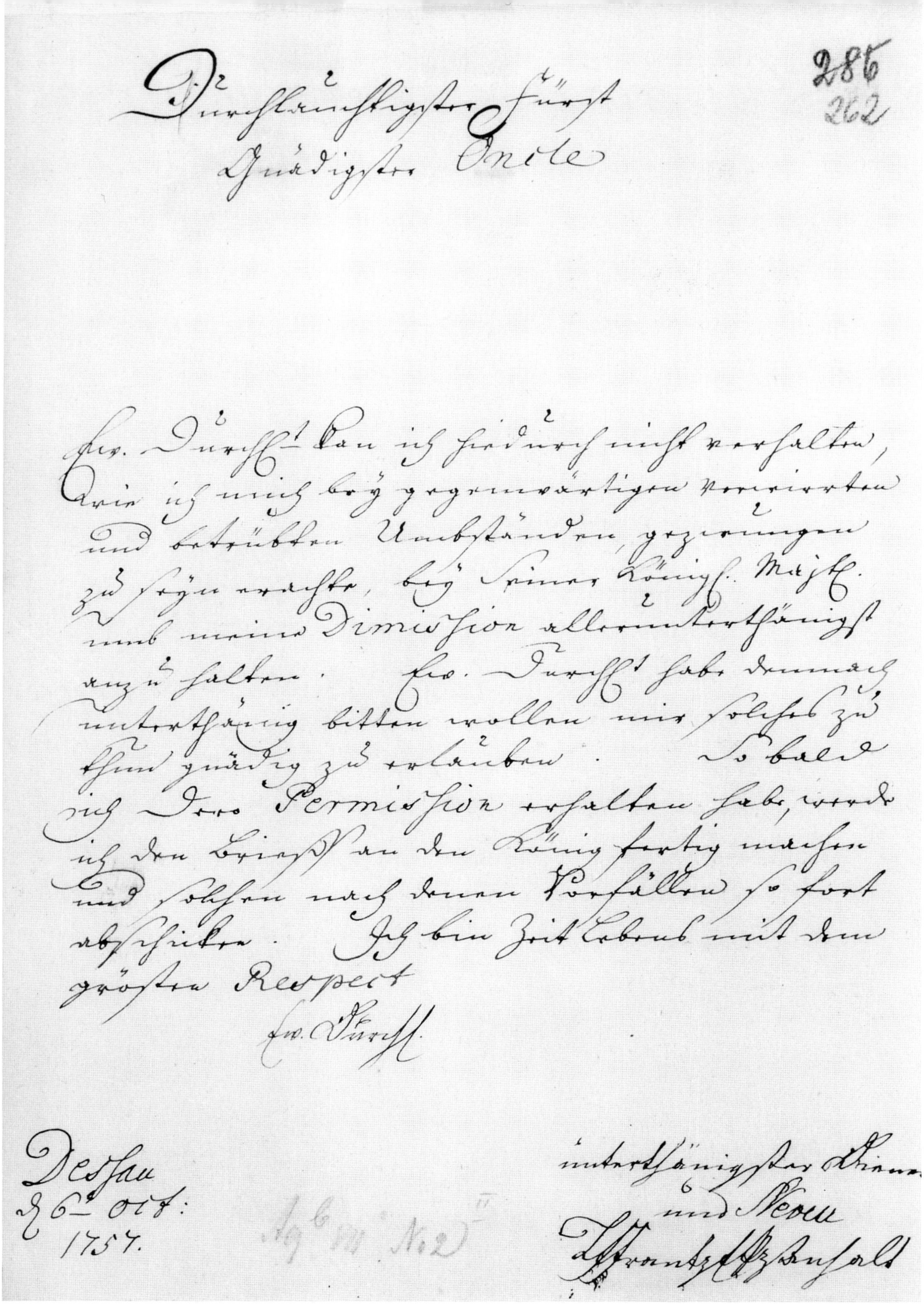

Durchlauchtigster Fürst
Gnädigster Onkle

[handwritten letter in German cursive]

Dessau
26. Oct:
1757.

unterthänigster Diener
und Neveu
[signature]

Petition by Crown Prince Leopold Friedrich Franz of Anhalt-Dessau for permission to leave the Prussian army, addressed to his uncle and guardian, the reigning Prince Dietrich, on 6 October, 1757. He received a favourable answer on the following day.

Reinhard Melzer

The land of the Princes of Anhalt

This book describes the extraordinary cultural achievements of a modern and enlightened state. They astonished Europe in the late 18th century and made the principality of Anhalt the centre of attention. It was an outstanding epoch for this little country in the central Elbe region, as it was rarely a focal point for great historical events. Most of its history was marginal, as is shown by its appearance in Anton von Werner's famous picture painted in 1885, *Die Proklamation des Deutschen Kaiserreiches* (The Proclamation of the German Empire): Crown Prince Leopold Friedrich von Anhalt (1831-1904) is placed on the extreme left-hand edge of the picture, with part of his head cut off. Along with 20 other German princes and representatives of the free cities of Lübeck, Bremen and Hamburg, he is cheering Wilhelm, the Prussian King and

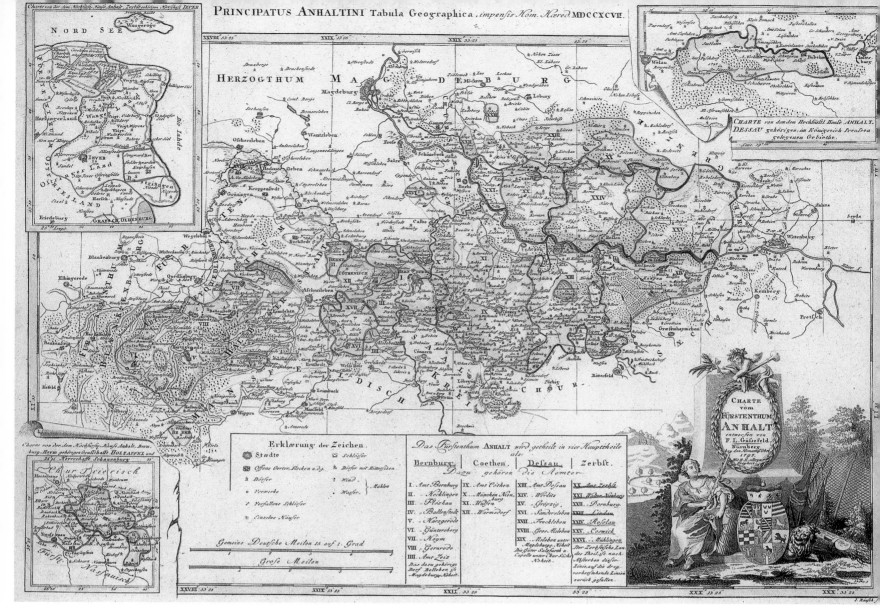

now German Emperor. This sealed the foundation of the German Reich as a federal state on 18 January, 1871. The Duchy of Anhalt, founded just eight years previously, with an area of 2294 square kilometres and 293,298 inhabitants, was in 13th place among the 25 federal states; it had only one vote out of 58 in the Bundesrat (Upper House of Parliament). Anhalt was a small German state that could not exist in its own right and in which a minister attended to business "that in Prussia would be dealt with by a rural administrative officer" (Treitschke). But it was a county that could rightly be proud of its cultural achievements and also derived its identity from these. And at that time it could already look back on four hundred years of history that were closely linked with the Ascanian line of princes.

Because of its central position, its early transport links – the Anhalt Station in Berlin was a symbol of this –, its geographical proximity to Prussia and the high degree of rapid industrialization, Anhalt was absorbed into the Reich faster than other small German states. A varied and tormented history still awaited this country after 1871; it even lost its name for 38 years, from 1952 to 1990.

The area between the Harz and Fläming, where the country of Anhalt was later to be, was settled at an early stage. This is proven by finds from the Palaeolithic period near Mosigkau (Dessau) and Werdershausen (Köthen district). Old Stone Age hunter-gatherers moved through the region, and the corresponding sites of finds become more widespread into

Principatus Anhaltini Tabula – the Anhalt principalities with their enclaves in East Prussia, Jever and Holzapfel, printed in Nuremberg in 1797.

Lucas Cranach the Younger, *Das Abendmahl* (The Last Supper), 1565. This shows a Last Supper with reformers and Princes of Anhalt. The three brothers, Johann (at the back, second from left), Georg (in the Supper scene, to the left of Christ) and Joachim (front left) can be seen, as well as Johann's son, Joachim Ernst (left of column). Prince Franz brought this large panel picture back into the church to adorn the new prince's throne in 1779. This also confirmed his legitimacy as spiritual head.

26

the Neolithic period. For example, iron objects from the so-called "house urn culture" (10C – 6C BC) were found.

Anhalt attracted historical attention between 29 and 7 BC, when the Greek writer Strabo reported on the Germanic tribes settling on the Elbe. At the time of the migration of the peoples in the 5th century, the great Thuringian tribe established itself in central Germany, and the land between the Harz and the Elbe was also part of this territory. This empire fell in the year 531 in a decisive battle against the Franks on the Unstrut, and Slavic tribes moved across the Elbe and as far as the Saale. Around 919, when Henry became German king, the land on the central Elbe was, for just under 200 years, at the centre of the developing German Empire and formed the point of departure for the armed seizure and Christianization of the West Slavic settlement area east of the Saale and the Elbe. Many noble lines grew up here, including the Wettins from the lower Saale area and the Ascanians from the Ballenstedt region. Both reigned in Saxony and Anhalt until 1918, and only lost their power as a result of the November Revolution.

While the Wettin Konrad the Great was made Margrave of the Mark of Meissen and the Lausitz in 1136, the Ascanian Albrecht the Bear (c. 1100-1170) was given the Nordmark. Under him – he was also Duke of Saxony until 1142 – the Ascanian line reached the pinnacle of its territorial power, but they broke their territories up through divided inheritances. Even Albrecht divided between his sons: Otto I (1126-1184) became Margrave of Brandenburg, Hermann (d. 1176), Count of Orlamünde and Bernhard (1140-1212), Duke of Saxony (later Electoral Saxony). Bernhard again divided his share of the country up between his sons in 1212: Heinrich I (c. 1170-1252) was allotted the Principality of Anhalt (he was the first to call himself Prince of Anhalt) and Albrecht I (d. 1261), the Duchy of Saxony. The latter divided Saxony again, into Saxony-Lauenburg and Saxony-Wittenberg. So Brandenburg, with the Altmark, Orlamünde, Anhalt, Saxony-Lauenburg and Saxony-Wittenberg were once Ascanian property. The Ascanians died out in Brandenburg in 1319/20, and the Hohenzollerns took over the Electorate in the Mark in 1415. The Ascanian line came to an end at almost the same time in the Electorate of Saxony-Wittenberg (1422). There, too, it did not prove possible to secure the inheritance for the House: the Margraves of Meissen were granted the Saxon Electoral Crown. The Counts of Orlamünde died out in 1487,

and the Saxony-Lauenburg line ended in 1689. In fact, the Ascanians retained only the Principality of Anhalt (in approximately their former freehold land), which had come into being through the 1212 division, with the associated stewardships and protection rights over the monasteries of Gernrode and Nienburg. Anhalt's later core territories, Zerbst and Lindau, were added in 1307. As the Ascanians had obviously not succeeded in introducing primogeniture to their house, their power and influence dwindled within a few centuries. So, in the 15th and 16th centuries, Anhalt's geopolitical situation was extraordinarily complicated; it was now nothing, but a little country between the great territorial powers of Brandenburg and Saxony, who on top of it all, were competing in a threatening manner for influence in the Archbishopric of Magdeburg. This situation now determined the fate of the Principality of Anhalt for centuries, remaining valid until the Reich was founded in 1871. Anhalt, too, was destined to undergo separation of inheritances. Heinrich I (1170-1251/52) split the land up into Aschersleben, Bernburg and Köthen. While Aschersleben fell to the Bishopric of Halberstadt in 1315, the rest of the country was successfully held together with Zerbst. Thanks to the laws of succession, Joachim Ernst was able to rule alone in the whole of Anhalt from 1570. After his death in 1586, his heirs agreed in 1603 and 1606 on a division into Anhalt-Dessau, Anhalt-Köthen, Anhalt-Bernburg and Anhalt-Zerbst, and independent royal seats developed in each. But the whole of Anhalt still had only one vote in the Regensburg Reichstag. It took 260 years for Anhalt to become a Duchy again, through fortunate succession. The Anhalt-Zerbst line died out as early as 1793, Köthen with Anhalt-Plötzkau in 1847

Left ‹ Lucas Cranach the Elder, Prince Johann IV (1504-1551), father of Joachim Ernst. The Reformation came to Anhalt-Dessau in his reign.

Right › Lucas Cranach the Elder, Prince Joachim (1509-1561), brother of Johann IV. The two 1532 portraits were formerly part of the extensive holdings of Cranach pictures in the Gothic House, Wörlitz.

and Bernburg in 1863, so that Leopold IV Friedrich of Anhalt-Dessau was able to call himself Duke of Anhalt from 1863. The course of the dynastic history of the country alone shows how limited the possibilities were for achieving political goals. Events and individuals, that are important for understanding the period dealt with in this book, are presented below.

The royal seat of the Elector of Saxony, and later university town, of Wittenberg became the condensation point for Renaissance and Humanism in north-east Germany after 1500. It was, above all, the starting point for the Lutheran Reformation. Anhalt, which lies north of Wittenberg, was influenced by this centre at the time, even though the Ascanian line of Altzerbst-Köthen successfully resisted it under the administration of Margarete Münsterberg (1516-1530). After the Peasants' War of 1512, the first anti-reform alliance of German princes formed at the Dessau court in 1525. It was only after Margarete Münsterberg's death in 1530 that all parts of Anhalt accepted the Reformation. The humanistically trained Prince Georg III, a close confidant of both Luther and Melanchthon, had done much to promote the introduction of the Reformation. The town of Dessau owed its Renaissance stamp, which was finally destroyed in the Second World War, in many parts to Saxon Electoral influence. This included, among other things, the building of the Schloss, its interior furnishings and décor, the decoration of the Marienkirche by the Cranach workshop, the building of the Marienkirche tower. Prince Georg's important scholarly library has survived, impressive evidence of his passion for artistically designed and lavishly bound books. This epoch, in particular, was the subject of one of Prince Leopold III Friedrich Franz's collector's passions in the 18th century; he initiated the Dessau-Wörlitz Garden Realm. In the reign of Joachim Ernst (1561-1586), Anhalt was successfully united, and Calvinism was introduced to the country shortly after his death. This determined future political developments: the special connections with the Netherlands and Brandenburg. Joachim Ernst founded the school, the Gymnasium illustre, in 1582, and the ambitious aspiration, to have its own reformed university, was fulfilled in the form of the Zerbst Gymnasium. Leopold III Friedrich Franz did not dissolve the Gymnasium illustre until 1798.

Anhalt provided two important princely personalities at the time of the Thirty Years War, Christian I of Anhalt-Brandenburg (1568-1630) and Ludwig of Anhalt-Köthen (1579-1650).

Christian I was one of the great political talents of the Ascanian line. He also became one of its military leaders, as initiator and co-founder of the Protestant Union (1608), under the Bohemian King Friedrich IV, the Winter King. But both men's European roles ended on 8 November, 1620, at the Battle of the White Mountain. Wallenstein's victory over Ernst von Mansfeld's troops at the Dessau Bridge in the Lower Saxony war against Denmark (1623-29) in 1626 was an important step towards imperial success and the Edict of Restitution in 1629. Ludwig von Anhalt-Köthen carried out important reforms in his country amidst the turmoil of this great war. In 1618, the important educationalist, Wolfgang Radtke, renewed the principality's school system, and Prince Ludwig became chairman of the "Order of the Palm Tree", which he co-founded in 1617. This made Köthen home to a society devoted to improving the German language and promoting knowledge and education. It was one of the first scholarly associations in Germany. The society had over 500 members when the prince died in 1650.

After the devastating war, it fell to Johann Georg II (1627-1693) in Anhalt-Dessau and to Carl Wilhelm (1657-1718) in Anhalt-Zerbst to attempt to re-order and revitalize their countries. Johann Georg II, with his wife, the Orange princess Henriette Catharina (1637-1708), successfully carried out a magnificent piece of reconstruction. The country was not just beautified under the influence of Dutch culture, art and intellect, but also reinforced and modernized economically. The Schloss (palace) and town of Oranienbaum and the wealth of Orange paintings bear eloquent witness to the renewal of the country at that time. Henriette Catharina brought an international public to Dessau: Italian merchants, Dutch builders, Bohemian glassmakers, Jews and French people. Carl Wilhelm also carried out his economic,

Left ‹ Prince Christian of Anhalt Brandenburg (1568-1630), a diplomat and warrior of European status during the Thirty Years War. Copperplate engraving by Martin Bernigroth, c. 1710.

Right › Prince Leopold of Anhalt-Köthen (1694-1728), patron of Johann Sebastian Bach. Copperplate engraving by J.C.G. Fritsch, c. 1757.

political and also denominational reorganization in Zerbst. The Schloss in Zerbst, destroyed in 1945, and the Trinitatiskirche were signs of the willingness to rebuild after the catastrophe of the Thirty Years War.

Prince Leopold of Anhalt-Köthen's (1694-1728) patronage did world culture a lasting service. From 1717 to 1723, he promoted Johann Sebastian Bach as his Kapellmeister (court conductor), musical advisor and travelling companion. A large proportion of Bach's instrumental works were written in Köthen. The composer spent many carefree years here, and married his second wife, Anna Magdalena. – Wherever the great cantor's music is played, Prince Leopold of Köthen will be remembered as well.

With Prince Johann Georg II of Anhalt-Dessau, who was a Brandenburg field marshal and the Elector's governor in the Mark of Brandenburg, the politics of Anhalt-Dessau came to be oriented permanently towards Berlin, Brandenburg and Prussia. Johann Georg was the directly related to the Elector by marriage, through his wife Henriette Catharina. Their son, Leopold, and the grandsons almost all served as field marshals in the Prussian army, namely Leopold Maximilian, Dietrich and Moritz; Crown Prince Gustav died as early as 1737 with the rank of general, and Prince Eugen served in Electoral Saxony. In this way, good salaries filled Anhalt's coffers. Prince Leopold of Anhalt-Dessau (1676-1747) served the first three Prussian kings in this highest military rank: Friedrich I, Friedrich Wilhelm I and Friedrich II. Leopold continued his mother's policies based on economics and tolerance.

He succeeded in buying up almost all the landed properties in his principality, so that he really was lord of the country and had absolute rule. He continued dike-building and cultivation measures on a grand scale. History has remembered him as an important military figure, but this prince was also interested in technology, and created the economic and cultural basis for his grandson's reforms. Thus Leopold III Friedrich Franz – undoubtedly the most important Anhalt prince – succeeded in the second half of the 18th century in raising the little principality to the status of a cultural centre of European rank. After Saxony-Weimar-Eisenach, Anhalt-Dessau was the second place to take over leading cultural positions in Germany for a while. Anhalt emancipated itself from Saxony and Prussia at this time, and sent out an abundance of new impulses in it own right. Leopold III

Friedrich Franz's successors tried to preserve what had been achieved.

In the 19th century, central Germany was one of the areas of Germany that was particularly shaped by advancing industrial development. Anhalt had a dense rail network from as early as 1839, including the Leipzig-Halle-Magdeburg line, the Anhalt railway from Berlin to Dessau, and the Potsdam-Magdeburg-Braunschweig route. The Elbe Bridge in Rosslau was opened in 1836. The Elbe, with its growing steamship trade, was also part of this transport network. The 1848 revolution led to the constitution of a pan-Anhalt parliament that controlled the ministries. The unification of all the sections of Anhalt, which had been in the offing for some time, happened in 1863 with the death of Prince Alexander Karl of Bernburg. This had a favourable impact on the economy. Dessau, Bernburg and Köthen became industrial centres even before 1900. Potash production in particular formed the basis of Anhalt's wealth, and the names Oechelhäusers and Junkers became symbols of a modern industry. On 12 November, 1918, when Prince Regent Aribert renounced the throne, the November Revolution ended Ascanian rule. Anhalt was governed mainly by Social Democrats under the Weimar Republic. When the Bauhaus moved to Dessau in 1926, the country underwent another cultural renaissance similar to those of Reformation times or in the period of Henriette Catharina and Prince Franz.

This period ended in 1932, when the NSDAP came to power in Anhalt. Germany had its first National Socialist prime minister here. After the devastating Second World War, in which Zerbst and Dessau were up to 80% destroyed, Anhalt was first occupied by the Americans in 1945, then by the Soviets. Anhalt was attached to the former province of Saxony, and the Land of Saxony-Anhalt, with Halle as its capital, was born in 1947. But in 1952, when the district structure was introduced in the GDR, Anhalt was absorbed into the districts of Magdeburg and Halle. The constitution meeting of the parliament in Dessau on 28 October, 1990, saw the rebirth of Saxony-Anhalt as a Land. And with the town of Quedlinburg, the Luther memorials in Wittenberg and Eisleben, the Dessau Bauhaus and the Garden Realm of Dessau-Wörlitz – the Land's four World Heritage sites – the eyes of the world are once again on Saxony-Anhalt.

By the Grosskühnau Lake.

I

ORANIEN
BAUM

Wolfgang Savelsberg

A baroque Orange exclave

Oranienbaum, one of the few largely surviving baroque ensembles of palace and town, is about nine kilometres east of Dessau. This architectural unit, which is particularly worth seeing, was founded by Henriette Catharina, Prince Franz of Anhalt-Dessau's great-grandmother. The fact that he included Oranienbaum in his Garden Realm, by redesigning a section of the park as an English-Chinese garden and extensively renovating and rebuilding parts of the Schloss, show in what high esteem the prince held it – even if he came here only seldom, when hunting.

At the same time as creating the town, Henriette Catharina of Anhalt-Dessau (1637-1708) started to build the residence and lay out the park in the early 1680s. This three-winged building, with its "cour d'honneur" (courtyard of honour) opening towards the town and a recessed main section, the "corps de logis" (living quarters), is typical of northern European palace

architecture. Its architectural concept goes back to the "hotel" building type developed in France in the 1620s, culminating in the Palace of Versailles, built from 1669 by Louis XIV to plans by Louis le Vau. But despite being structured in the same way, the Oranienbaum palace differs considerably from its famous models in its building ornamentation and articulation, its imposing straightness of line and simple roof forms. These stylistic characteristics point to the northern Netherlands, where a comparable, reduced vocabulary of form can be observed in 17th century town halls, churches and palaces. The princess also commissioned a Dutch master builder, Cornelis Ryckwaert, to erect the palace.

The houses of Anhalt-Dessau and Orange-Nassau ‣ The palace's architectural elements point to the northern Netherlands, whilst the name Oranienbaum (Oranien = Orange), in particular, confirms a close connection with the United Provinces of the Netherlands. The woman responsible for building this baroque ensemble, Henriette Catharina, came from the Netherlands. She was a scion of the mighty and noble European house of Orange-Nassau, which made a crucial contribution to the emergence and further development of the United Provinces. She had come to the principality on the Elbe as a result of deliberate marriage policy by her mother, Amalia von Solms, the ambitious spouse of the governor Friedrich Heinrich, intending to create and reinforce a connection between the House of Orange-Nassau and principalities of the reformed confession. Her marriage to Prince Johann Georg II of Anhalt-Dessau in 1659 was of fundamental importance to this little country, impoverished by the Thirty Years War, and represented a turning-point in its history.

Oranienbaum

The defining architectural element of the garden façade is the gallery with its sculptures. Ryckwaert found ideas for this in Honselaarsdijk, the summer residence, now destroyed, of Henriette Catharina's parents.

Amalia von Solms, at the age of 27, with her two eldest children, Wilhelm II and Louise Henriette. This portrait by Gerard van Honthorst was painted around 1629 and was accorded the place of honour in the Gothic House in Wörlitz, over the fireplace in the reception room.

This monumental portrait by Jan Mijtens, dated 1666, shows the four daughters of Friedrich Heinrich of Orange-Nassau and Amalia von Solms, with the Schwanenburg in Kleve in the background; Maria, one of the subjects of the painting, was married here to Count Palatinate Ludwig Heinrich Moritz von Simmern.

There had been political and intellectual contact between Anhalt and the Netherlands and the House of Orange since the late 16th century. Johann Georg, whose mother had already spent part of her youth at the Orange court in The Hague, spent some time in the Netherlands among other places on his Grand Tour.

The Anhalt princes' conversion to the Reformed faith in 1634, which made Anhalt into an eastern outpost of the Calvinist confession, had been of central importance in the turn towards the Netherlands. In fact, the differences in influence and significance of the two principalities could hardly have been greater. The House of Orange was one of the most powerful noble lines in Europe and conducted an exclusive court life that could measure up to the greatest princely and royal houses in Europe. Existing palaces were extended, modernized and decorated and furnished magnificently. From 1645 onwards, Friedrich Heinrich and Amalia von Solms saw to the establishment of a new residence in the form of the "Oranjezaal", the present queen's Huis ten Bosch Palace in The Hague.

A link between the two princely houses was not solely in Amalia's interest, but was also considerably promoted by the Great Elector, Friedrich Wilhelm. Johann Georg, born in 1627 in the middle of the Thirty Years War, was intended to succeed to the throne as the only surviving child of the Anhalt-Dessau princely couple, Johann Casimir and Agnes. The ambitious Crown Prince first entered the services of Karl X Gustav of Sweden, but was forced, by the sudden gain in strength of his country's immediate neighbour, the electorate of Brandenburg, to think of a volte-face. This suited the Hohenzollerns ideally, as they wanted to win the experienced and accepted military man over to their side and link Anhalt securely with the electorate of Brandenburg. This change succeeded not least because of the excellent prospect of marriage to the Orange princess, the younger sister of Louise Henriette, the wife of the Great Elector.

The web of Brandenburg-Orange-Anhalt connection was advantageous in every respect for the little principality. And Johann Georg's contacts with his nephew, William III, later to be King of England, were also not to be underestimated. William had promoted, among other things, the marriage of the Anhalt princess, Henriette Amalia, one of Henriette Catharina's daughters, to her cousin, Johann Wilhelm Friso. So the couple were granted the privilege, when William III died childless, to carry on the name of the Orange-Nassau line, which made an Anhalt princess the progenitor of the present royal Dutch house.

This 1666 portrait by Adriaen Hannemann particularly emphasizes Johann Georg II Prince of Anhalt's virtues such as courage and steadfastness, as well as the ideal of courtly elegance.

Like the portrait of her husband, this portrait of Henriette Catharina, also dating from 1666, probably a contemporary copy from an original by Jan Mitjens, hung in the Rittersaal in the Gothic House in Wörlitz – a sign of Prince Franz's respect.

Henriette Catharina in Anhalt-Dessau ▸ It cannot have been easy for Henriette Catharina to move to the Elbe from one of the most luxurious courts in Europe, and one of the most progressive state structures. In the early years of their marriage, the Anhalt prince and princess spent most of their time at the Brandenburg court, Johann Georg's place of service. The first of their ten children was born in Berlin, and they made important decisions about Anhalt-Dessau from here. They also promoted the development of political, economic and cultural links with the Netherlands in particular. The example of her sister, Louise Henriette, was also important for Henriette Catharina's subsequent work in Anhalt. Louise Henriette had had a model agricultural domain and the magnificent country seat of Oranienburg built in the little Brandenburg town of Bötzow with the assistance of Dutch colonists.

But it would be absolutely wrong to assume that Johann Georg and Henriette Catharina had turned their backs on their country because of Anhalt's many deficiencies. The couple finally moved there in 1667 and started to discharge their princely duties with commitment. Henriette Catharina in particular, who was considerably more solvent than the prince himself, devoted herself to a wide range of social, economic and cultural activities in her new home. She was particularly driven by her Calvinist education and its most important postulate, the vita activa. So, she sup-ported the Dessau infirmary of St. George with a considerable sum of money, had an orphanage built in Dessau and saw to building a home for widows in the Oranienbaum market place.

The economy was given a major boost, not least by the tolerant princely immigration policy, which was already practised in the Netherlands and Brandenburg-Prussia. Immigrants with a lot of capital, above all Henriette Catharina's countrymen, but also French Huguenots and Reformed co-religionists from other German countries, were drawn to Dessau. Henriette Catharina's granting of permission to build a synagogue in Dessau in 1687 is a clear sign of the political tolerance practised in relation to Jews, which was also maintained by subsequent princes. Catholics were also allowed to settle again, and a church was even built for Lutherans in Oranienbaum.

Dutch engineers made a crucial impact on economic development. They came to the country in Henriette Catharina's lifetime and then increasingly in the reign of her son, Leopold I. They opened up wide tracts of land for usage by building dams against the floods on the Mulde and the Elbe, and drainage plants. Agriculture grew, numerous towns were founded. As well as this, new cultivation methods that had already been tried out in the Netherlands and modern cattle-breeding techniques improved agrarian life. Prospering branches of the economy included above all brewing, as

This front view of Schloss Oranienbaum over-emphasizes the breadth of the complex and makes a spectacular impact. Copperplate engraving from the *Historie des Fürstenthums*, published by Johann Christoph Beckmann in 1710.

39

well as tobacco cultivation and processing. And a crystal and mirror-glass manufactory, with Bohemian and Venetian masters, also flourished for two short decades in the Mulde town, during the reign of the princess. As well as improving the economic situation, the princely couple also pursued an urban modernization programme for the town of Dessau from the 1680s. The most eminent example of this were the so-called Buden (booths), a well proportioned and functional arcaded structure with shops on the long south side of the Marienkirche; they were destroyed in the Second World War.

Baroque splendour – Schloss Oranienbaum ▸ Henriette Catharina and Johann Georg waited for over two decades after their wedding to build a palace that would meet their need for appropriate prestige and pomp. They chose the little town of Nischwitz, which had been abandoned in the late Middle Ages. There had already been new building here for Johann Georg's mother, Agnes of Anhalt-Dessau. A house, protected by ditches and ramparts, was built for her in the mid 17th century, along with a yard for domestic offices and a prayer house. From early on, Henriette Catharina had had her eye on this place, which had been given to her as a wedding present in 1659, as a site for a future palace, and had rechristened it Oranienbaum as early as 1673.

As the princely couple benefited from the outset mainly from the economic achievements and intellectual and cultural developments from the Netherlands, it is not surprising that when they were looking for an architect for the planned building project, the choice also fell on a Dutchman. Cornelis Ryckwaert trained with none other than the famous North Netherlands master builder, Pieter Post – who had had considerable involvement in projects such as the building of the Mauritshuis and the Huis ten Bosch, both in The Hague. Ryckwaerts had already made his name with two palaces, Sonnenbrug in the Neumark (now Slonsk, Poland) and Schwedt. He had been working for Anhalt since 1681. As well as the Buden in Dessau, he designed the "corps de logis" of the residential palace in nearby Zerbst, which was largely destroyed in the Second World War, and the Trinitatiskirche, also in Zerbst, one of Germany's first Protestant centrally planned churches. The architect, who had already accumulated experience of technical and military structures, designed a trail-bridge over the Elbe near Dessau, before starting to plan Schloss Oranienbaum in 1683. He died in 1693, before it was completed. It is assumed that his son, Adriaen, managed the project for a time, before the complex as we know it today was completed by Johann Tobias Schuchart.

The overall view of Schloss Oranienbaum from the market place shows the complex with the main building, the adjacent wings, the courtiers' houses and the domestic buildings, which were added in a later building phase.

The overall architectural concept behind the ensemble of palace, garden and town underlines the claim to power asserted by the Anhalt princely couple. The French-style U-shaped palace distances the complex from the bourgeois milieu. It is comprises the prestigious residential complex with the main building, the adjacent wings and pavilions and the domestic yard in front, demarcated on the street side by canal and balustrade. The geometrically planned town opposite the palace follows the ideal town plans developed in Italy, with which the idea of an ideal system for absolute monarchy had been linked ever since the early 17th century. In this way, the interplay of all the urban elements with the palace reflects the socio-political organization of the territory under rule, with the monarch as its undisputed head.

But there were financial constraints on enhanced prestige. So, Henriette Catharina must have been clear from the outset that her home could not compete with the monumental palaces of her Orange relatives in the Netherlands or Brandenburg. This explains why Ryckwaert borrowed only to a limited extent from great 17th century houses in Holland, such as Hoselaarsdijk, now destroyed, the Huis ten Bosch or the Brandenburg palaces of Oranienburg and Köpenick. Despite this, the complex as a whole is one of the most important German baroque palaces – especially as the near-

by Schloss Zerbst no longer exists, with the exception of a single wing that has fallen into disrepair.

From country palace to dower house ‣ As the building documents were buried with Henriette Catharina in her coffin – so tradition has it – there is no adequate source material for Oranienbaum's construction history. Only two historical documents dating from the 1690s give information about building progress and the condition of the palace at that time. One is a travel diary by the architect, Christoph Pitzler, and the other is a report by an unknown author, possibly a Dutchman working at the court, entitled *Von Oranienboom*. The description of the place in Johann Christoph Beckmann's fundamental work on the history of Anhalt, the *Historie des Fürstenthums Anhalt*, published in Zerbst in 1710, draws on the latter.

Pitzler, who already describes Dessau as a town built to a large extent in brick in the Dutch manner, is the only contemporary to attribute the authorship of Oranienbaum to Ryckwaert. Pitzler's factual description about the state of the original building is extremely revealing. He describes it as a two-storey structure with single-storey wings and two-storey pavilions on either side. He says the "corps de logis" was built of masonry, and the wings of wood. In front of

The garden side of Schloss Oranienbaum, seen from the snowy English-Chinese garden. The garden was developed from a baroque island garden, laid out at the time of Henriette Catharina.

the complex was an "outwork" with a completely enclosed courtyard. At the front entrance, Pitzler sees three gates, of which one led to the cowsheds. This description is supported by a sketch, very rough in places, certainly drawn from memory at a later stage, and not very detailed. It does not fit the description in all points. It indicates that the domestic wings adjacent to the pavilions were still missing at this time, with the exception of two transversely placed buildings at the side of the courtyard entrance.

The second source, of a slightly later date, notes that the building was not "brought to perfection" until 1698. But the author goes on to say that additional buildings were added to the complex "at the time". Study of the sources reveals that Ryckwaerts's first draft foresaw single-storey wooden wings on the sides of the "corps de logis". Recent inspections of the building also lead to the conclusion that the wings were built with a single storey only at first. But the same study also proves that this storey was, in fact, built of masonry. The intermediate buildings were not completed with an additional storey until about 1700, after the architect's death. The square pavilions were completed at the same time as the main building.

After her husband died in 1693, Henriette Catharina assumed responsibility for the state and chose the palace as her dower house. After she handed government of the principality over to her son, Leopold I, five years later, she lived in Oranienbaum until she died in 1708. This use as a permanent residence probably required the extension of the palace by the single-storey domestic buildings in front. The copperplate engraving in Beckmann's *Historie*, published in 1710, shows the complete ensemble.

Cour d'honneur and domestic courtyard side ‣ On the town side, the palace complex is complete by transverse stable buildings on both sides. These open to the road and the canal

beyond it with large, round-arched windows replacing the original open gallery. Adjacent to these are the long, somewhat lower domestic wings; their centre is accentuated by a superstructure with a round tower. The buildings end at the outer corners of the large, two-storey pavilions called "cavalier houses". These timber-frame buildings with many windows, on a square ground plan, have massive pyramid roofs. These were once covered with black tiles, and are topped by a central, heavily profiled chimney. The narrow wings are built along the same line, between the pavilions and the corps de logis. The roof cornice of the two-storey wings is in line with the floor height of the main building, but rises higher than the cornice of the pavilions, so that the connection between the two parts of the building does not seem to have been achieved very successfully. This irregularity alone shows that the first floor of the intermediate buildings was not part of Ryckwaerts's original plan.

The two-storey main building with its formerly black hip roof, which has two dormer windows and four symmetrically arranged chimneys, is considerably higher than the side wings. Eleven window axes articulate the massively stonebuilt structure with cellars. The entrance portal and the window above it are accompanied by a half-window on either side. The centre of the building is clearly accentuated by a slight projection, edged at the sides by strips of rusticated masonry. This section is topped above the roof cornice by a triangular pediment with coats-of-arms cartouches. The twin flights of sandstone steps lead to the entrance portal, which is flanked with Ionic pilasters, with a tympanum above. The façade is subduedly decorated. Apart from the base area and the corners of the building in rusticated sandstone, the only contrast with the ochre rendering (recent finds suggest a broken white as the first version) is provided today by the simply profiled framing of the windows in sandstone. In contrast with this, the wings are still decorated with rosettes between the upper and lower windows. The window shutters used to be another decorative element. These presumably covered the lower half of the originally more intricately articulated windows, at least on the ground floor of the "corps de logis" and the side wings. They were painted on the front and back with a Seville orange branch and an A for Anhalt, as a surviving shutter shows.

Garden façade ‣ The town side of the palace with its open, three-winged complex emphasizes the claim to power, but the rear façade conveys a completely different impression. As

These chased pewter and brass tea-caddies, dating from the period around 1700 and thought to be Chinese, are among the few craft objects surviving from the old inventory of Schloss Oranienbaum. Two lids in each case ensured that the aroma of the costly tea was preserved for as long as possible.

The contemporary architect Christoph Pitzler wrote this in his travel diary in 1690 about the stairs in Schloss Oranienbaum: "The staircase was double and indeed fine …," but added as a reservation: "… but all only in wood …"(!).

the wings and pavilions can scarcely be seen on this side, the building seems to be oriented entirely towards the garden. The protruding section is broader, and stands out more clearly in front of the building line. A portico with rhythmically placed columns and open steps leading to the portal are place in front of the building as a sophisticated architectural motif. Above this, a gallery makes it possible to come out into the open air and look at the garden. Additionally, six putto musicians on plinths on the balustrade emphasize the sense of gaiety and playfulness. There were originally two more terraces at the ends, providing direct access to the garden and making it possible to spend time in the open air. These access points were presumably closed in the 1690s when the palace was being modified as the dower house and, temporarily, as the residence, and replaced with lavatory shafts at these points.

The different statements made by the courtyard and garden sides are additionally emphasized by the sculptural decoration on the pediments. On the town side, the Anhalt and the Orange lion coat of arms (the lion is the Dutch heraldic beast) appear, which is to be interpreted as a symbol of the fortitudo (power and strength) emerging from the connection of the two lines. In contrast with this, on the garden side, flora and fauna alongside both coats of arms clearly indicate the fertile growth and beneficent developments brought about by this alliance. Even though the complex cannot match the size and splendour of Netherlands palace buildings, the plain, straight-lined quality of the architecture will have made Henriette Catharina feel at home. For example, the plain roof forms are far too characteristic of the Netherlands to be following French models. The narrow wings seem typically Dutch, as used by Jacob van Campen in 1639 for the extensions to the Orange Noordeinde Palace in The Hague, work also inspired by the new French hôtels. Even though it is found in numerous European palaces, the canal running round the whole complex is above all a motif familiar from

The Tea-Room, which is being restored at the time of writing (completion provisionally in 2007), here in a photograph taken in 1943, is the best-preserved room in the building from the period of Henriette Catharina, who commissioned the palace. The room has a lavishly decorated stucco ceiling, leather wall hangings and other original furnishings.

The leather wall hangings in the Tea-Room, made in the Netherlands c. 1700, were recently removed, revealing that the repeating patterns, which had previously been hung up with straps elsewhere in the palace, were being used here for the second time during Henriette Catharina's lifetime.

Oranienbaum

45

the Netherlands. Only the gallery on the garden side is an architectural detail borrowed from the Orange residence of Honselaarsdijk.

The interior. Extravagant luxury and a little of the Dutch homeland ‣ Henriette Catharina was particularly concerned to have something of her native Holland in the interior furnishings in particular. While the external appearance has remained almost unchanged, with the exception of the windows, which were modernized in the late 18th century, and the colour scheme, regrettably little remains of the house's interior furnishings. The costly interior was left to her daughters after Henriette Catharina died, and must have been removed from the building in its entirety. Other, comprehensive changes can be attributed to Prince Franz, who had several rooms repapered and refurnished in two modernization phases, in 1767 and 1789. Most of these were designed according to the prevailing Chinese fashion, inspired by pattern books compiled by Sir William Chambers, an English traveller to China. The interior was further changed and impoverished in the 20th century as a result of war, and over 50 years of foreign use as a Russian commandant's headquarters, accommodation for refugees and, from 1848 to 2002, as the Anhalt Land archive. But the latter did in part contribute to the conservation of the building.

Only the so-called tea-room (leather wall hangings room) and the tiled cellar (summer dining room) still provide evidence of the high quality of the original interior. Otherwise, the same sources drawn upon for the external architecture were again consulted for information about the interior furnishings and the use of the other rooms. So Pitzler, who visited the building when the wings and pavilions were still incomplete, found that "the country house … well furnished". But he was critical about architectural aspects, as for example when he said that the floors and staircases were just made of wood and the stucco was not very impressive. An anonymous author, who described the house about three years later, reported that there were "fine Netherlandish 'Tapezeryen' (tapestries), brocades, hangings, golden leather, imitation shields and paintings".
As well as this, the surviving inventories, accounts books and correspondence about deliveries from The Hague to Dessau over decades show how extravagantly luxurious the individual items of furniture and décor must have been. These books and lists carefully record what goods the Orange

The summer dining room contains five unique tiled tableaux of gods. Their manganese colouring makes them stand out effectively from the blue-and-white tiles around them.

Oranienbaum

princess received, and in what quantities. This shows clearly how greatly the spoiled governor's daughter needed luxury. All her wishes were fulfilled generously, alongside large gifts of money, especially while Amalie was alive. Apart from all the essentials for a princess such as jewellery, diamonds, clothes, shoes, medicines, bath oils, books or even several coaches with horses, she received large quantities of furniture for her house, Delft faïence, Chinese porcelain, silverware, decorative fabrics, lace, damask, crépon, silk, satin, embroidered quilts, East Indian fabrics, bed hangings, cupboards, chairs, mirrors and paintings.

As well as these deliveries, after her mother died in 1675 and later, through legacies from her sisters, Henriette Catharina had many other things she could call her own: a fortune in costly jewellery, varied and rare craft objects and numerous valuable paintings. The most detailed information about the interior decoration of the Oranienboom Palace is to be found in the *Inventarium of all legacies* ... This list also identifies the function of rooms when furnishing items such as "Tapisserie, gulden Lederbehangsel" (golden leather wall hangings) or "Anspiegeln and Cronen von Cristall de Roche" (rock crystal mirrors and chandeliers) are being allocated to particular locations: "König von Preuß. Cabinet" (King of Pruss. cabinet) or the "I. Hoheit presentz (cammer)" (Royal presence chamber) or "Frau Marggräfin Garderobe" (The Margravine's dressing room).

However, it is almost impossible today to understand how the rooms were arranged, as their functions changed many times to fit in with the palace's different roles – as a country seat, a residence, and a dower house. It is certain that "the great hall" on the top floor – the *Beletage* – was used as a banqueting hall or throne-room. It is in the middle on the preferred garden side and opens on both sides on to two large rooms, each with three windows, which were probably used for formal social occasions. Possibly they ended up as "cabi-

The walls and ceiling of the square tiled cellar, spanned by three cross vaults, are completely covered with Dutch tiles from various manufactories, decorated with varied, mainly biblical motifs.

nets" within two apartments, as in each case they are adjacent to smaller rooms, with direct access to the "lavatories". On one side is the princess's "cabinet", and on the other, that of the Prussian King Friedrich I. Henriette Catharina's nephew was one of the most distinguished visitors to the palace. It is also certain that the room on the ground floor north-east of the stairwell on the courtyard side was used as a reception or audience room. Here, three rooms are linked by the enfilade, customary in baroque palaces. This makes it possible to look right through a set of rooms when the doors, all aligned along a single axis, are open. It also gives access to one of the most distinguished places in the palace, the Tea-Room in the north wing. As no source material is available, it is only possible to speculate about the arrangement of the apartments in the "corps de logis", intended for King Friedrich I, family members and other guests, and consisting of "cabinet, chamber and dressing room".

One of the most elegantly decorated rooms in the palace, the "gallery", was presumably in the south wing. Two crystal

chandeliers, 27 mirrors and "Allerhand Pretiosen Vasen, welche klein, auß Agath, Cristall de Roch, Jaspis" (all kinds of precious vases, which were small, of agate, rock crystal, jasper) adorned the room. Its counterpart was the Tea-Room, which still exists today, on the ground floor of the north wing. Its faïence decoration was plundered in the war – 103 vases, flasks, pyramids, obelisks, jugs and lidded boxes from Frankfurt or Delft, mainly extremely rare – but the mighty stucco ceilings, the costly leather wall hangings, mirrors and chairs survived. Very few examples of leather wall hangings, as hung in the early 18th century, mostly from the Netherlands, can match the quality found in the Tea-Room in Schloss Oranienbaum. The principal models for the lavishly decorated and furnished room were the porcelain cabinet in Oranienburg and the famous rooms in Henriette Catharina's parents' residences, designed by Daniel Marot.

The well-equipped kitchens described in the Inventarium and other documents also suggest how lavishly the house was fitted out. For example, there was a "Conditorey" for the manufacture of sweetmeats, a jam kitchen for preparing the citrus fruit grown at the palace, which has also survived intact, and another kitchen especially for the princess. The description of the interior of the "grotto" in the garden gives an idea of the extravagant luxury and excess of decorative and furnishing items. This building, which may have been on the north side of the northern domestic wing, no longer exists. It was built of black and white marble and had several rooms, including a bathroom and a princely bedroom. It is said that 36 (!) paintings, along with other precious items, hung in the antechamber to the bathroom alone. In another room, a figure is recorded of 254 pieces of Delft ceramics on four étagères, quantities that are almost incomprehensible today. The "tiled cellar", which has changed very little, is a treasure. It is in the basement under the portico, was accessible from the garden, and was used as a dining room on warm summer days. It is unique for such a large, completely tiled room to be used for this purpose; even in the Netherlands, one only finds considerably smaller, completely tiled rooms in a few 17th and 18th century palaces, such as the Het Loo Palace in Apeldoorn. They are usually used as kitchens, in some cases as orange kitchens.

The surviving decorations and the records make it clear how very keen Henriette Catharina was to preserve some of the lavish courtly atmosphere of her youth while she was in far-away Dessau. Setting up guest rooms, above all for her chil-

The ceiling stucco on the top floor of the palace, dating from c. 1685, is of great art-historical importance. It was probably the work of Giovanni Simonetti, the most outstanding early and high baroque stucco artist in central Germany.

Right hand page ‣ The Teegesellschaft (Tea-Party) by Abraham Snaphaen, dating from 1686, shows Henriette Catharina's daughters in a room of the kind that could well be imagined in Schloss Oranienbaum in the 17th century.

dren, shows how important contact with her immediate family was. Henriette continued to see herself, similarly to her mother before her, residing in the Huis ten Bosch, as the centre of that family. And setting aside an apartment for the King of Prussia and her readiness to receive visitors from Saxony, which was so close to Oranienbaum, of whom the Augustus the Strong, the Elector, was probably the most famous, goes one step further to show how important it was for her to maintain connections with her Brandenburg kinsfolk and thus secure her closest allies.

Henriette Catharina was able to look back in her old age on a full, rich life. She had rendered considerable service as the mother of a large family and as the ruler of her state. Her son continued her rationally determined, responsible qualities, so that at the end of her reign, Anhalt-Dessau, formerly weakened and impoverished, had become a flourishing country. It was Henriette Catharina who used the opportunities available to her to prepare the ground for the enlightened statesmanship that Prince Franz was to introduce a few decades later, and which was to produce the famous Garden Realm. Franz was very well aware of the credit due to her. He had a complete ceiling painting of the apotheosis of the House of Orange removed from the Stadtschloss in Dessau and refitted in the prestigious summer hall in the Gothic House in Wörlitz. Under it, marble busts of Friedrich Heinrich of Orange-Nassau and his son Wilhelm II, by François Dieussart, from the Oranienbaum garden grotto, were placed in neo-Gothic framed niches. Showing respect in this way does not only show how proud Prince Franz was of his origins. It is at the same time also to be understood as a memorial, that the enlightened prince was setting to the House of Orange, in the very house in his Garden Realm that brings Europe's most famous rulers together in over 100 portraits.

The bronze door-knocker on the door facing the garden side is one of
the many original components that make the house so charming – the
lion is the symbol of the House of Orange.

Dutch garden and English Landscape

The first phase of the Oranienbaum garden was created in accordance with plans by the Dutch architect Cornelis Ryckwaert (1662-1693). He was commissioned in 1681/83 by the Anhalt princess, Henriette Catharina, to create the Dutch-baroque ensemble of town, palace and garden. The choice of location for the dower-house could probably be traced back to the hermitage, then in a state of disrepair, which Princess Agnes of Anhalt (1606-1650) had had built near the village of Nischwitz. The task of creating the gardens for the newly founded palace, planned from 1673 and sealed by the laying of the foundation stone in 1683, was placed in the hands of one Jacob de Grande from 1687 to 1704. Presumably he, like the architect, was a Dutchman. As in the palace, work in the garden proceeded only very haltingly; the architect Christoph Pitzler's 1696 travel diary confirms that the northern sections, with the canal and the island garden, were still missing at this time. In any case, the

system of ditches around the palace island, excavated by Dutch hydraulic engineers, only became possible when the Schleesen and Goltewitz brooks were diverted to Oranienbaum in 1708/09. The plans had been altered frequently by the time the princess died and the garden was still not completed. Her son Leopold (1676-1747) brought the work to a conclusion and in 1714, with 60 specimens, also laid the foundation stone for the major collection of citrus plants, which had a crucial impact on the effect made by the garden. The last of these plants was not lost until late spring 1961, when it perished due to an error by the gardener responsible.

A very vivid plan of the garden based on a precise earlier survey, dates from 1719. A. Berger's coloured pen and ink drawing shows the complete Dutch-baroque ensemble of city, palace and garden, 36 years after the foundation stone was laid. The only

earlier depiction of the whole complex is the one made by Bosse in 1695. The garden, which existed from 1719 onwards and was mature by 1783, was made up of eight distinct parts, and this structure was retained until the landscape changes made at the time of Prince Franz. The core of the first complex was the palace island, surrounded by a moat and running from east to west. On the town side it was attached to the market by a drawbridge. The palace with its stable buildings surrounded the "cour d'honneur" and a square for coaches. Between this complex and the ditch were house-gardens, in which decorative cabinets originally surrounded by trellises, an orange garden and a playground were arranged. This is also where the first oranges were placed, around a pool of water by a grotto.

From the palace island, a narrow bridge ran south and north into the kitchen and canal garden respectively, and to the west,

The best view of the central part of the formerly transversely structured Dutch parterre is from the gallery of the palace. Prince Franz restricted it to a third of its original area and simplified the articulation and decorative elements of the initially very differentiated two-dimensional and

formal designs. The baroque dolphin fountain, reconstructed in 1998, forms the centre of the remains of the parterre area, which is decorated with potted plants.

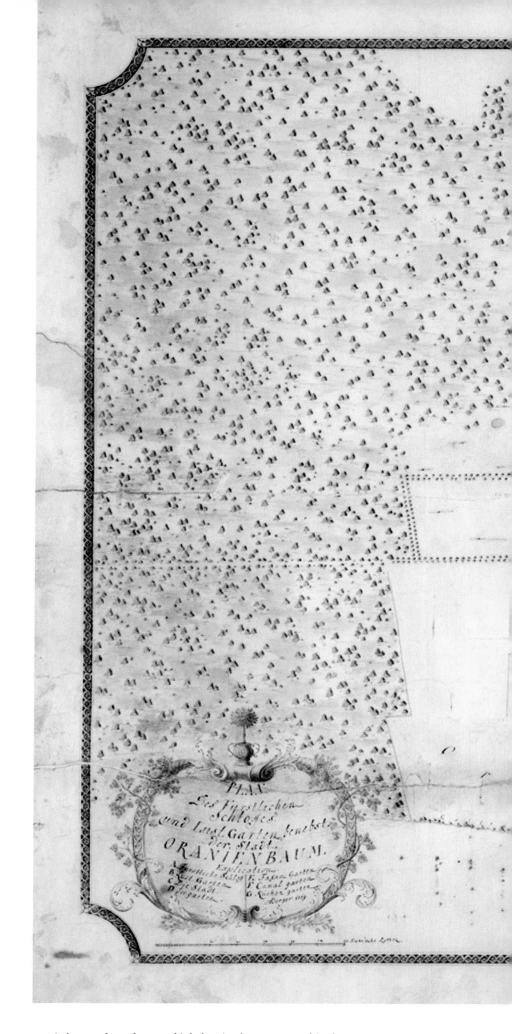

Oranienbaum, coloured pen and ink drawing by A. Berger. This plan, drawn in 1719, shows the Dutch baroque ensemble of town, palace and garden upon completion.

a broad stone bridge led to the broderie parterre. This creative highlight of the garden, on the main axis of the palace, was structured into four regular compartments and decorated with box edging, beds and sculptures. Towards the wooded areas in the west, the garden was edged with "Franzbäume" (trimmed fruit-trees with small crowns); this is where the princess picked her own fruit when practising her jam-making skills. A dolphin fountain provides the accent in the parterre. Restoration of this was made possible in 1998 with the support of the Dutch government. South of the parterre was the maze, and on the north side the very elaborate island garden (also pool garden), based on Dutch and Italian ideas. The three islands are surrounded by a rectangular system of canals and linked by bridges. The centre island is round, the outer ones are square. On the west side the garden was bordered by a fenced area of woodland; here, game was kept for hunting purposes. A hermitage from the previous complex was to be found in it.

Prince Franz neglected Oranienbaum; its regular design ran counter to his views on landscape design. In his day, it was mainly used for hunting in autumn. Prince Franz started to redesign the periphery of the garden in about 1793, thus creating a transition to the surrounding countryside. He turned the austerely structured island garden into an English-Chinese garden. Franz made use of the conditions provided by the previous arrangement, in which three regularly structured islands, enclosed by a canal, were accessible over bridges. The English architect and garden theorist William Chambers's requirement that "one and the same character should always dominate all parts of the composition", led to the tripartite island garden being modelled as a Chinese island landscape. The gaps between the islands were filled in and the garden planted accordingly. The canal on the south side remained unchanged at first, but the canal on the north bank was widened to form a pool and the shoreline acquired natural, curved lines and was drawn back. The earth from the canal excavations was used to fill in the gaps between the large islands, but some of it was used for modelling on the northern periphery and for the pagoda mound. In this way, the view across the open countryside was restricted to just a few aspects, and concluded the Chinese garden on the north side. When the pagoda mound was being built, an ice cellar and a tunnel vault were constructed at ground level on the site of the original pheasantry, and the mound was raised to the height of the foot of the pagoda. The differentiated expanse of water and the islands, decorated with stones, made it possible to fit in various

Chinese House, also called the Tea-House, in the English-Chinese garden in Oranienbaum. The Chinese character "ji", which can be translated as "happiness", is written above the door of the entrance porch facing the island.

Right-hand page ▸ Seville orange (Citrus aurantium). Citrus cultivation, which is difficult even for experienced gardeners, has been one of the essential skills required of those tending Oranienbaum ever since. They are grown as potted plants and intended to decorate the garden in summer.

For use and adornment: orangeries

Ludwig Trauzettel

The word "orangery" refers on the one hand to the structure in which the tender southern plants are accommodated, and, on the other hand, to the current stock of any collection of such plants. Orangeries have adorned northern gardens since the Renaissance. They made it possible to bring flora from southern areas to the cool north, demonstrating their owners' interest in botany as well as their wealth. Anyone who could afford to construct a building just for plants, to provide the necessary heat and care for their cultivation and decorate the table with exotic fruit, must have had more than adequate funds. Here we are not just talking about oranges and other citrus plants; the term "orangery" covered all the plants that could not be cultivated all the year round in the open air and were thus protected indoors under temperate conditions for a time. The fashion of the day and availability of the plants led to collections that were built up over centuries.

The history of orangeries started with the so-called "temporary" plant houses erected over citrus cultures planted in the ground in the winter to afford them some meagre protection from frost. To save the twice-yearly construction work these entailed, the plants soon started to be grown in tubs and cultivated in winter in ventilated, lit and heated orangeries. Unlike Oranienbaum, where the orangery was used only for keeping plants, baroque orangeries were generally also used in summer for magnificent court festivities. Even though each of the Anhalt-Dessau gardens contains an orangery, these buildings fell out of fashion elsewhere with the development of the landscape garden. It was only the invention of cast iron and the development of modern heating technology in the late 19th century that brought a new heyday for the cultivation of exotic plants. However, there are no metal and glass hothouses in Dessau-Wörlitz.

Today, very few orangeries are still used for their original purpose, even though orangery culture is a crucial factor in garden conservation and essential to the understanding of old garden culture: baroque effects and sense of space can be conveyed to today's visitors only by setting out orangery plants and through the original cultivation techniques. The only surviving orangery replanting tower in Germany to survive outside Oranienbaum, is in Darmstadt. This technical building monument, restored in 1996 together with the orangery, was needed for re-potting the huge old citrus plants.

Of the many citrus species and types, the Seville orange (citrus aurantium) was best suited for cultivation in orangeries north of the Alps, as this species flourished well in this climate and could also be used. In 1882, the Oranienbaum court gardener Dietrich Kleewitz reporting harvesting 2425 of the finest fruit. The regular yield led to commercial use of parts of the citrus plants in the 19th century. Fruit and blossoms were used to make liqueurs and confectionery. The coveted orange sugar was made by boiling the plucked flower petals in sugar solution. And the Friedrich company of Oranienbaum has been producing stomach bitters from orange-blossom since 1864. Hallervorden reported that every year, despite the sale of many kilos of blossom, the oranges still blossomed and fruited among the dark foliage of the citrus crowns.

Inside the orangery, the typical Anhalt "baker's oven heating", which runs from behind the walls, and the ventilators in the ceiling provided an ideal climate for the overwintering of the valuable plants.

The window rack, with the warmer temperatures under the ceiling, offered a space-saving position for the tender young plants, which needed a lot of light.

Chinese-style bridges and gave the garden a lighter quality, illumination for its mirror effects and an exotic feel. William Chambers's book, *Designs of Chinese Buildings, Furniture, Dresses, Machines, and Utensils*, published in 1757, had already been used for ideas on furniture, wall hangings and spatial design for the Chinese designs in certain palace rooms in Wörlitz and Oranienbaum. His three major works were once again referred to for the new design of the Chinese garden in the 90s. As well as the five-storey pagoda and the Chinese House, furniture, Chinese figures and two Chinese gondolas were intended to help reinforce the exotic effect suggested by Chambers and to meet his demands for variety and sublimity in this garden experience. The Chinese character was particularly underlined by the erection of the dominant, upward-tapering pagoda and the Chinese House, which stands half in the water. The construction of these buildings was overseen by the prince's director of buildings Georg Christoph Hesekiel (1732-1818), following instructions and sketches by Prince Franz. The Oranienbaum court gardener Wilhelm Neumark directed the changes to the gardens between 1793 and 1797.

During the reign of Prince Franz, the previously strictly baroque maze garden, as well as the Chinese garden, were adapted to the rural design style and restructured by tree planting. This meant that the original north-south orientation of the three linked

Baroque garden art

Ludwig Trauzettel

Baroque gardens are also called French gardens, as the best-known example of feudal and absolutist garden art was developed under France's King Louis XIV (1638-1715) in Versailles. They are formal gardens, characterized by regular, geometrically articulated outdoor spaces, usually oriented towards the royal palace.

From the Middle Ages, design forms in the garden were dominated by geometrical principles. In the baroque phase, these climaxed in the fact that the garden and its design elements were matched to strict architectural forms. The outside areas were seen as an extension of palace architecture. The view taken at the time was that plants grew too freely and independently for this, and consequently trees and hedges were trimmed to conform with the architecture. Natural flowing water was forced into geometrical pools at the designer's will. This was intended to express absolute rule, in other words domination of nature as well.

In Versailles, the greatest work of the royal landscape gardener André Le Nôtre (1613-1700), the central point of the whole complex is the king's bedroom in the central section of the magnificent palace. All the paths, sight lines and symmetries relate to this focal point in the architecture. Forced to be part of a system in this way, nature was brought right up to the central palace building and then inside it; conversely, the garden became an outdoor continuation of the palace architecture's axes.

The emergence of the French garden meant that landscape gardening achieved recognition as an art genre in its own right – it became an acknowledged science. Thus, green exterior architecture developed into an art whose spatial framework within the complex was structured by parterres, boskets, avenues, canals and architectural decoration. The baroque avenue took the gardens of the day into the surrounding landscape and woods, thus expanding the garden into the country. The garden itself was intended to create levels and, especially, to reflect the sky with its linear structures and long water axes. The mirror effect and the illusion that the main axis was connected with the line of the horizon reinforce this. Hence French baroque complexes are oriented essentially in one direction, via this main axis from the palace outwards into "infinity".

France's influence on 17th and 18th century European gardens cannot be denied, but nevertheless baroque gardens in other European countries developed in different ways according to the prevailing conditions there. Palaces in the Netherlands were usually surrounded by wide moats, in the fortress tradition and because the terrain was usually wet, had to be drained before any building could be done, in other words were built on an artificial island. The individual parts of the garden, the parterre, fruit and vegetable gardens, were grouped around this. These gardens have no main axis stretching to infinity; rather, they are often articulated transversely, as the Oranienbaum garden was at first.

The island garden in Oranienbaum, originally called a pool garden, is a typical element of the Dutch garden tradition. Geometrical islands are arranged adjacent to each other within a rectangular overall plan of a divided-off section of the garden. The fact that in Oranienbaum the central island area is round, is seen as a possible Italian Renaissance influence (Villa Lante).

In the Netherlands, for topographical reasons, baroque avenue art had the function of structuring space, as there was scarcely any opportunity there to create spaces through terracing or steps. The mistress of Oranienbaum appointed architects and gardeners from Holland to create the garden here, presumably prompted by ideas and specimen designs by the Dutch artist Daniel Marot (1661-1752) and his garden at the Zeist palace, which she had got to know on her visit to Holland in 1696/97. So, when she died, the still incomplete gardens were an example of Dutch baroque landscape architecture, in which were incorporated Ryckwaert's basic designs, with his emphasized transverse axis and the three adjacent garden areas.

parterre areas was abolished. From 1812, Carlo Ignazio Pozzi built the 178 metre orangery, but this was not completed until 1818, under Duke Leopold Friedrich, because of the turmoil of war. The adjacent service area for horticultural work came into being, to meet the needs of the increased number of potted plants. In the 19th century, over 550 citrus plants were cultivated, after the original collections had been complemented by the stocks inherited from Schloss Friederikenberg.

New design in following decades again changed the effect made by the garden. Two important parts of the complex as a whole were lost. The site of the former canal garden, north of the Schlossinsel, now accommodates a school, and the kitchen garden is occupied by residential and commercial buildings. The work of the first garden director of the Joachim Ernst Foundation was of major significance for the restoration of horticultural art in Oranienbaum. Hans Hallervorden (1872-1965) tried to restore the original baroque structure to the remaining central areas between 1927 and 1938, after years of nothing but forestry work and the associated return of the gardens to a state of wilderness. He got rid of changes that had been introduced lat-

er, and altered the appearance of the complex, without removing the design changes made by Prince Franz. His work concentrated first on reinstating baroque structures and peripheries in the area of the "cours d'honneur" (court of honour), the parterre and the garden axes. Basing his work on the "Berger plan", which he had turned to for assistance, 2240 metres of hedge was replanted.

This restored the effect of a baroque structure, but emphasizing and planting the central Dessau axis changed and distorted the character of the gardens as a whole. The trend towards cultivation, introduced by Hallervorden and pursued into the 1980s, was replaced by efforts to restore horticulturally valuable developments following the character of particular periods of origin. This is still behind the work today. So the basic structure of the English-Chinese garden is once again discernible since restoration took place between 1991 and 1994. The intended restoration of baroque design to the Schlossinsel (Palace Island), which will be possible only after the palace itself has been restored, is to be concluded in the west with the replanted baroque avenue of limes.

In 1994, the bridge of rocks in the Chinese garden in Oranienbaum was reconstructed from a copperplate engraving in Johann Christian Grohmann's garden magazine, published in 1799. When the erratic stones in the artificial cliff slipped about a hundred years earlier, the bridge collapsed and was forgotten.

Oranienbaum

The pagoda, also called the bell tower because it is decorated with little bells, was erected between 1794 and 1797. Prince Franz had it built on the edge of the Chinese garden as a viewing tower and view-point.

It stands raised on an artificial mound above an ice-cellar that was originally filled with broken ice from the stretches of water in the Chinese garden.

61

Reinhard Melzer

The town of the golden oranges

The town of Oranienbaum is not an organism that developed over the centuries, but rather was created all at once. It is a planned complex, and owes its existence and design to a princely desire to build. Henriette Catharina had the old village of Nischwitz pulled down and the little baroque town of Oranienbaum built in the Dutch style; its size and ground plan are governed by the palace. Thus it is related to many residences completed at the same time, such as Karlsruhe, Ludwigslust or Oranienburg. The town with its basic geometrical pattern, dominated by the emphatic positioning of the palace, is a manifestation of the ruler's claim to power and like all these planned towns, reflects an order seen as sent by God, expressing the Utopia of a blessed power in community life that extended from antiquity to the 18th century. "The purest embodiment of Dutch culture in Anhalt is the town and palace of Oranienbaum" (J. Harksen).

The old place-name was replaced by "Oranienbaum" in 1673. The town started to grow when the foundation stone for Schloss Oranienbaum was laid on 8 July, 1683. The Dutch master builder, Cornelis Ryckwaert, was responsible for planning both the town and the palace. Johann Christoph Beckmann wrote appositely in his work *Historie des Fürstenthums Anhalt* in 1710: "The little town is in itself quite regular, and the buildings are also arranged in a form; the market is in a straight prospect down from the palace, in the middle of which there is also a pleasing fountain." The little town developed opposite the palace, following a regular right-angled structure. It was as wide as the palace and garden, and arranged around the market-place, which was planted with double rows of lime trees. At the centre of the urban structure is the symbol that has stood in the market place since 1719 – a sandstone urn with an orange-tree in it. The town

could not spread far to the east because of the immediate proximity of the borders of Electoral Saxony. For this reason, Prince Leopold built the church and other quarters between 1707 and 1712, as the southern conclusion of the transverse axis, at right angles to the palace and at the same distance from the market place. This is a special feature in the town's planning structure, as actually palace and church should be on the same axis. The individual buildings in the 12 quarters were of uniform and prescribed height. Only a few buildings were allowed two storeys. This served to emphasize the palace and the church as features of the town. The building of the church concluded the baroque town expansion.

The little Lutheran church to the north of the palace was not built until 1750, and is not part of this town plan.

The church was conceived for both the town and the court. In 1707, Prince Leopold and his family officially laid the

The Schlosskirche, built between 1707 and 1712, with the protruding entrance section on the north side. It is one on the most important Protestant preaching churches of the baroque period, and has survived largely intact.

63

and has been paid far too little attention. Essential to the form was the introduction of the reformed denomination in Dessau in 1596, the revocation of the Edict of Nantes in 1685, which brought the Huguenots to Germany, and the close family ties with Holland and Electoral Brandenburg brought about by marriage. Calvinism relates differently to the house of God from other denominations. "The key to reformed church architecture is the conviction that Christianity does not need dedicated spaces for its worship ... reasons of appropriateness to function alone govern church architecture, and only use makes a space sacred ... For the Reformed Church, the church building is not where God resides ... it contains the space in which the congregation can comfortably carry out its worship. And the pulpit has shifted into the centre of this building because of the overwhelming value of the interpretation of the scriptures and instruction through the word. The altar is merely a table on which communion is taken and baptism celebrated; it is not the place of sacrifice" (Cornelius Gurlitt). The Oranienbaum church emerged from this reformed spirit. Frequent reference has been made to Anhalt architecture's dependence on Holland. But for church architecture in Anhalt, and especially for the Protestant centrally-planned church, Huguenot influences seem to have been rather more dominant. An important predecessor of the pure preaching church, the "Temple de Lyon, nommé Paradis" , in other words the famous 1564 Paradise Temple, provides the original form. Otherwise a pure, elliptical ground plan as in Oranienbaum, whose internal structure, without additions of any kind, is not broken up, having only a simple, continuous gallery, is not to be found anywhere else outside the area. As this form was built five times in Anhalt in the reign of Prince Leopold, it does not seem to have emerged by chance, but expresses a conscious architectural intention, which certainly came from Leopold. Walter Mai wrote: "... the church in Oranienbaum is impressive because of its deliberately simple but spatially sensitive design, apparently based on the idea of the French Huguenots' prayer room, and bringing this model into German baroque architecture."

foundation stone for this church, which was important for his reign in both urban and art-historical terms. As was also the case with the founding of other churches, the prince linked the new building with a votive intention, namely that "in memory of and as grateful thanks for the many happy successes granted to him in his glorious military campaigns, a larger church (was to) be built in a more convenient place." The church was consecrated in 1712. The only changes to its interior appearance came about when an organ was installed in 1766/67, along with its organ choir, thrusting convexly into the interior space, and when renovation was undertaken in 1905/06. Otherwise, the church has largely been faithfully maintained in its original form. The building has an elliptical ground plan, with the altar and pulpit in the narrow eastern curve. The church, like the Georgenkirche in Dessau, the village churches in Norkitten, Wadendorf and Alten, is a centrally-planned Protestant preaching church. This special form had developed in the country under Prince Leopold – a centrally configured structure on an elliptical ground plan. This was an independent achievement in 18th century Protestant church architecture in Central Germany,

The elliptical church interior with surrounding gallery and the organ choir, added later in 1766/67.

Right-hand page ▸ The stylized wrought-iron orange tree in the market place in Oranienbaum symbolizes the fruitful link between the two houses of Orange-Nassau and Anhalt-Dessau.

Reinhard Melzer

The "Alter Dessauer" (The Old Dessauer)

The lands of Anhalt were ruled by over 46 princes from the 16th century, and some of them have won an enduring place in general historical awareness through their lifetime achievements: Prince Leopold of Köthen (1694-1728), a patron of Johann Sebastian Bach, and his ancestor Ludwig (1579-1650), the founder of the "Order of the Palm". And Prince Leopold III Friedrich Franz of Anhalt-Dessau (1740-1817), the creator of the Garden Realm and Christian I of Anhalt-Bernburg (1568-1630), a diplomat and warrior in the Thirty Years War, also count amongst them. The most popular of all Anhalt's rulers is undoubtedly Prince Leopold I of Anhalt-Dessau (1676-1747), whose life and deeds were closely linked with the rise of Brandenburg/Prussia to become a great European power. And because German national history has long been written from a Prussian perspective, Leopold's works acquired national dimensions. So until 1945, the Hall of Fame

in the Berlin Zeughaus contained a large painting of the Battle of Turin and a bust in his honour, and even today his deeds are part of German history's treasury of images and anecdotes. These include, for example, a prayer that the elderly field marshal probably never uttered in this form. He had been driven on by denigrating letters from Friedrich II, the young King of Prussia, and is said to have called out, furiously and god-fearingly at the same time, before his troops at the Battle of Kesselsdorf on 15 December, 1745: "Oh God, stand graciously by me today, or if that be not Thy will, then at least do not help that rascal, the enemy, but see to it all." Leopold I of Anhalt-Dessau, the "Alter Dessauer", is still as popular as Frederick the Great and Augustus the Strong. Leopold's fame and historical significance are based on his military career, as he is seen as one of the most important early 18th century generals. This has meant that his extraordi-

nary achievements as the ruler of his country have been forgotten. It was his restructuring in economic and social fields that laid the basis for reforms by his grandson Prince Leopold III Friedrich Franz. This grandson was also responsible for the terse but apposite description of the prince on a marble relief from the monument in the Wörlitz gardens. "Creator of the Prussian warrior breed. Statesman."

Leopold was born on 3 July, 1776 in the Dessau Schloss, as the ninth child of Johann Georg II and Henriette Catharina, a princess of Orange-Nassau. Through his mother, Leopold was first cousin of the first Prussian King Friedrich and the English King William. His parents had long hoped for a son to secure the Dessau-Ascanian male line. In 1695, at the age of 19, he fought for the first time at the siege of Naumur in the War of the League of Augsburg (1688-1697), and was appointed major-general there.

Oranienbaum

Hermann Prell, *Leopold von Dessau und die Anna Liese*, 1888 oil painting. This scene is based on an anecdote according to which the prince, returning from his journey to Italy in 1695, did not go back to the palace first, but rode past it to his childhood sweetheart, the daughter of the apothecary Föhsin.

After the death of his father in 1693, his mother became regent on behalf of her son, who had not yet come of age, but his father's Anhalt regiment was put under his command immediately. Leopold did not start to govern his country until 13 May, 1698. In the same year he married Anna Louise Föhse, the daughter of a Dessau apothecary, who had been his companion since childhood. This marriage, which was not in keeping with his social standing, but happy, contributed considerably to his popularity and legend. Emperor Leopold I raised Anna Louise to the princedom of the Reich in 1701. This meant that Leopold's and Anna Louise's children – they had ten – were legally capable of being heirs. King Friedrich I of Prussia made Leopold Governor of Magdeburg in 1701. The city was Prussia's most important fortress at the time; in times of danger, both the court and valuables were moved from Berlin to Magdeburg.

Leopold did not serve only Prussia, but the Emperor and the Empire as well. He was appointed to the prime post of Imperial Field Marshal in 1745. This meant that in the course of his life, as well as being ruler of his country, he had held the most important military offices and honours: regimental commander, governor, Prussian Field Marshal (from 1712), Imperial Field Marshal. And he had played a crucial role in

wars as sub-commander and as a general, acting independently: the War of the League of Augsburg (1688-1697), the War of the Spanish Succession (1701-1713), the Nordic War at the Siege of Stralsund (1715) and the first two Silesian Wars (1740-1745). His reputation as a war commander of European status was made at the two battles of Höchstädt, in 1703 and 1704. In the Battle of Cassano in 1705, the fearless, brave, but also fame-seeking Leopold sacrificed over 1000 Prussian troops, which almost cost him his command of the army corps, and in 1706 he led the Prussian troops at the relief of Turin. Leopold and the Prussian Crown Prince Wilhelm both took part in the Battle of Malplaquet in 1709, at which the Duke of Marlborough defeated Louis XIV's troops. From then on, Leopold and the later King Friedrich Wilhelm I were firm friends, which meant that the Anhalt prince not only greatly influenced the monarch, but also Prussian history. The Soldier King's successor, Friedrich II, was much less in sympathy with Leopold, even though he called him "the great war mechanic of the Prussian army". Leopold was already a military legend when Friedrich came to the throne. And so tensions arose very quickly between the young king, eager for action, and the methodical field marshal. The king gradually withdrew Leopold's privileges. Even though he

Johann Joseph Freidhoff, after an original by Antoine Pesne, *Leopold I Prince of Anhalt Dessau at the Victory of Aire Ao in 1710*, mezzotint from the Chalkographische Gesellschaft Dessau, 1798.

Like all the sons of Prince Leopold I, Leopold II Maximilian also served in the Prussian army (as a field marshal). His son, Prince Franz, incorporated this 1748 painting by Pesne into the pictorial programme for the dining room in the Wörlitzer Landhaus.

was the highest-ranking officer he was not used for the invasion of Silesia (16.11.1740), and he was not given command of an observation army until 1741 – on the borders of Brandenburg. This less than honourable treatment led Leopold to resign his commission in 1742. His resignation was not accepted. Leopold played only a peripheral role in the second Silesian War as well, until he was given command of over 30,000 men on 7 November, 1745, with whom he invaded Saxony. The decisive victory at Kesselsdorf then provided a glorious end to his military career. Leopold died in the palace at Dessau on 9 April, 1747.

As governor of Magdeburg, he had directed the expansion of the city to make it Prussia's largest fortress. The city, which still seemed medieval at the time, was broken up inside the fortifying walls and the previous urban structure replaced with broad, light, regular streets and parade grounds, and also prestigious baroque buildings. As a member of the royal building commission he exercised considerable influence over the design of the city. The Fürstenwall (Prince's Rampart) and the Neuer Markt (New Market) with its baroque palace made a particular impact on the cityscape. He arranged for the Dutch fortress architect Gerhard Cornelius von Walrave to be entrusted with building the fortifications. Leopold was always interested in technological solutions, and he is to be thanked for building up an effective troop of engineers in the Prussian army. He was directly responsible for the following military innovations: the iron ramrod, marching in step and the concentrated use of platoon firing. As ruler of his country, Leopold was responsible for many reforms in his 50-year reign, which rightly earned him the title of "statesman", bestowed by his grandson. Shortly after his accession, he withdrew the right of co-determination from the landed classes in 1698 and insisted on principles of absolute rule. He instituted a new census in 1702 and was thus able to levy new taxes and increase state income. The introduction of excise (indirect taxation of consumption) in 1704 served the same end.

Leopold also continued his father's pro-Jewish policies. He settled increasing numbers of Jews and conferred privileges on wealthy Jews. Moses Mendelssohn was born in the local Jewish community in 1729.

There is no doubt that the land cultivation measures taken were the prince's most significant land policy achievements. Villages and outlying farms were established under the protection of the newly constructed Elbe barriers, thus pursuing "Peuplierung", the settlement of the land. These new places included Lennewitz in 1700, Alten in 1704, Kochstedt, Naundorf-Waldersee and Dellnau-Mildensee in 1706, Horstdorf in 1708, Siebenhausen and Ziebigk in 1709, Kleinkühnau in 1710, Lingenau and Niesau in 1713, Marke in 1727, Münsterberg in 1745, Brandhorst in 1747. When the Kapengraben was constructed (1706-08), the whole of the Wörlitzer Winkel could be opened up for agricultural use. The Kapengraben and the great Elbe barrier of 1707 and 1735/38 respectively are lasting land cultivation achievements.

Extensive building activities that have not yet been adequately researched, developed in the prince's long reign. One striking feature is the many churches he had built: the Johanniskirche in Dessau in 1702, the Stadtkirche in Radegast in 1703/04, the village church in Rehsen in 1707, the Stadt- and Schlosskirche in Oranienbaum in 1704-12, the Georgenkirche in Dessau in 1712-17, the village church in Horstdorf in 1712-14, the village church in Meilendorf in 1717, the village church in Jonitz in 1722-25, the village church in Tornau in 1723, the village church in Norkitten in 1731-33, the village church in Wadendorf in 1735, the village church in Alten in 1743, the village church in Riesigk in 1746. Young building timber was used for these houses of God, which is probably why they were very unstable, and many of them had to be rebuilt. Prince Leopold III Friedrich Franz took advantage of this to build his churches, characterizing his Garden Realm, in the neo-Gothic style.

Prince Leopold worked particularly hard on beautifying Dessau's buildings. As well as the excise wall, which was erected in 1704, he added the Wasserstadt on the other bank of the Mulde in 1706. Above all in 1712/13 he started to develop Leipziger Strasse and Dessau's new high street, Kavalierstrasse. Buildings like the "Holland" (chancellery building), the riding school, the pleasure gardens and individual town houses in Kavalierstrasse made the town look like a baroque residence. He had the north wing of the Renaissance palace complex pulled down, thus opening his palace up to the town.

From 1706, Prince Leopold started to buy up debts on the overburdened noblemen's estates in his country. This meant that Anhalt-Dessau lost the tranche of rural feudal aristocracy that was typical of the times. Leopold transformed their agricultural businesses into a leasehold economy. Anhalt-Dessau became a gigantic area of tenanted farms. Even though this practice was not as successful as Leopold had promised himself, Anhalt-Dessau was nevertheless a prosperous, small German state when he died.

II

MOSIGKAU

Wolfgang Savelsberg

Schloss Mosigkau –
a rococo pearl

"The little Sanssouci" ‣ Schloss Mosigkau is only a few kilometres west of the centre of Dessau. It is the only late baroque
palace building in Central Germany to have survived largely
intact. It is celebrated as the most architecturally perfect
building of the rococo age in Anhalt, and popularly known
with affectionate respect as "the little Sanssouci". Even
though this building, started in 1752, cannot measure up to
the grandiose splendour and dimensions of the Potsdam
palace built only a few years before by Frederick the Great,
the unexpectedly high artistic quality of the interior and the
works of art exhibited are still surprising. Some of the artist-
craftsmen who worked in Mosigkau were from the school of
the most important Potsdam sculptors and stucco artists
Friedrich Christian Glume and Johann Christian Hoppenhaupt, or followed their approach, and so the sculptural and
interior decoration show close parallels with the rococo of

the age of Frederick the Great. Stylistic comparisons also display hints of the architectural style of Georg Wenzeslaus von Knobelsdorff, Frederick's architect and the builder of Sanssouci. It is to be assumed that the woman who commissioned the building of Mosigkau, Anna Wilhelmine (1715-1780), was in touch with the famous Prussian architect a few years before building started, as he had been commissioned by her brother, Leopold II Maximilian Prince of Anhalt-Dessau, to rebuild the residence in Dessau.

A "maison de plaisance" comes into being ▸ The right conditions for the glittering palace and gardens were created when Prince Leopold I of Anhalt-Dessau presented his 27-year-old, unmarried daughter, Anna Wilhelmine, with the Stubenrauch estate on the western edge of the village of Mosigkau in 1742, with all its rights and associated lands.

The handsome annual apanage of 15,000 reichstalers that the father willed to his daughter when he died, will have reinforced her intentions to build the palace. Anna Wilhelmine was particularly interested in architecture and had an outstanding knowledge of fine art. This, and an intense desire for prestige and esteem, probably influenced by the lavish building work undertaken by the grandmother, Princess Henriette Catharina, who built Schloss Oranienbaum, may have led Anna Wilhelmine to tackle this large, ambitious project. As well as this, her lack of attachment and concomitant liberation from family duties may have been an additional motive for her commitment. More recent research makes it increasingly clear that the princess not only organized the entire building process, but also involved herself to a considerable extent in planning the interior design of the building.

Mosigkau

When travelling through the village of Mosigkau on the way from Dessau, two orangeries appear on the right-hand side, and between them the eye is led through the wrought-iron south gate along the central axis to the south façade of the palace.

The architectural concept had to be adapted to a plot of land that was wet, and with a width of 72 metres by a length of 440 metres, extremely narrow, and thus anything but ideal for such an elaborate complex. According to a garden plan from the building period, which survives only as a photograph, the precise centre of the plot, which runs north-south, was chosen for the palace buildings, which have survived in their entirety, so that the "corps de logis" could be placed transversely like a bar. The almost square courtyard was to be developed to the north. Two free-standing pavilions placed at right angles to the main building and two adjacent domestic wings set back by the width of the pavilions were to provide the architectural frame. An elaborate pleasure garden was planned on the south side, while tall pillars topped with urns, with wooden lattices in between, were to separate the courtyard from the "Great Garden" on the north side. However, Dessau's Master Builder, Christian Friedrich Damm, who was commissioned to build the palace from 1752, deviated from the first design, drawn up by an

unknown architect, in several points. The architect had intended there to be a gallery and an orangery in the middle section of the main building, with the staircases in the side wings. Damm took the orangery out of the house and placed the staircase in the middle instead, apparently to gain more living accommodation. Additionally, the planned half-storey above was transformed into a full storey.

These changes of plan permit conjectures about the role Anna Wilhelmine intended the palace to play. She had previously meant the building to be merely a pleasure palace for certain summer celebrations and entertainments, but the new concept suggests that she wanted to use it for more frequent and longer stays with a number of guests in the warm season. Technical restrictions on heating made it impossible to live here after October. As a summer residence, it corresponded with the châteaux developed in France in the 18th century, modelled on Vaux-le-Vicomte, built near Paris by Louis le Vau around 1657. These and the garden palaces that developed from them linked the advantages of a prestigious house with comfortable apartments and the unofficial pavilion offered by garden architecture. This building type represented an ideal synthesis in which a new 18th century ideal, the "commodité", could be realized, the idea of living in a relaxed fashion without major ceremony. So Mosigkau, as a small residential palace in the country, can be called a "maison de plaisance" or "maison de campagne", according to the definitions formulated by Jacques-François Blondel, the leading 18th century architectural theorist. But the combination of intimate small rooms, offering everything needed for courtly pleasures like games, dancing, concerts, literature, supper, tea and conversation, with official rooms like the audience chambers shows that Mosigkau matches these types only to a limited extent. Neither do contemporary reports state that the house was ever the scene of great feasts and extravagant entertainments. This would scarcely have been in keeping with the seriousness of the lady of the house and her general frugality.

A palace takes shape ‣ Schloss Mosigkau was conceived as a complex with three wings. The two storeys of the rendered "corps de logis", eleven window axes wide, with a mansard roof on a U-shaped ground plan, occupy the south end of the almost square court of honour. This is framed on the narrow sides by two lower, two-storey, free-standing pavilions and single-storey domestic wings, adjacent and staggered outwards.

The orange tree in the portrait of Princess Anna Wilhelmine, painted around 1745 by Christian Friedrich Reinhold Lisiewsky, symbolizes her proud Orange origins. It also alludes to her valuable collection of orange plants.

The course of the building work can be reconstructed from bills, material deliveries and work contracts. The first preliminary work started in autumn 1752. In the following spring a start was made on laying the foundations, which consisted of oak trunks and large granite erratics, which were needed because the subsoil was so wet. The high groundwater level presumably ruled out cellars as well. Work on the walls started in August, and the roof was added late in 1754. In the following year, work continued with interior decoration and the domestic wings, which were more urgently needed than the pavilions.

The gardens came into being at the same time as the palace buildings. Their basic conception was probably planned at the same time as the palace. Realization work probably started shortly after the appointment of the gardener, Christoph Friedrich Brosse, in 1754. Two years later, in departure from the original plans for the palace, work started on building the two orangeries at the sides of the south exit from the garden, as is shown by old accounts for delivery of the necessary materials, dated 1756. A first small gardener's house must have been built at this time as well. Its site, only a few metres

west of the orangeries, had been chosen so that the gardener could carry out his heating duties in winter several times a day and also at night. The simple building was either extended or completely rebuilt about 20 years after this.

Overall, the work had progressed so far in 1757 that Anna Wilhelmine was able to move into the palace.

The palace complex ‣ A mere five years of building had produced a palace complex that was only marginally inferior to Oranienbaum. The courtyard side in particular, which visitors come to first through the official east entrance, was impressively monumental. Here, Anna Wilhelmine, entirely in the high baroque spirit, was determined to achieve a prestigious, regal effect. As in many other 18th century German residences, the courtyard side, as an echo of the Grand Siècle, was keen to follow the great model of Versailles. And the dynamic staggering of the individual buildings, along with the lantern that originally topped the main section, does indeed make an impressive impact. The long, low domestic wings, which used to accommodate the stables on the east side, and where the castellan's apartment was later located

The general view from the north makes it clear that, despite the substantial size of the Mosigkau Schloss complex, the predominant impression is one of rural charm, captured here in a painting by Leopold Ahrendts, c. 1825.

on the west side, are simply rendered and plain in form. Considerably more architectural effort went into the two-storey Kavalierpavillons (nobleman's pavilions), which housed the kitchen and laundry, as well as some apartments. The buildings have some cellars and high mansard roofs, originally with dormer windows. The rendered pilaster strips between the windows on the upper floor and the rustication of the lower storeys are still conservative late baroque design devices, while the fact that the pavilions are detached from the "corps de logis" by the width of the building indicates the departure from the centralized system that was already starting in the rococo period.

The two-storey "corps de logis", with its eleven axes and massive mansard roof, refers back to traditional building patterns. Much is similar to the reticent yet imposing air of Saxon palaces in the first half of the 18th century, typical of those designed by Johann Christoph Knöffel, for example. One unusual, indeed spectacular, feature is the monumental portico, reminiscent of Knobelsdorff's Stadtschloss in Potsdam (1744-1751). Its four Ionic half-columns rise through two storeys, to be topped with sculpture above the powerful pediment. Another innovative effect is achieved by the rococo

reduction of baroque decoration on the façade. François Blondel had recommended this more sparing use of architectural articulation and sculptural ornament in his 1737 work on the "maison de plaisance". The only decoration on the walls is the sandstone framing for the windows and the round pilaster strips on the corners, repeating the column motif. The impression of lightness is also not lost by the two side sections of the building, which are drawn slightly forward along three window axes. At the level of the terrace, which is accessed by six steps, thick, fluted sandstone slabs have been added all round the building to emphasize the base, providing a band to tighten the delicate wall. A large mansard roof with four dormer windows rises above the powerful cornice. Originally, the roof was adorned with eleven dormer windows in the lower roof zone and four bull's-eye windows in the upper one, as well as four symmetrically placed chimneys and the high lantern.

A link with the outside – the garden façade ‣ The south façade of the palace, facing the pleasure garden, conveys a very different image from the northern, courtyard side. Its intended effect was different in that it was accessible only to

In 1952, the garden historian and designer Heinrich Sulze tried to reconstruct the parterre in the Mosigkau pleasure garden in this watercolour, drawing on all the available historical sources.

noble acquaintances and close family members and friends of the princess. Visitors coming for business or official reasons or even as petitioners could at best see this side of the house from a distance, and then not completely, from the south gate. Unlike its northern counterpart, the southern façade was intended to impress with its grace and elegance, rather than its monumental quality. This is achieved by devices, including cutting out all ancillary buildings, and by the fact that the three side window axes project only slightly. But the impression of lightness and transparency is conveyed above all by the five French windows of the gallery room that opens the house to the garden. This new relationship between inside and outside is a defining characteristic of rococo summer palace architecture: the palace building and the garden came into being as a homogeneous whole, as two parts of a complete work of art, depending on and related to each other. Just as the building related to the garden through its façade, the garden had to have a direct effect on the rooms, to fuse with the interior decoration, as it were. The portal motif with double half-columns and projecting top is also used on this side, to a certain extent as a recognition feature.

The sculpture programme ‣ Sculptural decoration was a fixed component of all princely palaces and gardens in the baroque and rococo periods. The extensive and varied Mosigkau sculpture programme includes the work above the portals, the larger-than-life sculptures on the sides of the north and south terraces and other statues in the garden, and not least the numerous urns and ornamental urn tops on the courtyard pedestals. In terms of both form and content, Anna Wilhelmine allowed herself to be guided freely by programmes like those of the palace complexes in Potsdam (Sanssouci) or Saxony (Grossedlitz). As well as this, the Mosigkau sculptures suggest that the princess had read widely to form a comprehensive impression of the possibilities afforded by sculptural decoration. Her sound knowledge helped the Mosigkau sculptures to show artistic quality through their imitation of ancient models and ensured a thoroughly considered approach for the whole programme.

The figures on the open steps on the north and south sides are by Johann Wolfgang Träger, who trained at the Academy in Vienna, in whom the princess made a particularly lucky choice. With Minerva (Greek Athena) at the north entrance

The effect made by the south façade of the palace is completely different from that made on the courtyard side. A different design for the courtyard and garden sides was expressly recommended in contemporary French architectural treatises for buildings of the "maison de plaisance" type.

The maze is one of the few such hedge structures in Germany to have survived with its original structure intact. This photograph shows the view from the water-tower, built in 1908/09 on the edge of the western part of the garden to provide water for the gardens as a whole.

79

to the palace, Anna Wilhelmine already confidently ascribes excellent qualities to herself – the goddess stands for wisdom and intelligence, but also for the sciences and arts, above all architecture and sculpture. And the Apollo placed on the opposite stringer – based loosely on the famous ancient Apollo of the Belvedere – was the god of light and art, the protector of the muses, and above all, of music and song, which was completely in tune with the intentions and demands of the woman commissioning the building of the Mosigkau summer palace. The massive ornamental sculptures above the portal gables were created by the Potsdam-trained Dessau sculptor, Nathanael Eppen. The northern one, in keeping with its direction, shows an allegory of autumn and winter between an upward-thrusting initial cartouche with a rocaille-like frame, a blue background and a gilded monogram. On the left sits winter in the figure of a woman by the fire, pointing to masks on the ground. On the right, autumn, as a laughing putto, carries a heavy garland hung with grapes. In the south, the gable sculpture is appropriately decorated with allegories of spring and summer. These are attended on the terrace steps stringers by the ancient goddesses, Flora and Venus. As symbols of spring, of flourishing nature and gardens, and of love, harmony and

beauty, they are directed towards the pleasure gardens with a wealth of appropriate associations.

The pleasure garden at the Mosigkau palace ‣ Following rococo principles, the Mosigkau garden is closely linked with the architecture and is part of the entire work of art. Thus, the building and the parterre are linked from the inside to the outside by the large windows in the garden room, and likewise from the outside to the inside. Something similar is achieved with the sculpture programme, which starts with the ornamental work over the porticoes and continues via the terrace sculptures to the sculptures in the garden.

Planning the garden ‣ Because the palace and the garden were intended to form a design unit, they had to be planned and realized simultaneously. For this reason, Anna Wilhelmine commissioned the first designs for the gardens as soon as building began, though little was actually implemented from these plans. Essentially, the gardens were established in the two years after the shell of the building was completed, from 1755 to 1757, after the "art and pleasure gardener" responsible, Christoph Friedrich Brosse, had taken up his post. A 1780s' map of all the properties in Mosigkau gives a general idea about the historical situation, and an inventory and a detailed description of the garden dating from 1784 a much more precise one. However, in its present state, it is only in some areas that we still get a faint hint of the ambitious conception, the remarkable variety and the richness of this rococo garden.

As the long-term intention is to restore the garden to its original condition, it seems worthwhile to form some picture of this. The 18th century horticultural ideas were strictly limited by the course of the stream and the cottage gardens adjacent to the east and the farm estate buildings and road forming the western border. But leaving aside the limitations on the space, Anna Wilhelmine had very different ideas about designing her rococo garden than those prescribed for half a century by the strict formalism of French baroque gardens. Even in the period from 1715 to 1750, it was possible to see a gradual breakdown of the dominant baroque garden structures shaped by André Le Nôtre's gardens in Vaux-le-Vicomte and Versailles, extended to gigantic proportions and transformed into pure art. These structures were replaced by more intricate, complex ground plans, *more natural* in the eyes of the day, though, in the early stages, nature

This large sandstone urn, lavishly decorated with rocaille and leaves, marks the site of a carousel that was one of the many amusements in the Mosigkau garden.

meant no more than a greater variety of motifs, scenes, perspectives and views. The Mosigkau garden evolved in this period of transition from the baroque garden to the English style landscape garden.

The pleasure garden ‣ An axis 170 metres long leads from the palace as the central point of the entire complex to the southern perimeter of the garden. The gate is bordered on either side by two orangeries, placed like gatehouses. These were built as timber-frame structures, and replaced by the present one in the mid 19th century. And they are still used as winter quarters for a small, very valuable collection of potted plants, some of which have even survived from the time the palace complex was built.

The two most important sections of the garden were created between the "corps de logis" and the orangeries, in the form of the parterre and the adjacent bosket zone. Brosse placed the parterre, a garden area structured by symmetrically arranged beds, by the south façade of the house, beyond a fourteen metre wide open space. The parterre consists of three sections on either side of the central path. A broderie parterre, decorated ornamentally with sand in many colours, gravel, lawns and box, is followed by a rondel with a central mound of flowers. The concluding feature is a slightly lower area of lawn that was later used as an area for placing the orangery plants. The six quarters were fringed on the outside by a border of flower-beds, framed by box hedges. Small topiary-work yew trees, six putti and eight approximately life-size sculptures were places inside these. The whole parterre was surrounded at the sides by an arbour, set higher and arched at the top, which separated the formal gardens from the cottage gardens and the domestic building. In line with one of the most important rococo horticultural precepts, windows in the arbours and in the pavilions built of slats permitted views of this once especially elaborately designed garden area. Only hints of it survive today.

It is much easier to make out the design of the so-called bosket zone today, which consists of four areas of hedge of approximately the same size, adjacent to the parterre. Eight hedged boskets, whose function we no longer know, once presumably bordered the parterre. They offered various amusements, such as the carousel in the eastern quarter, which has now been replaced by a round flowerbed with a sandstone urn. There was also once a little well-house here, a painted "prospect", probably formerly accessed via a sight line, a "bird-game" about which no further detail is given

The Chinese House, built in 1775 on the foundations of the old manor house, forms the centre of the western section of the garden. The pavilion's pyramid roof was originally topped by a Chinese figure, painted in colour, with a sunshade hung with little bells.

The austere staircase, considerably altered in the late 19th century, still
gives no idea of the perfection and elegance of the adjacent show rooms.
Today it is hung with an extensive selection of portraits of the princes of
Anhalt.

and a few little cabins with benches in them. The next quarter contains an almost square fishpond that came from the garden belonging to the former manor house. It is reached from the central path via an arbour that was also a centre for other amusements. These included two ball-games surrounded by beech hedges, a skittle alley and a "game of chance" about which nothing more is known. On the other side of the main path is the entrance to the maze, which represents one of the most popular baroque and rococo garden elements. Its winding hedged paths, 320 metres long in all, ended in a rondel with three trimmed chestnut trees, now replaced by a tall plane tree. The 70 (!) plum trees trimmed into spheres that were originally planted in the hedges have not survived.

The area beyond the stream to the east was used as an orchard and vegetable garden. The western section was occupied by the old manor house until the garden started to be laid out. After this was demolished, Brosse's successor, the gardener Georg Friedrich Brätsch, redesigned this area. He created an intricate and varied garden with about nine quarters, which used to contain the *Comedien Platz*, a hedged theatre. The only item surviving from this part of the garden is the "Chinese House", now considerably weathered, reflecting the taste of the times and the love of chinoiserie. It is obviously based on the Chinese House in Potsdam, completed only ten years earlier (1764), but the Mosigkau version was much more modestly equipped. Anna Wilhelmine and subsequent occupants of the palace used to take their tea in the house, which had Chinese furniture and red wallpaper. Later, an "English part" was created in the southern section of this area of the garden, obviously based on the Wörlitz landscape garden, with a mound planted with poplars and firs and a hermitage.

Plantation – house garden – north garden ‣ This western part of the garden is bordered on the north side by the estate's domestic area. Behind this extended the "French plantation", a good view of which was afforded by the western rooms in the "corps de logis". It was an orchard, planted with over 250 (!) small fruit trees planted in the shape of a star, and about 1500 square metres of "kitchen land" level with the main courtyard.

North of the palace complex was the "Great Garden". A wrought-iron fence (originally a wooden fence), framed by masonry pillars topped with richly decorated sandstone urns, divides it off from the courtyard. The path that forms the central axis for the whole complex continues from here over the stream to the end of the garden, which is marked by two gateway columns, and is fringed today by a row of walnut trees on both sides. An avenue of pyramid oaks leads to the enclosed cemetery for the noble ladies' home, occupying about 600 square metres, in the north-east of the garden.

Redesign of the gardens began in 1780, after the "Hochadeliges Fräuleinstift" had been established in Schloss Mosigkau as a home for noble ladies, after the death of Anna Wilhelmine in 1780. In 1784, Johann Gottfried Schoch came on the scene. He was a gardener with a totally different theoretical approach, inclining towards the idea of English landscape gardens, which he had already realized in the other gardens in Dessau-Wörlitz. The typical rococo elements gradually disappeared from the garden, or were considerably simplified. Under Leberecht Abel, who held the office of gardener to the Fräuleinstift from 1805, the Mosigkau garden was finally completely redesigned following the English model. Evidence of this is provided, for example, by the little garden seat in the form of an ancient temple that was placed by the wall of the domestic building belonging to the estate and later moved to the end of the path starting at the west end of the palace, the original main entrance.

The Second World War brought much more disastrous consequences for the Mosigkau palace garden. A start was made on restoring the complex only after the museum was founded in 1951, and work can only proceed gradually today, above all because of the stock of old trees, some of which are rare.

The interior – pomp and intimacy in the "maison de plaisance" ‣ The difference between baroque and rococo can be demonstrated particularly vividly in terms of the interior of the Mosigkau palace. For example, in Mosigkau the contrast, typical of the rococo, between more sparing decoration outside and a lavishly decorated interior is very striking, as recommended by 18th century French architectural theory. The idea that led to reduction in the spirit of covenance (appropriateness) outside produced extremely lavish and sophisticated interior decoration. As well as this, the Mosigkau ground plan shows that the representative and symbolic symmetry of baroque palaces had been more or less abandoned and replaced by a more comfortable arrangement of the individual areas, appropriate to the functions of the rooms.

Following Anna Wilhelmine's ideas on the use of the palace, the house was divided into official spaces and residential apartments; the two areas were related to each other. The vestibule and the rooms intended for show and entertainment, with the exception of the western corner cabinet, were in the central section of the palace, on the pleasure garden side, following the principles of the "maison de plaisance". The princess used the west wing to meet her particular residential and state needs, while the east wing housed small rooms for guests, the lady-in-waiting and the mistress of the household. The mezzanine above the garden room and the attic rooms were intended for the female servants.

It is still possible to form an impression of the original furnishings in some parts of the palace today. For example, the state rooms have survived in their original condition, or have been restored over recent decades to the condition they were in when the palace was built. But considerable changes were made to a series of small rooms, particularly in the east wing, since the princess's testamentary dispositions changed the complex into a "Hochadeliges Fräuleinstift "(Home for aristocratic gentlewomen). The ladies in the home had the rooms altered to meet their needs. Individual spaces were divided to create apartments with up to four rooms, which meant that the elaborate wall cladding and the rest of the decoration were lost. But three detailed inventories from Anna Wilhelmine's lifetime are available for restoration purposes, providing information about the original furnishings and equipment and the functions of the individual rooms.

Living and ceremony in the west and east wings ‣ Visitors enter the plain stairwell with its twin oak flights, hung with a series of Anhalt portraits, through the entrance in the middle of the "corps de logis". The stairs have been greatly changed by rebuilding and renovation. They lead into the west wing, where the apartments on both floors were largely kept to meet the princess's needs. The ground plans of the two sets of rooms are laid out in the same way. Two doors, opening up from a long rectangular anteroom facing the courtyard, provide access to a closed set of rooms oriented north-south. The three main rooms are linked by the enfilade that is usual in baroque palaces: when all the doors lying on the same axis are open, they provide a view through the complete sequence of spaces.

The rooms of the ground floor quarters relate to each other not just in terms of the spatial sequence, but also due to the fact that the panels, doors and shutters have been left unpainted. The right-hand door leads into the "corner room facing the palace square", which has not yet been restored,

now known as the Hofkavalierzimmer. The original furnishing with gaming tables suggests that the room was provided with pastimes for those waiting for an audience with Anna Wilhelmine in the adjacent room, the "middle chamber". She also used this audience room to perform her official duties. She was responsible, among other things, for the lower jurisdiction in the Mosigkau area, and she also had three estates to administer. In keeping with its use, the room was furnished plainly and functionally. The oak panelling was accompanied by a wall covering in green "Trojett" (droguet = silk fabric), which has been replaced today with a green silk damask wallpaper.

The next room, the "corner room facing the garden", is, in its simple elegance, one of the most beautiful and impressive rooms in the house. It is no longer possible to establish precisely what role the Braunes Kabinett, as it is known today, played in the sequence of rooms. It is possible that the princess used it for discussions with the inner court circle and as a study. Like all the other rooms, the wood panelling, which covers all the walls here, is left unpainted. Unlike comparable rococo rooms, the cladding, which is made of pear-wood in the lower sections and of alder in the upper sections, as are the shutters, bears no elaborate ornamentation. So the wall creates its effect, essentially in the spirit of early baroque room design, through a rhythmic sequence of simple, closed compartments. This plain design is presumably connected with the lavishly ornamented, gilded frames for the Gallery of Beauties, consisting of twelve portraits of women, a collection type developed in the late 16th century. These were distributed evenly across the walls without windows, and made any other wall decoration superfluous. The comfortable effect made by the "corner room" is further enhanced by the sandstone fireplace decorated with rococo ornaments and placed diagonally in the north-east corner. The opposite corner is dominated by a corner cupboard with writing desk, lively in form, and veneered, containing costly porcelain and Viennese writing utensils made around 1730. Two windows facing south and one facing east make the little room very light and provided a view of the garden. A room facing south and west like this was reserved for the personal use of the master or mistress of the house in other contemporary palaces as well.

The quarters on the floor above are arranged according to the same ground plan as the ground floor, but different furnishings and lighter, brighter colours generate a completely dif-

ferent effect. In the sequence of rooms on the lower floor, the unpainted panels and dark wall coverings create warmth and dignity, while here, wood painted in light colours and delicate colour shades, and also powerful colour chords, make for a lively and cheerful atmosphere.

The "Upper Room" in the stairwell leads first into a long anteroom. It is now adorned by a canvas wallpaper dating from about 1763 by the Dessau painter Johann Wolfgang Buch, which was brought here in 1962 from Schloss Oranienbaum to replace the lost wallpaper by the same artist. The northwest room, also without its original furnishings, the "corner room facing the Schloss-Platz", now contains baroque period furniture and paintings, including the one by Jan Mytens showing the daughters of the Dutch governor Friedrich Heinrich and his wife Amalia, dating from 1666.

The next room, the "mittelste Kammer", is almost in its original, 18th century condition. It was a private audience cham-

ber, and thus accessible only to high-ranking visitors. Its magnificent décor aims to create an effect of status and power. It is dominated by the "crimson red damask wallpaper with fold beading and corners", which contrasts powerfully with the white-painted wooden panels. The strong red of this wall covering, like the stucco ceiling, finished to the highest standard by Carlo and Benigno Bossi, aimed to make a lasting impression on visitors. These two artists, about whose biography very little is known, were members of the famous Lombard dynasty of stucco artists, who made a name for themselves in the 18th century with outstanding stucco work in Dresden, Bayreuth and the Würzburg residence. The choice of these excellent craftsmen is a clear statement of the princess's insistence on the highest quality and artistic perfection when decorating and furnishing her house. She also had the five portraits of her siblings hung over mirrors and doors, in order not to detract from her appearance at audiences. The interior is completed by the slender, rocaille-decorated, cream-coloured faïence stove, which was fed from the

The sandstone mantelpiece in the Braunes Kabinett carries a set of blue-and-white faïence vases, above which an excellent still life by the Flemish painter Jan Fyt is set into the panelling.

Mosigkau

The Gallery of Beauties with twelve portraits of English ladies-in-waiting in the "Braunes Kabinett" is the work of Remigius van Leemput, a studio colleague of Anthony van Dyck, after his portraits. It was presented to the Orange family in 1642 by the English queen, Henriette Maria.

cloakroom behind it. It seems certain that the last room in the sequence, the "corner room facing the garden", above the Braunes Kabinett, was reserved largely for private use. This is suggested by the proximity of the dressing room and the choice of family portraits for paintings.

On leaving Anna Wilhelmine's apartments for the east wing of the palace, a completely different ground plan from that of the imposingly organized west wing can be discerned. To gain space, an east-facing corridor divides both floors. The upper floor, which was intended for guests and the first lady-in-waiting, consists of two apartments, each with two rooms and a closet. The lower floor accommodates an apartment with three rooms for the mistress of the household on the north side and a small room belonging to the ceremonial sequence on the south side. As the three apartments were occupied by gentlewomen from 1780, a great deal of conversion was done here, impinging on the original building.

The ceremonial area ▸ Visitors are taken from the stairwell to the ceremonial area through the door opposite the entrance portal. In the centre is the light-flooded garden or gallery room, which immediately captivates the viewer with its beauty and lavish appointments. It is a good 20 metres long, and opens into smaller rooms on both sides. It is followed to the west by the "yellow-silvered cabinet" and to the east by the music cabinet, which leads into the last room of the ensemble, the so-called chapter room or "Chinese room". All four rooms relate to each other as an enfilade, and face south over the pleasure garden. At the west end of the sequence in the yellow-silvered room is a mirror, which continues the enfilade visually. Access to the Braunes Kabinett behind, in the west wing, is via a double door, set to the side. The straw-yellow painted panelling, contrasting with the silver shade of the applied beading, ornamental carving, rocaille and palm trunks and also the festoons of flowers, fruit and animals in natural colours, gives the yellow-silvered cabinet a cheerful, intimate atmosphere. The silver tone appears for a second time in the six gaily carved frames containing pictures by the contemporary painters Adam Manyoki, Antoine Pesne and Cornelis Troost. The five paintings above the doors, of which three depict a cycle of the ages, with a boy, a middle-aged man and an old man reading, symbolizing wisdom, take up a popular baroque stylistic device. As well as these, delicate double wall candelabra with porce-

lain flowers and a portrait of a Brandenburg prince over the sandstone fireplace decorate the room. The sparse furnishings, consisting of four silvered tabourets (stools) upholstered in yellow satin and a console table attached to the wall under the mirror, lacquered in the colour of the panelling, suggest that the room was used as a place for amusing conversation. There is no other room in the house, in which the influence of Sanssouci is so clearly visible. The guest-room, known as the Voltaire Room in the Potsdam palace, is painted in a similar colour, and the rooms created for the Prussian king by Johann Christian Hoppenhaupt have comparable ornamental decoration.

The "marbled cabinet", the small music room on the other side of the garden room, is the same size as its yellow-silvered counterpart, but presents a completely different effect. The walls are completely clad in grey-green stucco marble and give the room a cool elegance, underlined by the delicate ceiling stucco on a green background, extending from the continuous rocaille borders via diagonal palm trunks symmetrically to a central rosette. Garlands with stucco wind and string instruments in the areas above the doors show the space's function as a music room. The house organ, commissioned by the aged gentlewomen from the Dessau organ-builder Zuberbier in 1837, was not originally intended for this room, but for the gallery room.

At the eastern end, the sequence of ceremonial social rooms concludes with the "Chinese room", also known as the chapter room, which is lit by four windows. As in the other small rooms in the east wing, the furnishings are influenced by the rococo inclination towards chinoiserie. By analogy with the original furnishings, which have not survived, the room is now adorned with different Chinese lacquer cupboards. They contain a number of rare Chinese porcelain items and other craft objects like Chinese tea-caddies and smokers' stands owned by Anna Wilhelmine. The curiosities include a table with Amsterdam or Harling tiles from the porcelain cabinet in Schloss Oranienbaum. The table's frame consists largely of Chinese vases and bowls. Following the restoration that is currently taking place of the leather wall-hangings room in Schloss Oranienbaum, the table will be taken back to its original location there. The original "white silk *Pequinge Tappete* (Peking wallpaper)" with delicate floral ornaments has survived, though it is very faded. It had to be removed so that the wall cladding could be restored.

The mirror, placed in the yellow-silvered room to make it look larger, reflects an above-door painting, which was repeated for this location by the Prussian court painter Antoine Pesne in 1743, after the original by

Nicolas Lancret, which was part of Frederick the Great's collection (now in Schloss Charlottenburg in Berlin).

The complex, lively rococo stucco, enriched with motifs from music, science, flora and fauna, extends into the vaults of the ballroom.

Mosigkau

90

The picture gallery ▸ The "Bilder Gallerie" is the high point of the whole palace complex. It combines the light-hearted atmosphere of the adjacent small rooms with a sense of dignity and festivity. The recessed wall areas are completely covered with paintings. They are framed in polished yellow and pale grey stucco marble, whose play of colour harmonizes with the ceiling's apple-green ground and the extremely lively and complex stucco. The original oak parquet and magnificent smoked glass chandelier complete the imposing furnishings of this high room. Five French windows, reinforced by four large mirrors on the opposite side, allow bright light to flood into the south-facing gallery and create an intimate connection between the interior and the garden. The large, semicircular window and door apertures and the floral motifs in stucco and paintings fuse the building and garden architecture to form a universal work of art, reflecting the new relationship between interior and exterior in rococo summer palace architecture, as can also be seen outside, in the garden façade. The lucid articulation of the space shows high mastery of interior architecture. It is based on four entrance doors in round-arched niches placed opposite each other, the two fireplace and console table zones with large, full mirrors and above-door decorations on the long walls, and the lavishly filled painting niches. The execution of the light stucco work with rhythmically accumulated, complex rocaille, creatures, palms, fountains and instruments, attributed to Johann Carl Lindner and Johann Michael Hoppenhaupt, also reveals great richness of ideas and a high level of craft skill.

The importance of Schloss Mosigkau lies mainly in the paintings in the Garden Room. The status of the picture collection derives not only from the considerable number of outstanding works, but also from the way they are displayed, which is still largely original. Most of the paintings, preponderantly Flemish and Dutch, were part of the so-called Orange Inheritance. The princess was able to acquire some contemporary pictures from the estate of her aunt Marie Eleonore von Radziwill. The selected paintings are not hung according to theme or symmetry. In the customary baroque manner of hanging art, the large-format pictures are arranged on the upper part of the walls, the small ones in the lower areas. Even though it is not possible to establish any connections in terms of subject matter, Anna Wilhelmine at least seems to have tried to own a work by each of the great Flemish masters, and from the important schools of Dutch painting. As well as this, she clearly wanted to have a varied mixture of the main painting genres, in that she brought together mythical and biblical histories, allegories, portraits, still lifes and landscapes.

Chinoiserie

Wolfgang Savelsberg

The term "chinoiserie", first used in France in the rococo period, describes decoration following the "Chinese taste" that was very popular in the late 17th and 18th centuries. However, many artistic expressions of this Chinese fashion remain merely formal reflexes, through lack of a real ability to come to terms with Chinese culture.

This distant land first entered the European consciousness when sea-routes to Asia were discovered in the 16th century. Chinese products reached the continent, and travellers' tales conveyed an idea of China as a country of light-hearted, playful enjoyment of life, and of highly developed cultural achievements. Maritime trade was considerably boosted in the 17th century when East India Companies were founded in England and Holland, meaning that large quantities of Asian goods like silk fabrics, lacquer work, soapstone, tortoiseshell and porcelain could be transported to Europe less riskily.

The world of Chinese forms and motifs was enthusiastically embraced in Europe. Even before 1700, faïence factories in Delft, Hanau, Frankfurt and Berlin were redesigning Chinese models to suit European tastes. From the mid 17th century, chinoiserie can be found on displays for collections of genuine Chinese works or on furniture influenced by "Indian" taste. The first Chinese lacquered cabinets and consoles with porcelain appeared in the residences of the northern Dutch governors, as Holland in particular had early access to Asiatic products because of its maritime trading supremacy. In Oranienburg, the first completely equipped porcelain cabinet was even set up in 1662.

Rococo, in particular, developed a marked feeling for the world of foreign motifs, and thus, chinoiserie became increasingly popular in France, Germany and England in the 18th century. Idealized scenes of Chinese life covered the walls in lacquer painting, silk embroidery or stucco, and Chinese porcelain was displayed on consoles or in cabinets. Entire rooms in palaces were decorated and furnished in the Chinese style, including outstanding examples in Berlin and Potsdam by Johann August Nahl the Elder and Johann Christian Hoppenhaupt. Chinoiserie affected the architecture of the day in the form of countless pagodas, as in the Chinese teahouse in Sanssouci in Potsdam or in Schloss Pillnitz. Countless pattern books provided artists with models for their chinoiserie. For example, Thomas Chippendale in England published the first pioneering work with furniture designs containing a large number of Chinese motifs. The work by the architect Sir William Chambers, completed after his visit to China, includes a compilation of drawings made by direct observation. This provided a fundamental nucleus for faithful imitation of Chinese motifs in the late 18th century and was used in gardens among other places, including those at Oranienbaum.

The "Hochadeliges Damenstift" (Home for aristocratic gentlewomen) ‣ Princess Anna Wilhelmine was able to take advantage of the summer residence for 23 years, from the time she moved in until the end of her life. She probably spent more time in Mosigkau than was intended before building started. This farsighted woman decided at an early stage that her "great house" in Mosigkau, with three estates and other properties and capital of 70,000 talers, should become the seat of the "Hochadeliges Fräuleinstift zu Mosigkau", a home for gentlewomen. She had set this idea down in her will a year before she died, and added a detailed set of regulations for the home, according to which not more than six unmarried ladies and an abbess of the Protestant faith should live in the palace. There were also regulations about attending services, holding sessions of silent prayer,

and Bible reading. Only a few months after the death of the Anna Wilhelmine on 2 April, 1780, the home was founded and confirmed by the ruling prince, her nephew Leopold III Friedrich Franz, Prince of Anhalt-Dessau, for her birthday on 12 June.

The prince had enclosed pews for the ladies, which had been built in the church in Mosigkau, which dates from around 1400. The exterior of the church was considerably altered by erecting an unusual double-towered façade in the English style.

In the course of the 165 years of the home's existence, until it was expropriated in 1945 as part of the GDR's land reforms, a total of 46 ladies made their home here.

Among others, an unhappy outcome to a relationship with the 17-years-older poet Mathisson brought the 21-year-old Annette von Glaffay into the Mosigkau home. After she was elected abbess, this active, artistically versatile woman was able to introduce many innovations to the home. For example, from then on, the ladies took on social responsibilities such as caring for the sick and looking after the poor. A girls' school was also established. Silkworms were bred in the upper, south-west facing chamber, and the mulberry trees needed to feed them were grown in the garden.

After 1947, the few remaining ladies in the home were allowed to live in ancillary buildings in the palace, but the home itself acquired the status of a cultural foundation, from which a museum emerged that still functions today. In common with only a very few small palaces in the GDR, men and women acting responsibly and with artistic sensibility were fortunately able to save this exquisite palace from being used for other purposes, as was so often the case.

Home music-making did not only play an important part in Anna Wilhelmine's court life, as numerous motifs in paintings and stucco ornaments show. During its time as a home for gentlewomen, when the organ in the music room was built (1837), music was also made for entertainment and religious uplift.

This wooden panel by Peter Paul Rubens and Jan Brueghel the Elder is believed to have been presented to the House of Orange by the governor of the Habsburg Netherlands around 1630, in the spirit of a hoped-for peace. Flora, the goddess of flowering nature, and Zephyrus, the god of the west wind, were seen as symbols of renewal.

The Orange Inheritance

Wolfgang Savelsberg

The most important and most valuable works of art in the Dessau-Wörlitz Garden Realm came from the "Oranische Erbschaft", the "Orange Inheritance", which is the traditional term. But in art history, it is customarily used to describe the paintings that came to Berlin in the 18th century when the Prussian King Friedrich I asserted his claim to inheritance upon the death of his cousin, the Dutch governor and English King William III of Orange-Nassau in 1702, taking possession of the Orange residences with the richest painting collections.

When the "Orange Inheritance" is wrongly alluded to in the context of the Anhalt pictures, this refers mainly to the many paintings owned by the Orange-Nassau princess, Henriette Catharina (1637-1708), wife of the Anhalt prince, Johann Georg II. They came from the estate of her mother, Amalia von Solms. The collection of paintings, craftwork and jewellery left after her death in 1675 was immense. According to her will, the four daughters (who were alone eligible to inherit the movable fortune) received 250 paintings, to which should be added hundreds more that were not included in the estate lists. There was also a considerable quantity of jewellery, silver and gold objects, costly porcelain, fur-

niture, numerous tapestries and other rarities.

The largest part of the collection is in the form of Flemish paintings. Amalia and her consort Friedrich Heinrich had largely acquired paintings by contemporary 17th century Flemish masters like Peter Paul Rubens, Anthony van Dyck, Jacob Jordaens, Jan Brueghel and their contemporaries and successors. Gerard van Honthorst and Jan Mijtens were court painters in the service of the governor, and so the Dutch paintings include many portraits by them. As well as these, mention should be made of paintings by Adriaen Hanneman, Cornelis van Poelenburch, Govert Flinck, Rembrandt, Jan Lievens and Nicolaes Maes, Caspar Netscher and Karel Du Jardin. Dutch patriotism largely accounts for the fact that there are almost no Italian paintings in the collection.

As Henriette Catharina's sisters and also some of her daughters died before her or without female issue, the Anhalt princess came to own a large proportion of the estate because of the particular testamentary disposition. She decorated the Dessau residence and Schloss Oranienbaum, which she had had built, with this wealth of paintings and craftwork. One of Henriette Catharina's daughters, Marie Eleonore, Duchess of

Radziwill, inherited just as fortunately as her mother. Because of the special testamentary process, about three-quarters of the collection came into her possession during her lifetime. When she died in Dessau in 1756, her unmarried niece Anna Wilhelmine, daughter of Prince Leopold I, acquired about 80 pictures, a large part of the collection, for her palace in Mosigkau, which was under construction at the time. Shortly before attaining his majority, Leopold III Friedrich Franz, subsequently Prince of Anhalt-Dessau, bought numerous other paintings for the country house he was later to build and the Gothic House in Wörlitz, where some of them still hang today. A third keen purchaser was Anna Wilhelmine's sister, the ambitious collector Henriette Amalie, whose pictures now form an important part of the holdings at the "Anhaltische Gemäldegalerie" in Dessau. Apart from a number of works for the residence in Dessau that went to the Soviet Union as spoils, and sales of especially valuable pictures by the ducal household in the 1920s and 1930s, most of the wealth of paintings have remained in Dessau-Wörlitz.

Left-hand page ‹ Portrait of Amalia Margaretha von Brederode. This
originally hexagonal painting by Gerard van Honthorst was enlarged
so that it could be used above one of the doors in the yellow-silvered
cabinet.

This portrait of Prince Wilhelm II of Orange-Nassau, painted in
The Hague in 1631/32, is one of the highlights of the Orange treasury
of pictures. Anthony van Dyck shows masterly skill in giving the boy,
who was just under six years old, a childlike and yet dignified air.

The gallery room in Schloss Mosigkau contains one of Europe's rare
"baroque" collection of hung paintings, which has survived almost
intact. The pictures include outstanding pieces by Rubens, van Dyck
and Honthorst, and also other important 17th and 18th century masters.

The noble ladies' apartments in the home usually included a kitchen, a bedroom and a living room. The bedroom was divided from the living room by a wall that was built in additionally, as in this reconstructed example.

Right-hand side ▸ The entrance to the cemetery of the gentlewomen's home. The home gardener was commissioned to plan a burial place just a year after the "Hochadeliges Fräuleinstift" was founded.

III

WÖRLITZ

Ingo Pfeifer

The prince and his architect

Friedrich Wilhelm von Erdmannsdorff was born to a high Electoral Saxon court official in Dresden on 18 May, 1736, and educated there at the academy for the sons of noblemen. On 10 August, 1765, when he left Wittenberg, where he had studied mathematics, history and philosophy, to pay his respects to the Anhalt heir to the throne, Prince Franz, on the prince's 16th birthday, probably neither man sensed that this encounter would lead to a lifelong friendship.

Love of the arts, enthusiasm about antiquity and the idea that people could be improved by training and education brought the two young men together. This was not affected by the outbreak of the Seven Years War, in which the Anhalt prince became involved as a Prussian officer in what was now hostile Saxony. Erdmannsdorff tried to escape the turmoil of war, which inflicted grave damage on his Saxon home, by embarking on a Grand Tour to Italy. He reached northern

Italy in 1761, and visited Venice and Florence. Here this young man of fine sensibilities, shaped by baroque Dresden, encountered the works of the Italian Renaissance for the first time. He started to paint himself, and practised drawing. But he also spent time in the galant circles of theatre and poetry, until lack of money forced him to return after a year. Even at this early stage, Erdmannsdorff decided that he would make his new home in Dessau.

Shortly after the end of the war in 1763/64, the young prince and his noble friend travelled to England together for the first time, where they saw numerous country houses – including those by Inigo Jones, the first exponent of Palladianism in England – and a number of parks. It was on this journey that the prince developed his love of landscape gardens and Erdmannsdorff, his interest in architecture. On returning home, they chose Wörlitz as the starting-point

for a landscape design that was later to embrace almost the entire principality. The Grand Tour they started just a year later was to be a joint educational experience that made a profound impression on them, and on which they drew throughout their lives.

This journey finally made Erdmannsdorff into a professional architect. He took drawing lessons from Charles-Louis Clérisseau, who taught many neo-classical master builders. He learned model-making from the antiques restorer Bartolomeo Cavaceppi, and the two young men from Dessau familiarized themselves with ancient art and culture under the guidance of Johann Joachim Winckelmann.

Erdmannsdorff visited Italy on several more occasions, developing a passion for Rome in particular. He also stayed in the Eternal City from 1770 to early 1772. He acquired art objects for the rooms of Schloss Wörlitz, which was under

Architecture and landscape gardening combine harmoniously in the Elbe meadows at Wörlitz, with the beautiful and the useful complementing each other.

It was the creator's intention that both pleasure and education should derive from this garden.

construction at the time, and sent designs for its interior to Dessau. He was a close friend of many artists living in Rome, including the painter brothers Jakob Philipp and Georg Hackert, Anton von Maron, Giovanni B. Piranesi and Angelica Kauffmann. He met some of them again on his last visit to Rome in 1789/90. The master builder and the prince were bound above all by a desire to make their activities useful to the general good. Erdmannsdorff made it his duty to translate his princely friend's ideas and wishes into architectural forms. Though he never enjoyed official rank in the Dessau court as an architect, he felt responsible for all the building enterprises. The Enlightenment idea, which goes back to antiquity, of combining the useful and the beautiful in order to create true works of art, fitted in with their joint convictions. As art in Winckelmann's spirit was supposed to give pleasure as well as to instruct, they always saw works of art as educational instruments as well. The landscape garden with its many garden scenes offered itself as the ideal medium. Here different architectural styles, modern agriculture and ideal works of art could be experienced in harmonious union. The prince thus felt that opening up his Wörlitz garden to all expressed his educational intentions. It should be possible in this ideal landscape, in which the different social classes could meet, to offer natural and moral education in the spirit of Jean-Jacques Rousseau.

Even though Erdmannsdorff seldom left Anhalt-Dessau, his influence could be sensed beyond the principality. He worked in Prussia for three years only, but he made his mark on architecture there for a whole generation. One of the people he particularly influenced was Friedrich Gilly, who later taught Karl Friedrich Schinkel and Carl Gotthard Langhans, who built the Brandenburg Gate.

In November 1786, shortly after the death of Frederick the Great of Prussia, he was called to Potsdam to work as architect there. He was commissioned by the new king, Friedrich Wilhelm II, to produce a new neo-classical design for the room in which "Old Fritz" had died in the palace of Sanssouci. Thus, Erdmannsdorff became the exponent of the new building style that also symbolized a major turn of events in Prussian history. As well as this, he was admired for his ability and practice of providing precisely detailed material as a basis for stucco and ornaments. The next year, he was entrusted with redesigning the royal apartments in the

The Grand Tour

Ingo Pfeifer

Visits to the major cultural and political centres in Western and Southern Europe were among the highlights of training and education for the European nobility from the late 17th century. They were supposed to improve their knowledge of languages abroad, refine their manners and undergo their first experiences in the theatre of diplomacy. The term "Grand Tour" was coined for this sort of educational journey. For a long time the prime destination was Paris and the court of Louis XIV, whose ceremonial was seen as exemplary for all absolute rulers. From the 18th century, Rome increasingly shifted to the centre of interest. This city became the destination for British travellers in particular after the Scottish pretender to the throne, James Edward Stuart, moved his permanent residence from Paris to Rome. But the emphasis gradually shifted from the originally political and religious content of the tour towards addressing Italy's rich artistic and cultural tradition. The architecture of the Renaissance and antiquity attracted the attention of the Grand Tourists (see Palladianism, p. 121), along with the Italian aristocracy's large private art and antiques collections. Dabbling in drawing and model-making, writing poetry and music, but also studying antiquity and acquiring works of art were now key features of the journey. Throughout the tour, which usually lasted for several months, guided visits were made to the most important collections and palazzi in the city, and also to art studios and theatrical performances. And an audience with the Pope was a highlight of the tour, not just for Roman Catholics.

German princes and, by the late 18th century, members of the bourgeoisie followed the British example from about 1760.

The classical route from Germany was via Innsbruck and Verona to Venice, and from there to Bologna with its famous university. From here there were two ways to Rome: either the historical pilgrims' way via Florence, Sienna and Orvieto or the route via Ravenna, Ancona and Spoleto, which is the one the Dessau travellers chose. A detour from Rome to Naples was also part of the usual programme, to see the excavations in Pompeii and Herculaneum and risk an ascent of Vesuvius.

Continuing the tour via France and on to England, as Prince Franz did, was a novelty and an exception for German princes for a long time.

Previous page, left ◂ Portrait of Erdmannsdorff, painted by J.F.A. Tischbein in 1796. Previous page, right ◂ Immediately after the first visit to
England, the English seat was built from an original in Stourhead.

Anton von Maron painted Prince Franz of Dessau in Rome in 1766.
The Roman ruins in the background and a Grecian urn at his feet evoke
his enthusiasm for antiquity.

Berlin Schloss, as his work in Sanssouci had been greeted with such enthusiasm.

The master builder stopped travelling after the death of his wife Wilhelmine von Ahlimb, a lady-in-waiting to the Dessau princess, in December 1795. He applied himself with great commitment from then on to educational projects intended to shape the taste of large groups of the population. For example, commissioned by the prince, he developed a plan from about 1796 for a school of drawing, which was to lead on to a "teaching establishment for mechanical crafts and fine art". The financial and educational ideas that came into play here also played a part in the foundation of the Chalkographische Gesellschaft in 1796, a copperplate printing press under princely protection. Erdmannsdorff was artistic director of this enterprise, which was organized like a modern joint-stock company, and responsible for the publications programme. The graphic works printed here were supposed to disseminate the new aesthetic ideas and influence public taste. His plans came only partly to fruition, but his ideas were astonishingly modern, even reminiscent of the concept behind the Bauhaus, which moved to Dessau 130 years later.

These two tasks drained Erdmannsdorff's final reserves of energy. He died in Dessau on 9 March, 1800, profoundly mourned by his many friends.

Prince Franz was always aware what an important role Erdmannsdorff played for him as a friend, adviser, and also as a critic. After his death he said: "If I had not had Erdmannsdorff at my side, who always encouraged and refreshed me when I threatened to tire, there are many things that I would not have begun, and others that I would have abandoned. I have him to thank, the country has him to thank, for conducting and perfecting most of everything that is there, and that gives people pleasure."

Erdmannsdorff on architecture

Ingo Pfeifer

Erdmannsdorff started to address questions of architectural theory at an early stage. He was quick to come across the *Ten Books of Architecture* by the Roman author, Marcus Vitruvius Pollio, when studying proportions and decorations. The latter's treatise is the only surviving work on ancient architectural theory.

Motivated by English and French translations, Erdmannsdorff had started to translate the Latin text into German as early as 1764. This translation was later completed by his friend August Rode, thus providing a new, accessible German edition of this work, 200 years after Walter Ryff's version.

Vitrivius still held that the categories firmness, commodity and delight were of equal value in architecture, but in the late 18th century, greater emphasis on structural and functional elements led artists to take more interest in the technical aspects of architecture, and those relating to materials. The development of natural sciences like mathematics, physics and chemistry, promoted at the latest in the mid 18th century by the Enlightenment, increasingly brought these disciplines into the field of architecture.

In line with his universal approach, all building projects, be they palaces or farmhouses, were of equal value. His view was that they all demanded the same care and the application of the same principles. So Erdmannsdorff was not just the architect of the first neo-classical building in Germany, the country seat in Wörlitz, but also responsible for many minor architectural features in the garden landscape between Dessau and Wörlitz, right down to the domestic buildings for the Wörlitz demesne or the village schools in Griesen and Riesigk.

As an architect, he was always drawn to the "indispensable and generally useful" arts and crafts. "Among these we include mainly all those that are employed for the making of our homes, likewise the many different devices that have become necessary to meet our needs and provide for our comfort, indeed all those that work to measure and compass, chalk-line and set-square, balance and plumb-line."

Thus Erdmannsdorff is emphasizing the clear precedence of architecture and interior decoration (furniture and crafts) over all other artistic genres, especially over the "fine arts". Erdmannsdorff's image of the artist is influenced by his view that aesthetics and mechanics, art and know-how, belong together. Here he is visibly putting the emphasis on the mechanical-useful side, but agrees that it cannot exist without aesthetic "improvement". A work can only achieve perfection when the two elements are combined.

Towards the end of the century, Erdmannsdorff found his way out of a view of art shaped by rules to a free art, determined by the artist himself. "In the free arts, only few ... precepts based on generally valid reasoned conclusions are to be revered as immutable laws. ... Guided by his genius, he builds his forms and orders his relations in accordance with his own taste and his own judgement." Erdmannsdorff wrote these sentences in his foreword to the *Architektonische Studien*, a work intended to be used by young artists as illustrative material in their education.

At the same time as Erdmannsdorff emancipated himself from slavish imitation of nature and ancient art, he also abandoned the idea that art needs rules and instructions. "Yet art would be greatly diminished and its boundaries very restricted if one were to see fit to consider such rules, given as examples, as unchangeable instructions to artists," he wrote in 1797. He once summed up his artistic credo like this: "The closer the thinker and the worker, the scholar and the businessman, the philosopher and the artist come to each other, the better all their enterprises will proceed."

The portico of the Wörlitz Schloss with its dedicatory inscription:
FRANCICVS PR. AEDIF. INSTRVXIT. LVDOVICAE CONIVGI. DIGNISS. D.
(Prince Franz built it, furnished for Luise, his most worthy consort).

Ingo Pfeifer

Schloss Wörlitz – a neo-classical masterpiece

A new era begins: the country seat as a seminal building for neoclassicism ▸ On approaching the house at Wörlitz, the surprising feature is its lucidity and the harmony of its architectural design. The prince intended that his new house in Wörlitz show visitors from the moment they arrived, what aesthetic ideas and philosophical approaches he intended to follow. This needed a new artistic and architectural concept. Wörlitz was not to be a palace intended for summer pleasures, of the kind that European rulers built well into the 18th century, but a house in the style of the rural villa, appropriate for a prosperous, enlightened citizen-prince. The private man was to be in the foreground now, not the prince as a public person responsible for the state. Comfortable living and functionality in the rooms were much more important to the client and his architect than superficial pomp. A baroque façade design, blurring

the ground plan disposition and the function of the rooms, would have been wrong here. And a building like a town palace would also not have fitted in with the prince's ideas. So the architect Friedrich Wilhelm von Erdmannsdorff was faced with the task of designing a building of a quite different type.

Erdmannsdorff sought and found ideas in the country seats and villas designed and built by the Italian architect, Andrea Palladio, in the 16th century. His architecture, which borrowed from ancient forms and was appropriately adapted to life in the country, had been an important source of inspiration for the building of aristocratic country seats here and in England since the 17th century. As in the models he was following, Erdmannsdorff placed a portico of four columns with a triangular pediment in front of his well-proportioned building. A wide flight of open steps leads up to the main portal beneath it. From here, visitors enter into a circular entrance hall decorated with sculptures. All the rooms are grouped around an adjacent, open inner courtyard, borrowed from Roman building traditions, in such a way that the Great Hall, with access to the garden, can be directly reached from it.

With this Wörlitz house, whose outer forms present an almost modern-looking view of the functionality of the building, Erdmannsdorff introduced a new building type into German architectural history. It became Germany's first neo-classical building.

As an architect, Erdmannsdorff was not only responsible for the exterior, he also designed or acquired the individual items of furniture and decoration, so that everything fused into a perfect work of spatial art. Design and furnishings are well-considered in terms of the individual rooms, the art-

With its restrained proportions and reserved façade decoration, the building seems to be a translation into architecture of Winckelmann's postulate of "edle Einfalt und stille Größe" (noble simplicity and quiet greatness).

The visitor is met by plaster casts of ancient sculptures in the entrance rotunda of the palace. The Apollo Belvedere symbolizes knowledge, education and beauty, as well as indicating the prince's passion for antiquity.

works are selected to fit in with the overall educational programme.

The insertion of two simple, narrow oak stairways in the interior, forming a stark contrast with the magnificent, sweeping stairwells of the baroque era, underlines the fact that the claim to power has been withdrawn.

As well as the social and private rooms on the ground floor, which were occupied by the princely couple themselves, the middle floor of the house contained six apartments, each with living rooms and bedrooms, for family members and the court. The special position occupied by Erdmannsdorff at the court can be seen from the fact that he, too, had rooms of his own at his disposal. Accommodation for the servants was provided in the low intermediate floor under the roof, whose narrow band of windows runs round three sides of the house.

Erdmannsdorff did not only follow the theories of the ancient architect Vitruvius and his successor Palladio with their instructions about the positioning and arrangement of buildings and rooms, he was also inspired by ancient forms, ornaments and materials. He chose individual elements, such as door designs, friezes or entablatures from various ancient buildings, so that they could be combined with each other in a new way in his buildings. Examples of individual details can be found by leafing through the 18th century publications in the architect's library.

For example, we can find models for the design of the doors and window jambs in the Wörlitz house in Robert Wood's book, *The Ruins of Balbec otherwise Heliopolis in Coelosyria*, about the Roman temple in Syria. Erdmannsdorff's early creative period is characterized by the use of precisely copied ancient building parts or decorations. Here, ancient forms were not just a reference to completed study, but also expressed a new, enlightened and educated life. Erdmannsdorff's "archaeological classicism" started a new epoch in German architecture: it was the first time in architectural history that the results of archaeological studies had been used as a basis for developing a new style.

An idea takes shape ‣ It was decided as early as 1765 that a new garden should be located in Wörlitz. Work started three years later on pulling down the late 17th century baroque hunting lodge to make room for the new country seat. Erdmannsdorff had already started work on his designs for the new complex in 1766. Working from a first idea, which already featured the number of floors that

would later be built and the columned hall with open stairs, he kept bringing his designs closer to the neo-classical ideal. The baroque hipped roof originally planned was replaced by an attic storey at an intermediate stage, and then by the gable roof that was finally built. Moving away from the original draft plans, he reduced the height of the second floor and added the open inner courtyard to the ground plan, with the rooms grouped around it. The foundation stone was laid on 5 April, 1769. A small sandstone tablet in the south-west corner of the house carries an inscription referring to this important date. The building inspector Johann Gottlieb Daumann took over direct control on site.

The building was dedicated on 22 March, 1773 with a celebration at which almost all those present were dressed in ancient costume and Prince Franz asked his consort to take possession of the house that had been built for her. The dedication decorates the pediment frieze of the portico as a Latin inscription. The tablet above the entrance portal, carrying the words: "Love and friendship have built it / May unity and peace inhabit it / Thus domestic joys will not be lacked"

The ceiling in the second Chinese room, the "Day Room", is adorned with a gilded sun and four dragons. These symbols, and also the furniture, were designed from patterns by William Chambers.

refers to the prince's desire to be able to conduct harmonious family life here with his consort.

There was still some decoration to be done in the interior after the dedication. In 1783/84, the prince additionally had a belvedere built on the attic storey at the rear of the building. This contains a room decorated with wooden mock palm-trees and supports a small, accessible platform. The four sandstone urns that originally stood on the attic storey were taken down and were placed at the rear driveway and in the garden. The atrium, which had been open until then, was given a glass roof some time in the mid 19th century.

Chinoiserie at the time of the Enlightenment ‣ Visitors entering the Schloss and expecting furnishing and decorations in the ancient style in accordance with the house's outward appearance, may be surprised at first when they move from the round entrance hall into two rooms furnished in Chinese fashion. But this chinoiserie is not a play with forms, driven by taste, as is the case with rococo. It expresses an educational interest, which was not directed only at antiquity, but at ancient Chinese art and philosophy as well. It was the

English above all who brought this distant land's lore and art to Europe in the 18th century. The architect Sir William Chambers played a particular part in this. He visited China himself in 1748/49 and, on his return, published a lavishly illustrated book called *Designs of chinese Buildings, Furnitures, Dresses, Machines and Utensils*. Erdmannsdorff not only knew this book, but also the Briton's numerous buildings, including the Chinese pagoda in London's Kew Gardens. The clear geometrical forms of the Chinese furniture and wall ornaments corresponded perfectly with the views of the Dessau architect, who had been trained to appreciate antiquity. Hence it was easy for him to integrate decorations and furnishings of this kind into the building. The rooms form a creative unit, decorated with original Chinese wallpaper, woodcuts and porcelain. As with his architectural designs, Erdmannsdorff closely followed his models for the chinoiserie. So all the designs for the furniture, the wall ornaments and the lamps in the second Chinese room are to be found in Chambers's book.

Inspiration from England: Chippendale and folding furniture ‣ England also provided the stimulus for other pieces of

The curved and multiply-pierced backs of the chairs in the dining room adapt the forms of the popular Chippendale furniture. Tables that can be folded open to provide one large surface and an ice-cupboard hidden in a statue plinth emphasize the functional nature of the furnishings.

furniture, mostly made to designs by Erdmannsdorff, by the Dessau cabinet-maker Johann Andreas Irmer. For example, the upholstered pear-wood chairs with slightly curved, decoratively pierced backs, placed in the dining room along a long table made up of three folding units. Their relationship with English models by Thomas Chippendale (1718-1779) is striking, but these chairs are rather more subdued in their appearance. They were also referred to as "engländische Stühle" in an account dated 1769, even though they were made in Dessau. They are now known as "Prince Franz chairs", and are to be found in all the Anhalt-Dessau palaces, in pear-wood or ebony, and covered with leather, horse-hair or silk.

The numerous, extremely practical items of folding furniture are also based on English models. For example, folding beds for servants were concealed under one of the windows in the first Chinese room, and behind blind doors in the ballroom. A high degree of functionality and space saving were characteristics of British furniture design. Because there was so little space on ships, the maritime nation's cabinet-makers constantly developed new types of folding furniture. As the salt water of the world's oceans would have damaged a

painted finish and metal decorations, the surfaces were protected with wax and resin only, and brass rather than iron was used for the fittings and hinges. These characteristics are also to be found in the Wörlitz furniture.

Erdmannsdorff as a furniture designer ‣ On the main floor of the country seat in Wörlitz, the original furniture has survived intact over time, which is rarely the case. Items of furniture in particular, which Erdmannsdorff designed specially for each room as components of the décor as a whole, determine the room's appearance. The lavishly decorated wall tables in the two long rooms are impressive examples. The fluted legs, painted white and gold, have vines winding around them, with leaves and grapes underneath the tabletop. The ensembles are completed with chairs, stools and sofas covered in green silk. These tables were made by the cabinet-maker Johann Andreas Irmer, working with the sculptor Johann Christian Ehrlich. Similar chairs and sofas, though without the coloured paint, are to be found in the corner rooms. Their visible wood underlines the elegant forms of old vase paintings, borrowed from ancient furniture. Here, the chairs are combined with tables whose legs

The dining room mantelpieces are decorated with vases in the ancient style from Josiah Wedgwood's English manufactory.

Italian coastal scenes and ancient ruins on the lavishly decorated ceiling
of the first corner room identify staging posts on the Grand Tour.

The ballroom, the largest room in the house, is an impressive reminder
of the Grand Tour. It is dominated by paintings based on originals by
the Carracci brothers from the Galeria Farnese.

rest on gilded pine-cones and whose frames are adorned with rosettes and laurel wreaths. The table-tops are veneered with varied yellow marble from North Africa.

The furniture in the princess's chamber deserves special attention, as it is of very high quality. Four chairs are grouped around a delicate oval table on slightly curved legs. Two small cupboards and two adaptable games tables complete the ensemble by the cabinet-maker Abraham Roentgen, whose workshop in Neuwied am Rhein enjoyed a reputation that went far beyond the bounds of Germany in the 18th century. This was based, above all, on good workmanship, variety and the outstanding marquetry work on the furniture, all of which feature impressively on the Wörlitz pieces. Walnut veneer is laid on a pear-wood support. The ornaments and decorations in dyed maple, mahogany and various root timbers were set into the veneer. The top of the small oval table is decorated with rose blossoms and curved bands. This lightness and playful elegance is also to be found on the tops of the multi-purpose tables. Here, objects associated with female activities – pen and notepaper, playing cards, and a racquet with shuttlecocks are combined to form an ensemble and framed with plant tendrils. The three table tops, one on top of the other, indicate that the table does not serve one

purpose only. Swinging a leg round 90 degrees covers the flap that has been opened up at the back. The surface that becomes immediately visible upon opening, covered with green baize, was used for playing cards. The next two changes reveal a chessboard and a board for Trick-Track (a historical board game). A reading desk can also be set up, and a roller cover at the side conceals an inkwell and storage space for the game pieces.

Ornaments that recur on all pieces of furniture and bring the ensemble together are the leaf clusters on the legs and a garland with a medallion on the frames.

Ceramics à la grecque ▸ A collection of early ceramics from the important English manufactory belonging to Josiah Wedgwood is one of the special treasures to be found at Wörlitz. Wedgwood, who lived in Staffordshire in the English provinces, drew Queen Charlotte's attention to his innovative products around 1765. A light-coloured body reminiscent of porcelain, the lightness of the material and a markedly lower price, very quickly made his "Cream Ware" popular in England. With a sure artistic instinct, Wedgwood recognized a new trait in his customers' taste: their increasing interest in ancient art meant that they were increasingly

The slender, curved lines of the furniture take up ancient formal motifs. Their colours match the wall hangings in the room.

trying to furnish their homes à la grecque. The magnificent volumes about Sir William Hamilton's collection of ancient vases provided Wedgwood with ideas for his own products, and also with a name for his new manufactory, opened in 1769: "Etruria". The name was also intended to be a programme – the revival of ancient ceramics.

But simply copying ancient forms was not enough for Josiah Wedgwood. His relentless search for new material qualities and colour variants led him to develop "Black Basalt Ware", made from a compounded clay, and his famous "Jasper Ware", stoneware coloured with metal oxides, which is still synonymous with Wedgwood products in its blue-and-white colour combination.

Presumably Prince Franz had come across Wedgwood products while in England on his Grand Tour in 1766. He took his first delivery from England in 1772, and was delighted. Nothing seemed more suitable to him than these ceramics for furnishing his new neo-classical country seat in Wörlitz. Vases based on ancient originals were placed on the two fireplaces in the dining room. Other decorative vases of different sizes and figured candleholders in "Black Basalt Ware", some made to designs by William Chambers, and showing the highly artistic ambitions of both the manufacturer and

the purchaser, decorate the mantelpieces in the two long rooms. The small reliefs in Black Basalt Ware with portraits of British poets, which were kept in the Wörlitz library as collectors' pieces, are further proof of the manufactory's versatility.

The two most famous pieces in the Wörlitz collection are the small figure of a Ganymede in Black Basalt Ware in the first long room and the *Somnus* in the princess's bedroom. A sculpture in the Bargello in Florence provided a model for the statuette of Ganymede. Benvenuto Cellini had completed it as a full sculpture from an ancient torso in the 16th century, and it was very popular in the 18th century. The figure, put together from several shaped pieces, was probably originally produced in large quantities, but only the Wörlitz specimen has survived. The mastery of Wedgwood's modellers can be seen particularly in the figure of *Somnus*, a sleeping boy, based on the marble original by Alessandro Algardi (1598-1654) in the Galleria Borghese. The piece measures about 64 x 36 centimetres, and adorned the pediment on the princess's bed from 1773. It consists of several skilfully assembled parts. It is one of the largest and earliest Black Basalt Ware works ever produced in the manufactory.

Green, white and gold are the dominant colours in the second long room. Valuable paintings from the Orange Inheritance and Wedgwood ceramics on the mantelpiece complete the interior.

All the furniture in the princess's chamber, with the exception of the little oval table, was specially created for this room to designs by Friedrich Wilhelm von Erdmannsdorff in 1771/72. This was the first neo-classical furniture to be made in the Roentgen workshop.

Italian reminiscences ‣ Sunny Italy was and still is the land longed for by all Europeans north of the Alps. Here, travellers on the Grand Tour visited the most revered ancient sites, and here they came across the admired villas of the Renaissance. Anyone who had ever travelled to Italy wanted to be reminded of what had been experienced there.

The first corner room in the Wörlitz house is the room that most brings these memories to life. Its colour scheme, with an interplay of light yellow and green, seems to invoke the sunny south, and also corresponds with the colours in the surrounding landscape garden. Painted depictions of various Roman ruins and allegories on the stucco ceiling allude to the city of Rome and its historical origins. The paintings over the door are by Francesco Zuccarelli (1702-1788), showing Cicero discovering the tomb of Archimedes and a scene with Bacchantes, also relate to antiquity, as does a cycle by Andrea Locatelli (1695-1741) consisting of four pictures of the Diana myth. Small pictures by Giacomo van Lint (1723-1790) are inserted into the fine stucco on the outer walls; they show buildings in ancient Rome and its environs. Two busts of Roman empresses and an ancient statue of Venus complete the furnishings.

The magic of Italy is also to the fore in the neighbouring long room. Large paintings by the Flemish artist Frans van Bloemen (1662-1742), who worked in Italy, show southern landscape with picturesquely composed ancient ruins. Some of them can be identified precisely, others are products of the artist's imagination. These views combine the charm of the Italian landscape with an interest in ancient art. In reality, such things were seldom found so close together, but in compositions like this they can be fitted together to form an ideal. These pieces create an image of a harmonious antiquity rescued for the present day, intended to be reflected in the Wörlitz gardens when one looked out of the window.

Souvenirs of the Grand Tour ‣ Rome, the religious centre of Christendom, has attracted travellers from all over the world from time immemorial. When the pilgrims were joined in the city by an increasing number of Grand Tourists looking for antiquity, a new branch of craftwork emerged to produce souvenirs. Everyone who travelled to Italy wanted to take a small or larger piece of antiquity home. This need could be met in terms of architecture by Antonio Chichi's (1743-1816) famous cork models, or large-format copperplate engravings. Bartolomeo Cavaceppi and other craftsmen tried to meet travellers' wishes for sculpture with genuine, modified or copied marble pieces, and numerous painters offered views of the city or pictures with scenes from ancient mythology.

Anyone who could not afford the rapidly increasing prices for original ancient items had to make do with plaster or bronze copies on a smaller scale. We find examples of every variant in the Wörlitz Schloss. The prince bought genuinely ancient pieces from Cavaceppi, and also a total of ten marble copies of ancient busts in their original size, which were displayed on the tables in the corner rooms and on the cupboards in the Wörlitz Schloss library. The little bronzes, about 30 to 35 centimetres high, that were shown on the mantelpieces in the Grosser Saal (Great Hall), are outstandingly important. They were created by the Roman silversmith and bronze sculptor Giacomo Zoffoli (c. 1731-1785). His reduced copies link ancient artistic tradition with fine material and craftsmanly dexterity. He was almost second to none in his masterly understanding of reproducing even the

A putto carrying off a club and a lion's skin, the attributes of Hercules. This little image at the foot of the bed in the princess's bedroom alludes to the fact that even the greatest heroes can be overcome by the power of love.

tiniest details of a garment's folds or a hairdo in his miniature sculptures. As well as this, he gave his bronzes a greenish, ancient-looking patina.

Plaster sculptures as the simplest variant on the Rome souvenir are to be found in the upper part of the wall in the second corner room; here in the niches stand four famous figures of antiquity on a reduced scale, including Flora and the Farnese Hercules.

The large pictures in the ballroom are a special kind of souvenir. They are copies of ceiling frescoes by Annibale (1560-1609) and Agostino Carracci (1557-1602) in the gallery of the Palazzo Farnese, dating from around 1600. Love in all its many forms, often between gods and human beings, determines fate in these scenes from ancient mythology. Erdmannsdorff was particularly drawn to the Carraccis as their painting style, in the Renaissance tradition, fitted in with his aesthetic ideas. Set in wall cladding of coloured stucco marble, they dominate the room, which gains additional light from above from two windows. It was otherwise lit by 100 candles; their holders are scarcely visible in front of a painted frieze with amoretti and acanthus tendrils.

A small collection of stones and pieces of marble in concealed compartments in the library cupboards is one of the more unusual pieces of memorabilia, reflecting the prince's interest in geology. Accompanying labels identify the places where the finds were made in the course of the journey.

Antiquities – one of the prince's passions ▸ "There is absolutely nothing comparable with antiquities, and I prefer a single one of them to ten modern statues." This statement by Prince Franz is borne out by his collection of ancient sculptures. It was not particularly difficult to acquire ancient sculptures in Rome in the second half of the 18th century. On the contrary, it was "really difficult to resist the temptation, so long as one still had qualche danaro in one's pocket," as the Dessau harbinger, Georg Heinrich von Berenhorst, noted in his diary. Prince Franz bought his first antiquities in Italy as early as 1766, and Erdmannsdorff later dispatched more from Rome. Of the eleven ancient sculptures on show in the Wörlitz house as part of the furnishings, almost all probably passed through the hands of Bartolomeo Cavaceppi, the most important dealer and restorer handling antiquities in the Rome of his day. They include the Venus with shell in the first corner room. Here, the Italian had put an ancient head that did not belong to it on an ancient torso, and had completed the arms and the shell freely. This was common

practice in the 18th century, as only figures that were entirely complete met the aesthetic demands of that period.

The most important antiquities are displayed in the Wörlitz library. Busts of a Tyche, a Diana, and the torso of a wounded Amazon stand in the three niches between the bookcases. The last has become known as the "Wörlitz Amazon", because of its archaeological significance and artistic beauty. Prince Franz acquired the sculpture in Rome from the English art dealer Thomas Jenkins. The usual additions to create a complete figure were not made, even though the torso consisted only of the upper part of the body and the surviving head. Obviously the restorer had such respect for this masterpiece that he only carried out minor repairs and the purchaser was also aesthetically satisfied with the sculpture in this form.

The rare, small statue of a drunken Hercules on the commode in the prince's bedroom occupied a special place in the Schloss Wörlitz antiquities collection. Winckelmann mentioned it with great respect in one of his writings. The acquisition of an ancient bell-crater, the only vase in the prince's collection, can also be traced back to Winckelmann. This mixing vessel for wine was illustrated in the first French edition of Winckelmann's *Geschichte der Kunst*.

Today, the library cupboards are filled with other small ancient sculptures and ceramics. Some of them were among the works first displayed in the Pantheon or come from the collection of Princess Anna Maria of Prussia, who was born Princess of Anhalt. The pieces came to the Wörlitz house when she died in 1911.

The library – a place of knowledge ▸ The room connecting the princely couple's bedrooms contains the library. The walls are lined with lime-wood bookcases that have the doors to the adjacent rooms built into them so that they form a coherent design when closed. On three sides, large niches are let into the bookcases to accommodate ancient busts, while the fourth side of the area is left open for a stove that used to be there. Busts of the Roman emperors Trajan, Hadrian, Antonius Pius and Marcus Aurelius by Cavaceppi stand on the bookcases. These were the so-called peace emperors, who stood as models for the enlightened prince. 92 grisaille portraits of artists, scholars, poets, philosophers and theologians cover the walls above the bookcases right up to the ceiling. Here, the Berlin painter Johann Fischer used a very strict grid pattern relating to the room's architectural forms. Depictions of ancient authors are to be found in the

Right-hand page ▸ The marble torso of the "Wörlitz Amazon" in the bookcase on the north wall of the library is a Roman copy of a wounded Amazon of the "Sosicles type", dating from c. 150 AD.

Palladianism

Ingo Pfeifer

The European neo-classical architectural movement known as Palladianism, extending from the 16th to the 18th century, goes back to the Italian Renaissance architect Andrea Palladio (1508-1580). Palladio, who worked mainly in the Veneto, had made a thorough study of ancient Roman architecture and its proportion theories. Starting with the writings of Vitruvius, whose ten-volume work, De architectura, survives as the only ancient treatise on architecture, Palladio published Quattro libri dell' archittetura in 1570. This work introduced his numerous villas and town houses to a wider public, and thus made architects once again aware of ancient proportion theory and ideas about dimensions. Palladio's designs were based on an unusual application of colossal orders, in which the columns or pilasters in a façade rose through several storeys. Other features are columned porticoes, loggias and arcades. His rural villas, in particular, which followed Roman models by usually serving farming needs as well, have an often restrained, cubic central section and a colonnade with open steps, reminiscent of temple façades.

This architectural approach was taken up as a counter-design to Catholic, Roman baroque, above all in Protestant northern Europe, first in the Netherlands and in England. The British architect Inigo Jones (1573-1652) was the first to stimulate the spread of this style.

In the early 18th century, the English aristocracy rediscovered Palladianism. Political opponents to the erosion of liberal principles by the Hanoverian kings felt that villa culture and the glorification of rural life were appropriate to their social ideals. They transformed their regular, quiet baroque gardens outside London into landscape gardens, adorned with villa architecture modelled on Palladio. The architects William Kent (c. 1685-1748) and Colen Campbell (c. 1675-1729) created a number of country seats in the Palladian style, retaining ancient proportions and combining a central wing with living accommodation with the necessary domestic and farm facilities in the side wings. Comfort and elegance were more sought-after here than courtly pomp and affected ceremonial behaviour. This process was considerably promoted by Richard Boyle, 3rd Earl of Burlington (1695-1753). He had seen Palladio's villas on a visit to the Veneto and acquired some of the architect's estate. He laid out a landscape garden at his country seat in Chiswick, and built a Palladian-style villa there in around 1725. His social position meant that his creations very soon became models for other noblemen and citizens. Palladianism soon became the dominant architectural style in 18th century England and spread to the continent from there.

Cardinal Alessandro Albani, the owner of what was then the largest
private collection of antiquities in Italy, presented this marble statue
of the Drunken Hercules to Franz in 1766. It is a first-century Roman
version of a Hellenistic predecessor, dating from the third century BC.

upper area, and underneath them are the faces of the younger generations, down to the prince's contemporaries. Many of the portraits are painted from authors' portraits on the frontispieces of their books. Portraits that have come down archaeologically or also Raphael's *School of Athens*, a famous 16th century mural from the Vatican Stanze, in which the painter brought together imaginary portraits of the major ancient philosophers, were used as a basis for the ancient writers. Each wall, as August Rode tells us in his guide, was allotted to books and portraits from a certain field of knowledge: the north wall to poetry and rhetoric, the east wall to history and the fine arts, the south wall to philosophy and theology and the west wall to legislation and morality. As the books were sold after 1918, it is no longer possible to verify that they were arranged in this way.

Erdmannsdorff obviously found immediate inspiration for the iconographic design in Rome, in the Sala della Segnatura. This room decorated with early 16th century frescoes by Raphael, in which allegories of philosophy, theology, poetry and jurisprudence were brought together in mock architec-

ture, was used by Pope Julius II as a library. But Erdmannsdorff moved away from his model and combined philosophy and theology as worldly wisdom, thus making room for the academic discipline of writing down history, which was so important in the late 18th century. He described the design for the ceiling of this room in particular detail in a letter to the prince. This suggests that the golden sun in the middle symbolizes Apollo, the god of light and of the sciences. The signs of the Zodiac around it refer to astronomy as one of the oldest sciences, and stuccoed reliefs symbolize the other sciences. Here, a philosopher with muse appears as an embodiment of worldly wisdom; another muse, noting down the deeds of a hero, stands for history; the goddess of justice instructs an emperor, to indicate jurisprudence, and Orpheus, with the animals listening to his song, symbolizes poetry.

The Netherlandish paintings ‣ Prince Franz was proud of his Dutch-Orange roots throughout his lifetime. Hence, Netherlandish works of art always formed an important part

The bed in the prince's bedroom with a built-in writing desk was copied from an English model. Prince Franz also kept his favourite travel souvenirs in this room.

of his collections, especially as he was able to draw on the original Orange holdings. Just as his aunt Anna Wilhelmine had done for Mosigkau, the young Prince Franz also bought several pictures from the estate of his great aunt Marie Eleonore, Duchess of Radziwill, in 1756. It was not until 15 years later that some of them were to find a new permanent home in the prince's country seat. It is highly probable that the selection was made by Erdmannsdorff, who particularly admired the works of the Flemish school, mainly those of its principal exponents Rubens and van Dyck. Erdmannsdorff concentrated the pictures from the "Orange Inheritance" and some other Netherlandish paintings in the second long room and the concert room.

When going into the second long room, two pictures dealing with ancient subject matter draw attention: Peter Paul Rubens's *Marriage of Alexander the Great to Roxane* and Peter Thys's *Hermes discovers Herse*. The Rubens painting was owned by Amalia von Solms, and originally hung in her home in The Hague. Her husband, Friedrich Heinrich, probably gave it to her as a wedding present in 1625, which suggests an interpretation of the painting as an allegory on the couple's marriage.

The *Holy Family* by Jan Erasmus Quellinus (1625-1700) and *Hermes discovers Herse* by Peter Thys (1616-1667) had also been in Anhalt-Dessau ownership for three generations. The long room contains mainly works by Flemish masters, while most of the works in the adjacent concert room are by Dutch painters. A *Canal Landscape* by Salomon Ruysdael (c. 1600-1670) and two works by Jan Verkolje (1650-1693) are particularly worthy of attention.

The two portraits above the doors of the room are also important: Amalia von Solms and Friedrich Heinrich von Oranien by Anthony van Dyck (1599-1641). These two portraits are also from the extensive Orange estate. But as the two originals were sold by the duchy of Anhalt after 1918, their place is now taken by copies.

Hidden treasures ‣ Erdmannsdorff's concept for the interior decoration was not restricted to the prestigious rooms on the main floor of the Wörlitz country seat, but also included the rooms on the other floors. As the ducal family, who lived in the house until 1926, replaced individual pieces of furniture over the years in the less prestigious living rooms, the furniture here dates only partially from the time the house was built. Most of the surviving furniture dates from the first half of the 19th century. The original stucco decora-

tion and the wall and ceiling paintings have survived intact, however. Models for them include ancient paintings, as in the decorations for the small niche in the dressing room, for which Erdmannsdorff selected motifs from wall paintings discovered in Stabiae or Pompeii. They show the typical filigree column constructions with screens and garlands of fruit or flowers.

Contemporary copperplate prints were often chosen for the large-format wall paintings. Thus the dressing room on the ground floor contains a total of six wall paintings with views of English parks that the prince saw on his visits to England. They include Windsor, and also Wilton in Wiltshire and West Wycombe in Buckinghamshire, which have exemplary landscape gardens with neo-classical park architecture. The large wall pictures in four of the six living rooms in the first floor apartments depict the major Italian destinations on the Grand Tour. The five pictures in Prince Hans Jürge's living room show various ancient buildings in Rome like the Colosseum and the Pantheon. The ladies-in-waiting have Florentine city views in their living rooms, including the famous view from the Uffizi arbour, while Erdmannsdorff chose Venice as the theme for his living room. He probably felt particularly attached to this city through memories of his first visit to Italy. Naples appears as the fourth important destination in Italy in Prince Albert's living room. Six views of the Neapolitan coast with ancient temples and the famous

The famous antiquities scholar Johann Joachim Winckelmann, here in a portrait by Anton von Maron dating from 1768, was an important spiritus rector for Prince Franz.

road thrusting through under the Possilippo decorate the room.

Some Chinese decorative painting has survived in the room under the palm hall, while in the rooms on the mezzanine floor, which were originally occupied by servants, copper-plate engravings had been stuck to the wall as decorations, or flower tendrils were painted on.

Functionality and comfort: the technical equipment ‣ Erdmannsdorff was particularly concerned that his buildings should function correctly and be comfortable to live in, so he was keen to have modern technical equipment. For hygienic reasons, he placed the kitchen in a separate domestic building, and built an underground tunnel from there to the house. Two little hand-operated lifts in the two halves of the corridor created an invisible connection between the first two floors of the house and the cellar. They were used to transport firewood, night-soil disposal necessities and other items.

Contemporaries always admired the high level of technical equipment. The "water machine", which was made in England, was found particularly fascinating. It was used to distribute water from the well in the cellar to all floors of the house. Water containers rather like sarcophaguses stand in the corridors of the main and first floors. "If one opens the lid of the water container, one finds a vessel with a tap at one end of it, and by turning it on, water emerges as wished, drawn up by a machine from the basement. Water that overflows falls into a vessel that also has a tap in its floor, through which the water can be drained out into the courtyard, whence underground pipes take it to the lake." This comes from August Rode's report. At that time, running water on every floor was an almost incredible luxury. Setting up a "bathroom" in the cellar was unusual as well.

As well as these major technical achievements, many other minor things contributed to the house-dwellers' comfort. For example, the plinth for the statue of Ganymede in the dining room contains an ice cupboard for cooling drinks. Anyone who wanted to go up to the palm hall experienced the drama of a ship's staircase let into the ceiling of the room that could be let gently down against counterweights. And mention should also be made of the many small cast-iron stoves used to heat the rooms. These were portable, and could be set up quickly where needed.

Prince August Ferdinand of Prussia was one of the admirers of these technical refinements. Before he started building Schloss Bellevue in Berlin, he sent craftsmen to Wörlitz in 1785 to study the details of Erdmannsdorff's buildings there. The future palace builder pointed out: " ... 4. There ... in particular there are machines in the basement that pump water to the topmost floor. 5. The doors and locks that, when they are opened, fit into the wall and cannot be seen. 6. The machines should be seen that enable the night-buckets and wood to be transported up and down. 7. You will please notice all the commodes and compendious lockers and cupboards. 8. You must, above all, be sure to obtain models and drawings from workers there of all remarkable pieces, or if that is not possible, make drawings yourselves and deliver any such to me on your return."

The Wörlitz country seat, one of the most important European buildings of the 18th century, inspired a number of architects. Together with the gardens that surround it, it became the germ-cell of the Wörlitz Garden Realm. Erdmannsdorff's friend and biographer August Rode, praised the artistic completeness of this architectural work: "He seems here to have used everything that his art, science and imagination could deliver ... A magical charm flows out over it all."

On visits to Schloss Wörlitz, many 19th century princes and sovereigns added their signatures to a wall by a window on the top floor of the house.

Prints of engraved gems were not just popular souvenirs, but also
sources of artistic inspiration and educational objects. Prince Franz
collected over 2000 of them altogether.

The palm room was added in 1784, and takes its name from the unusual decorative elements. The room was used as a belvedere, with a narrow spiral staircase leading to a roof terrace.

Reinhard Alex

The Gothic House –
a refuge for the prince

The original building and its extensions ▸ Who could be more familiar with the prince's ideas about building than August von Rode, a highly educated cabinet councillor to Prince Franz of Anhalt-Dessau for many years, and topographer of the Garden Realm? His description of the Gothic House appeared in 1818, the year after Franz died. The introduction states: "The Gothic House was not built to any previously existing plan. At first it was just a little house with pointed arches for the gardener; the front as now, just without ancillary buildings; the surrounding wall without battlements and on the door inserted in it, a painted Capuchin monk, which made it look like a monastery. The present entrance on the ground floor and the present antechamber on the top floor, whose walls are adorned with Gothic churches painted on lime, were the only things that the man, who had it built, prepared for himself. Gradually, but at very

great intervals, this house was enlarged and as it were transformed into a knightly seat... . This is the cause of the great irregularity of this building, and of the darkness in some of its corridors and chambers."

Of course August Rode was discreet enough not to mention one very private reason why Prince Franz set up rooms for himself in the Gothic House, and so liked to withdraw here: the prince's liaison with Luise Schoch, the daughter of the gardener, who also lived here. She was later ennobled, and Franz also had children with her.

One's attention is constantly drawn, from near or far, to the vigorously articulated building on the edge of Schoch's garden, but its complexity comes to light only when one walks all around it.

If you travel in a gondola along the densely planted Wolf's canal from the Wörlitzer See, the canal façade of the building appears rather surprisingly on a bend, slightly raised above a sloping lawn. Opposite it, at some distance, the neo-classical Temple of Flora can be made out, and next to it, the neo-Gothic nursery ensemble.

In 1773-74, when Erdmannsdorff's palace was nearly complete and the Gothic House was being built, there was only one neo-Gothic building in Germany, the Nauen Gate in Frederick's royal seat of Potsdam. It was built back in 1755 to an English model. But it was the building in Wörlitz rather than the one in Potsdam that was to become significant for the development of the neo-Gothic style, which went back to the Middle Ages. Unfortunately, we do not know to what extent Friedrich Wilhelm von Erdmannsdorff was involved in building the Gothic House and its extensions. But we can assume that the master builder was involved, as certain stylistic elements, such as the rosettes on

Wörlitz

The Gothic House at Wörlitz is outstandingly important in German architectural history: it is an early example of the neo-Gothic style that then appeared extensively in the 19th century.

the garden façade, point to the style, which he made his own. And the interior ceiling decorations, combining Gothic-style decorations with neo-classical structures, are particularly strong evidence in favour. But the sparse written records mention only that the prince's building director Georg Christoph Hesekiel (1732-1828) was involved in building the Gothic House, even though his creative contribution is still unclear. Prince Franz himself must have exerted some considerable influence here, as he was very fond of the Gothic style, and there is evidence that he actually wanted to build Schloss Wörlitz itself in the Gothic style. Franz once said to his later biographer, the Wörlitz provost Friedrich Reil, when the conversation came round to Goethe and his knowledge of antiquity: "But as far as Gothic architecture and beautiful garden art are concerned he would have to concede the prize to me and throw in the towel. He had never seen England." But in fact, English influence can be discerned only in the later building phases, not in the original building by the side of the canal.

As Rode mentioned, the Gothic House was not very large at first. Parts of an earlier gardener's house were included in the square run of the walls. The flanking domestic wings cannot have been added until 1787/88. Their hipped roofs, which are highly deleterious to the original image with free-standing battlements, date from a conversion in about 1850.

The view on the canal side is dominated by the façade of the original building. It was created as a reminiscence of probably the most beautiful Gothic church in Venice, Madonna dell'Orto, a brick building with gleaming white marble articulation. The façade of the Gothic House is articulated very similarly to the basilica church type: with a raised nave and lower aisles, divided into three by buttresses topped with pinnacles. Cornices, blind arcades and arch friezes accompany the sloping roof sections. Of course the façade is not on the same massive scale as its model. The brick structure on the plaster areas, which are now painted yellow, was an imitation, and the prince had to make do with stucco rather than marble for the decorative elements, and the figures in the archways were simply painted on, rather than being sculpted. But it was possible to achieve what was intended in this way – making visitors to the Wörlitz Park aware of an important work of art from an epoch in the distant past. Some of the other neo-Gothic buildings, apart from the ecclesiastical ones, that came into being in the Garden Realm at the time were also set-pieces evoking associations. Their exteriors suggested quite different functions,

like, for example, the Palm House that can be seen some distance away, with gables that create the effect of a church with a nave and no aisles.

The New Tower, with a prestigious room on the top floor, clearly set back from the building line, was not added until 1789/90. The essential structures of its articulation again derive from a Gothic work, the Schweidnitz Tower of Breslau Town Hall. The tall, pointed helm makes an overall impact in terms of the Gothic House, as it provides an upward-thrusting accent for the breadth of the façade. The staircase tower on the south side was built only four years earlier, when the building was being extended. It was probably instantly clear that an architectural counterweight was needed within the arrangement of irregular building masses.

The garden side ‣ In his practical actions, Franz tried to bring alive a motto borrowed from Horace: "the useful with the beautiful". His wide-ranging reform programme was aimed not least at modernizing agriculture and at propagating efforts of this kind. For example, new varieties of fruit trees were planted in an area for agricultural specimens behind his home, along with mulberries for the silk-worm breeding that had become fashionable, and racks to dry clover, the new fodder for the cattle grazing amidst picturesque Gothic forms. But towards the end of the 19th century, the charming situation at the Gothic House changed fundamentally: even though fruit trees had been planted again, the picture was consistently, and still is, darkened by towering conifers, which considerably detract from the effect made by the building and its proportions.

The busts were brought from Oranienbaum to the garden room of the Gothic House. In the middle: Johann Georg II of Anhalt-Dessau, a piece dating from 1700 by Johann Michael Döbel, and on either side, two works by François Dieussart, c. 1650: Wilhelm II of Orange and Friedrich Heinrich of Orange.

The educationally-based idea of Enlightenment that pervades the Wörlitz Park, that of making available to everyone artistic ideas from near and far, can also be seen when looking at the garden side of the Gothic House, which is markedly influenced by impressions of English architecture. As Prince Franz lived in the "Schoch House" on his numerous visits to Wörlitz, and the art collections were getting larger, he decided that an extension was needed. So in 1785 and 1786 a long, not very wide section was added, ending in a transverse element on the garden side. At the same time, the window in the rear of the church was turned into a doorway, and the paintings on the former outer walls painted over. The main entrance was now via a staircase tower added to the original building.

The entire side of the garden façade is taken up on the ground floor by a garden room glazed on three sides, which also served as a green-house in winter. It was not until later that three baroque marble busts of the prince's great-grandfather, Johann Georg II, and relatives from the House of Orange came here from a grotto that had been removed at Schloss Oranienbaum; they were placed in elaborately

designed Gothic-style niches. The contemporary panel painting, mounted on the ceiling, shows Henriette Catharina of Orange-Nassau as Caritas, surrounded by family members. So in effect, this room became a gallery of ancestral portraits.

A quarter of a century after this garden section was built, 38 years after building started on the Gothic House, Prince Franz finally called for another, final extension: buildings of the same height were added between the longitudinal and transverse sections between 1811 and 1813. Wall paintings framed with round arches in both the outer and the inner walled courtyard decorated the outside walls and give them a "medieval" accent.

The asymmetrical ground plan, full of nooks and crannies, of this complex that emerged over so many decades, is reminiscent of the English castles and stately homes seen on journeys, and so is the design of the garden façade – unlike the "Italian" canal façade. Here, white plaster articulation contrasts with the dark red brick, and this also applies to the extensions completed in 1813. The rendered areas of the wall originally imitated brick, so that the design of the different walls harmonized. The emphasis on horizontal façade artic-

The design of the Gothic House's garden façade suggests English origins. A summer room occupies the ground floor. Behind the windows of the upper floor, with their numerous stained glass panes, are the Knights' Room and the Martial and the Spiritual Cabinets.

ulation, the arch forms, curved gables and a lively roof zone with rising pinnacled piers and chimneys are reminiscent of 16th century Tudor architecture. This was the final phase of the Gothic style in England, which was already showing signs of Renaissance influences.

On their various visits to England, Erdmannsdorff and Prince Franz had acquired a number of architectural ideas. They were impressed both by Palladian neo-classicism and also by buildings in the "picturesque" style, combining Gothic and other historical elements. There were numerous neo-Gothic buildings, especially in the landscape gardens. For example, the garden side of the Gothic House in Wörlitz shows a certain kinship with the 1741 Temple of Liberty in Stowe. On the their first visit to England in 1763/64, the Dessau travellers probably visited the politician and writer Sir Horace Walpole (1717-1797), for whom Strawberry Hill in Twickenham was built from 1748 onwards, a Gothic-style country seat with battlemented watchtower, coloured window panes, and neo-Gothic interiors and furniture. The Gothic "revival" in England shortly before the middle of the 18th century was greatly supported by pattern books; in particular, Batty and Thomas Langley's early work, *Gothic Architecture*, dating from 1742, in which Gothic elements are integrated into a neo-classical building system, was of practical use for neo-Gothic building in Anhalt-Dessau.

The rooms in the Gothic House and their furniture and fittings ‣ Unlike Wörlitz Park and most of the buildings in it, the Gothic House was Prince Franz's private residence and not open to the public; only a very few interested parties were allowed in from time to time. In 1797, the Weimar schoolmaster, archaeologist and later director of the Dresden antiquities collection Carl August Boettiger visited Wörlitz. He left a description of his impressions, from which a few extracts are quoted here: "We hurried to the Gothic House and looked, drawn on by deliberately planted flowers as signposts, through hewn-out trees across at the Temple of Flora once more, and thus arrived in front of the rear façade of the Gothic House, much adorned and a lively, higgledy-piggledy, colourful mixture of turrets, dentated windows and doorways, and all manner of Gothic-Saracen curlicues.... Simply passing through the entrance to the anteroom below announces what is to be expected here.... This puts you in the right mood immediately: you are strolling here through nothing but monuments of the old German past! Tables, chairs and all the other pieces of equipment have been studiously brought into harmony and agreement here. Everything is in rectangular, pyramid-pointed zigzag, and yet embellished with moderation. It is the height of taste in tastelessness. Some of the portraits hanging here are costly relics of old German art, and are themselves of some considerable significance for art history. The most exquisite things are to be found on the upper floor, where the corridor walls are adorned with old daggers, sabres, firearms, indeed even with a military Turkish horsetail. ... Certainly, it is not possible to leave the Gothic House without feeling respect for its owner. It is all due to his studies, his work, and, to a certain extent, chance, that it only gradually came into being ... and has grown to this extent, and has turned out to be quite fitting for this unruly agglomeration of protruding corners, bay windows, towers etc."

Rather like August von Rode in his 1818 description, Carl August Boettiger has captured the essence and meaning of the Gothic House perfectly. He paid tribute to the lavish furnishings and also the collection of "old German" paintings, with works by Lucas Cranach the Elder, his workshop and other Reformation masters. The collection is still significant, despite 20th century losses.

The room by the entrance. The decorations dating from 1570/80 were brought here after the Dessau Schloss was rebuilt. The full-length depictions of biblical figures are probably from the same room, and other paintings were added in.

It is especially remarkable that Prince Franz was one of the first collectors in Germany to pay particular attention to such works of art whilst still in the final years of the Enlightenment, which was shaped by its veneration for antiquity, and before the arrival of Romanticism.

Even though Boettiger praised the princely builder's intentions and achievements to the skies, he was trapped within the ideas of his day. Given a view of history that was shaped by the Renaissance, Gothic was still seen as a primitive form of artistic expression, and was thus assessed negatively.

As was customary at the time, the learned author spoke of "tastelessness", in the sense of a lack of artistic rules that characterized Gothic as an expression of a dark age. Goethe's paean of praise, *Von deutscher Baukunst* (Of German Architecture), attracted little or no attention when it was published in 1772 and praised Strasbourg Minster as an outstanding national historical monument, along with its presumed architect, Erwin von Steinbach. It was not until the turn of the century that "Gothic taste" was re-evaluated.

From the once almost impossibly large collection, unfortunately severely reduced in the 20th century, the greatest and most valuable set of items has happily survived intact: even today, there will scarcely be a visitor to the Gothic House, who leaves unimpressed by the effect of the glowing colours of the stained glass. Prince Franz's interest in stained glass probably derived from the influence of Lavater. Certainly it was he who mediated the first purchase as early as 1783. The extension wing to the Gothic House was about to be completed during Lavater's visit to Wörlitz in 1786, and the effect of this and the rooms added subsequently is largely created by tall tracery windows containing stained glass, framed by a multitude of ornaments.

"Ihr Denkmal' alter Kunst und Gottvertrauter Zeiten!
Bewundrung, Wehmuth, Muth und Hoffnung sehn Euch an
Zwar Kunst und Zeiten hin
Doch zeigt Ihr uns in Weiten
Was frommer Menschheit Fleiß und ernste Tugend kann
Wörlitz, 15 July 1786
Johann Casp. Lavater"

(You monuments of art and God-devoted days!
Our admiration, courage and hope regard you, tears
Though art and time must pass
You show us through the years
What pious man can do in earnest virtue's ways)

The Church Room. This room on the top floor acquired its name recently, because of the depictions of famous Gothic cathedrals Prince Franz had seen on his travels. The window was made into a doorway when the house was extended.

The façade of the Gothic House on the Wolfskanal. The central section of the building was built as a house for Prince Franz and the gardener Schoch and his family in 1773/74. The wings and towers were added later, and the Gothic House was extended as an irregular building ensemble.

Johann Kaspar Lavater (1741-1801) had known Prince Leopold III Friedrich Franz of Anhalt-Dessau and his consort Luise for a good ten years when he wrote these lines – evidence of the ideas that may have motivated the young prince when he was building, decorating and furnishing the Gothic House. Lavater, a pastor who worked in Zurich, had written numerous religious and philosophical essays and was admired by many contemporaries, though his main work, the *Physiognomische Fragmente* on interpreting character from facial features, was wildly controversial.

The Gothic House contains over 200 cabinet panes and fragments like this, dating from the time around 1500 to the mid 17th century. Most of them come from Switzerland, but some from Germany, Flanders and France. This branch of art was particularly highly esteemed in Switzerland. Craft techniques and artistic ability reached the peak of perfection there. The Wörlitz collection, with works from many important workshops, is one of the most outstanding outside the country of origin. It contains many panes showing family and trade coats of arms, and scenes from the Old and New Testaments stand side by side with depictions of the battle for liberation between the Swiss Confederacy and the foreign Habsburg rulers. The attentive viewer will come across many versions of familiar legendary events, such as the Rütli oath or William Tell's crossbow shot.

The prince was probably more interested in the historical than the artistic value of the objects he collected around himself. He was most particularly concerned to keep alive memories of the Ascanian line with its rich tradition and wide-ranging branches, and of events associated with it – hence the many portraits and busts, historical pictures, the abundance of every possible kind of memorabilia, trophies from the Turkish wars and elaborate furniture going back to Nassau-Orange's dynastic connections, like many of the paintings. Even older pieces of furniture and equipment from the palaces in Dessau and Oranienbaum were fitted into the rooms in the Gothic House because of their memorial value.

The Gothic House, effectively a "Knight's Seat", as August von Rode wrote, became Prince Franz's chosen location for a dialogue with history. Like many of his contemporaries, he felt that the Middle Ages were a period of order and harmony – at a time when signs of a looming change were

Top ▴ Holy Family and Instruction of Mary, c. 1510/12. Lucas Cranach the Elder's altar side-panels were moved to the Anhaltische Gemäldegalerie (Anhalt Art Gallery) in 1927. Bottom ▾ The Martial Cabinet was named for the images on the ceiling and in the paintings and stained glass.

Right-hand page ▸ The Swiss stained glass in the Spiritual Cabinet (top), dating from c. 1590, shows scenes from the biblical parable of the Prodigal Son. At the bottom is a depiction of the Rütli Oath on a panel dating from 1576.

Zug city pane, 1649. In the allegorical image, devils and angels are fighting for souls, and above them is a celestial carriage with Mary and the Christ-Child. With a magnifying glass, it is possible to make out the names of Swiss locations on the globe.

The knights' room. An expert contemporary visitor felt reminded here of the chapter house in a Carthusian monastery. The stained glass dating from 1572 to 1575, with Swiss municipal standard-bearers, all comes from the original Schützenhaus in Zurich.

emerging that were to culminate in the events of the French Revolution.

Furnished with something approaching countless works of art and memorabilia, the rooms in his private residence give the impression of a collection that seems to have grown constantly over a long period of rule by the old princely line.

Even the new furniture intended for the house was designed in the Gothic style, an innovation at the time. This was pursued particularly elaborately in the knights' room, where high-backed benches are set along the long walls. At one's leisure, one can take in the effect of the vaulted room with the old mantelpiece on the one hand and the stained glass on the other, along with the lavish collection of paintings in the room. In the middle of the room is a large collection chest whose top can be enlarged with pull-out sections. The lav-ishly decorated armchair in front of it conceals a stepladder, from which large-format drawings could be observed. Did Prince Franz work on his plans for the Wörlitz garden design here? It is entirely possible.

And perhaps it was also here that he developed his ideas for the last extension to the Gothic House, finally completed in 1813. This added a dining room and another library, and here again, costly stained glass adorns the tracery windows extending across the full width, copperplate engravings and depictions of medieval Anhalt heraldic seals dominate the ceiling decorations, and ornamented floors, painting and the Gothic-style furniture in the interior lend their impressive effect.

But the Prince of Anhalt-Dessau, who was already 72 years old, was to be granted only four more years to enjoy these rooms in his refuge, now familiar to him for four decades.

Neo-Gothic

Reinhard Alex

In architecture in particular, neo-Gothic describes a historicizing style based on expressive forms originating from the Middle Ages. It spread above all from England, where the Gothic Revival was very significant around 1750/60. Intellectually it relates to a return to nature and the past, and to the epoch's sensitive emotional world; it emerged particularly from the Gothic-style buildings in the new landscape gardens. A cult of ruins developed in awareness of the transience of all earthly things.

Owing much to views deriving from the Renaissance, Gothic was greatly despised at the time, seen as expressing the barbaric conditions of a past that had been superseded. First of all, individual design and decorative motifs such as arches, tracery structures or building ornaments were taken over, varied and transferred to walls, without anyone being in a position to copy the constructive features of Gothic, or even to recognize them. It is not uncommon in this early phase of neo-Gothic building to find neo-classical or Chinese stylistic elements appearing in the work as well. The painterly-looking style that this produced was known as "picturesque" in England.

For a time, neo-Gothic was associated mainly with aristocratic clients, but views changed after the awakening of bourgeois national awareness after 1800. Various European countries now saw Gothic as a national style, and particularly so in Germany, faced with the struggle for liberation against Napoleon. This could be seen both in the literature and painting of Romanticism, and in the work of the architect Karl Friedrich Schinkel. Efforts were made to conserve surviving monuments and Gothic was researched by art historians – a prerequisite for copying the style and the austere, sometimes quite dry historicism of later times. From 1842, when Cologne cathedral was completed by the Prussian king and the Catholic Church, and on into the 20th century, church building became the most important field for neo-Gothic architectural design.

In Dessau-Wörlitz, the Gothic House and the church in Wörlitz are the outstanding, but not the only buildings in the neo-Gothic style. In the last two decades of the 18th century and the early 19th century numerous other churches were built throughout the Garden Realm, as well as secular buildings for all kinds of purposes. They are among the early, previously under-appreciated evidence of neo-Gothic architecture in Germany, and thus of great importance within the development of architecture.

The Monument

Ingo Pfeifer

Anyone travelling from Coswig to Wörlitz will spot a strange building from some distance away. Topped by an ancient column, the Monument lies precisely on the axis of the Coswiger Chaussee. This continues to the palace, and turns off this line only a few hundred metres before the dike. If one moves from the dining room in the palace, where the little gallery of ancestral portraits is to be found, into the adjacent corner room, there is an uninterrupted view of the Monument through the left-hand window, and the appropriateness of the location is immediately apparent – the dedication runs: "To my ancestors. Franz". This unusual building, in erratics and rubble-stone, has an irregular ground plan and supports the Roman column on a plinth in the middle of the flat roof. It is a symbolic tomb and memorial for the reigning princes of the House of Anhalt-Dessau, and borrows its external forms from ancient funerary

The Monument is lavishly decorated inside, and its reliefs and niches are intended to be reminiscent of ancient tombs. The figurative paintings on the vault ceiling, with scenes from the lives of Dessau princes, were not completed by the Dessau theatre painter, Max Korn, until 1925.

143

like room. It was originally designed as a grotto, covered in shells and contained a large mirror, conjuring colourful reflected light on to the walls from the flood water in the Elbe meadows when the sun was shining.

If the exterior seems wild and rough, the long interior with its vaulted coffered ceiling is finely ornamented and decorated with great artistry. The walls are clad in greenish and reddish stucco marble. Large alabaster vessels stood on white marble consoles, and half-arched niches seem to be ready to hold urns. The model for the room's design was one of the Roman catacombs beneath the Villa Corsina.

The floor shows the nine fields of the large Anhalt coat of arms in circles of laurel and oak garlands, in plaster encrustations, The prince had head-and-shoulders portraits by the court sculptor Friedemann Hunold (1773-1840) mounted on the walls. They depict Prince Franz's predecessors. Each of the subjects is given an inscription with a short character description. The portrait of the young heir, Prince Friedrich, had to be added as early as 1815, as he died in 1814, even before commencing his reign. Franz's successor, Duke Leopold Friedrich (1817-1871), changed the Monument into a memorial for all the princes of Dessau, and had the bust of Prince Franz, by the Dessau sculptor Franz Woltreck, placed in the niche opposite the entrance in 1824. It was provided with an inscription by the poet Wilhelm Müller (1794-1827). Leopold Friedrich had his own portrait placed here in 1841, and the collection was then brought up to date with busts of all the other Dukes of Anhalt until 1918.

monuments. The column plinth is decorated with four reliefs of female figures, also borrowed from antiquity, and symbolizing the four seasons. The inscription under the allegory of summer also relates to the constantly recurring cycle of the year: "May hours and seasons always grant what is necessary". The path behind the building leads to a cellar-

The Monument. Prince Franz had it built in 1801-04, as the last building in the Wörlitz Park, on the embankment that forms the garden's northern border with the Elbe, between the Temple of Venus and the "Wachhaus zum Pferde".

The Pantheon

Ingo Pfeifer

The Pantheon was built by Friedrich Wilhelm von Erdmannsdorff from 1795 to 1797, and is one of the buildings adapted from ancient models. It is a dark red structure with a Corinthian portico in front, placed on the Elbe dike at the edge of the great Wallloch. Erdmannsdorff chose the name not so much as a quotation of its source, the Pantheon in Rome, but of the basic architectural form – a round main section of the building combined with a columned portico with a triangular pediment. The pediment relief shows the dispute between the Muses and the Sirens being settled by Minerva – an allegory of the clash between nature and art being mediated by science. The question of whether art should follow nature or improve on it was a central subject for the art theorists of the day. The inscription above the entrance "To lovers of nature and art", refers to this, and the garden design situation also

The Pantheon. Its cellar is also accessible from the lake shore, and contains copies of Egyptian sculptures. The position on the Elbe dike alludes to a comparison between the Elbe and the Nile – both rivers flood, making them both a threat and a source of life.

The group of Muses in the Pantheon. As the sculpture of Apollo was the smallest of all the ten antiquities, the life-size statue of Urania, the Muse of the sciences, was placed in the centre of the room in his place. Polyhymnia (mimic arts), Melpomene (tragedy), Euterpe (music) and Thalia (comedy) surround her. Calliope (epic poetry), Clio (history), Terpsichore (dance) and Erato (lyric poetry) were placed in the gallery. The figure of Apollo, identified as the leader of the Muses by his lyre, is in the gallery facing the entrance.

Wörlitz

The dome of the Pantheon is decorated with magnificently coloured paintings, based on ancient reliefs from the Nerva Forum in Rome. They show the various arts, indicating the originally planned use for the building.

Next page ▸ A comfortable flight of steps leads to the roof of the Pantheon. This affords a view of the Neue Anlagen (new gardens) and the adjacent Elbe meadows. The steps are protected by an umbrella that can be unscrewed and which also provides protection from the weather.

147

reflects this idea: architecture (art) rises on a rock pedestal (nature).

Inside, the building reveals itself as a centrally planned space with two storeys, lit from a skylight. The articulation with niches on the ground floor corresponds to a reconstruction variant on the ancient Pantheon, proposed by the archaeologist Alois Hirt in the late 18th century. Hirt had dedicated his study, published in 1791, to Friedrich Wilhelm von Erdmannsdorff. The stuccoed floor carries ancient symbols, but the ceiling is adorned with colourful paintings: scenes depicting the arts and sciences based on reliefs from the Forum of Nerva in Rome.

Plaster casts of ancient figures were intended, rather than the present sculptures, and the niches on the upper floor were to have contained cases of engraved prints of ancient gems, copperplate engravings and books. This would not have been an exhibition venue for a collection of antiquities, but a "museion" in the original sense of the word – a place for the Muses and for scientific study.

When Johann Joachim Winckelmann published his essay, *Gedanken über die Nachahmung der griechischen Werke in der Malerei und Bildhauerkunst*, in 1755, he was providing a theoretical basis for a new artistic movement aiming to find its own, up-to-date artistic expression through and with the arts of antiquity. Ancient works of art and copies of them became important elements of interior decoration in neo-classical living and social rooms within a very short time. Whether they were ancient originals or copies in plaster or marble, they conveyed an image of a new awareness by their owners. Portraits of Roman emperors were no longer used to represent and legitimize power, but were now seen as symbols of scholarship, wise statesmanship and enlightened thinking. Busts of Roman and Greek philosophers, depictions of the Muses and images of gods make allegorical references to their owners' interests and aims.

Prince Franz had proposed that the art agent Friedrich Rehberg (1758-1835), who worked in Rome, should purchase a reasonably priced group of marble figures for him, rather than the intended fragile plaster casts. These ancient figures, some of them very badly damaged, had been reconstructed as a group of Apollo and the nine Muses by adding heads, arms and attributes.

But the invasion of Italy by Napoleon's troops at first prevented the dispatch of the sculptures that had already been acquired, as a ban on exporting antiquities had been imposed. Some diplomatic intervention was needed before permission was finally given for transport in 1802. The figures were displayed in Wörlitz in October of the same year. The original plans for using the building had already been abandoned.

Other ancient busts and architectural items came into the Pantheon as well as the group of Muses. They stood on consoles on both floors until 1939, but were then taken to the palace as part of a raft of precautions. They were not returned for conservatorial reasons.

Another special feature is the building's cellar, which is built into the Elbe dike. It can be entered directly from the foot of the dike, as well as via the spiral staircase leading from the ground floor into the vault. Skilful lighting gives the space a devotional character. A Canopic vase – a vessel decorated with reliefs and topped by a human head – is placed exactly in the centre, in front of a fireplace-like niche. Beside him in the gallery are a total of three relief slabs depicting various Egyptian gods – the hawk-headed Horus (Osiris), dog-headed Anubis and the youthful Harpocrates. There is a statue of Isis in the gallery opposite the entrance. The inclusion of Egyptian gods suggests a true pantheon (temple of all the gods). At the same time, the sequence shows that ancient Egypt was seen as the basis of ancient culture, with Greece (symbolized by the group of Muses) rising upon it, and crowned by ancient Rome, indicated by the ceiling paintings. Thus the Pantheon once more reveals the all-embracing educational approach taken in the Wörlitz buildings and gardens.

The Wörlitz Vesuvius

Uwe Quilitzsch

The beautiful landscape of the Bay of Naples so fascinated Prince Franz on his visit to Italy that he wanted a small architectural copy of it for Wörlitz. He found models for this in the Roman emperor Hadrian's villa – Hadrian had replicas built of the most important places in his empire –, and in Sir William Chambers's publication, *A Dissertation on Oriental Gardening*. Here, the English author recommended expressing the sublime qualities of nature using artistic and technical resources. This was to be done by creating artificial volcanoes, waterfalls, earthquakes, artificial rain and thunder and lightning, all ready to reveal the primeval forces of nature to spectators on demand.

The Dessau ruler's close friendship with Sir William Hamilton may also have been crucial for the Wörlitz "Bay of Naples". The British diplomat had been accredited to the Neapolitan court since 1764. He was a passionate collector of

Aquatint, *Der Stein zu Wörlitz*, by Karl Kuntz, 1797. The eruption of Vesuvius was treated like a theatrical performance on the rocky "Stein" island in Wörlitz. It was intended to give 18th century viewers a sense of a powerful, threatening natural phenomenon.

The richly and elegantly furnished fireplace room in the Villa Hamilton, after restoration in 2004.

antiquities, and was interested in Vesuvius as a scientist. Prince Franz had visited him in Naples on his Grand Tour in 1766 and climbed the volcano with him; they conducted geological studies together.

So from 1788 to 1794, an imposing structure, the so-called "Stein" rock island, rose up at the eastern end of the Wörlitzer See, occupying an area of about 1000 square metres. The artificial rock was built around a brick masonry core, clad with field- and quarry-stones. Inside it were several levels with grottoes, temples, a columbarium and underground passages. Southern climes were evoked in the garden design by Mediterranean plants such as fig trees, dwarf almonds, agaves in tubs, and simple antirrhinums. Indigenous poplars and pines grew similarly to stone pines and cedars. Later, the soil around the rock was excavated to make the site a feature of the Wörlitzer See. The island thus created could be reached by ferry or gondola.

The island's main attraction, the 17 m high artificial volcanic cone, is visible from a distance across the flat countryside. The lava flow was imitated using glass-like slag that sparkled in sunshine or artificial light. The eruption was impressively staged after dark, as can be seen from the Chalkographische Gesellschaft's aquatint. Bangers and crackling twigs were used to imitate the sounds of an eruption. An artificial waterfall under the cone could be bathed in red light, looking like lava pouring into the Wörlitzer See. Under the volcano, the prince built a theatre in the shape of an ancient arena, with seats for several hundred people. The rocky island and its small neighbouring islands demonstrated the prince's and his architect's geological expertise. Towering "needles" of Saxon basalt tower up everywhere out of the ground. The choice of this eruptive rock was intended to underline the "volcanic" origins of this artificial landscape.

In the middle of this mountain massif is the Cabinet of the Night, a room that makes a unique impact. During the day, the room could be blacked out with shutters. Light was admitted to the cabinet only through star-shaped apertures and a skylight. The plaster sculpture of a Vestal Virgin on a black plinth, holding an illuminated alabaster vase in her hands, seemed to be floating in space. Underground passages led to a vault, copied from a Roman underground burial place, a so-called columbarium. In the niches here, the prince exhibited early historical urns and vessels found in the course of Wörlitz excavations. Thus he was able to show his respect for the mortal remains and gave the room an additional aura.

Erdmannsdorff undertook his last study visit to Italy in 1789/90, bringing back ideas for the "Stein" island. For example, he designed a smaller copy of the Villa Mappinola, Hamilton's observatory on the Bay of Naples. Prince Franz dedicated this building in Wörlitz to the British diplomat, as a monument to their friendship.

The Villa Hamilton is an architectural gem. The rendered brick building at the foot of the volcano covers about 90 square metres and is divided into three rooms, devoted to memories of Italy. The middle room, painted in Pompeian red, is filled with densely hung paintings. These include *Naples harbour with the English fleet at anchor* (August Rode 1798), a view of the famous ancient temple at Paestum and a number vedutas of Venice. The second room was set up as a graphic art cabinet, similar to the one in the Luisium palace. The most prestigious room in the villa has a fireplace and an extremely elegant neoclassical interior. Twelve coloured copperplate engravings show the famous Horae from Herculaneum. The easy grace of these ancient wall paintings was entirely appropriate to the stylistic sensibilities of neo-classicism; the wife of the British ambassador, Lady Emma Hamilton, had also chosen pictures like this as a basis for mimed performances.

The Prince de Ligne summed up his impressions of the Villa Hamilton as follows: "One is quite amazed that one was not swifter to discover a dwelling in one corner of this said rock, at the end of a platform adjoining a winter garden. It is a house that looks entirely simple and agreeable from the outside, but inside it is uncommonly magnificent. It is entirely in the style of Herculaneum ..." But the "Stein" as a complete complex, in fact an entirely bizarre construction for Wörlitz, had been criticized by contemporaries such as Carl August Boettiger, and according to his biographer, Friedrich Reil, Prince Franz himself was not entirely happy with his work. "It is a piece of work that has gone wrong, that has turned out differently from my intentions; too much and too many different things in the same place; I should have had more space ... Rode places me on a parallel with Hadrian in his description, which he should not have done, for I am nothing compared to him."

The Synagogue

Ingo Pfeifer

At the point where the garden meets the town, visitors are aware of a rotunda, articulated with pilasters and unassuming at first glance. This is the former Wörlitz synagogue, built in 1789/90 for the town's Jews, about 130 at the time. Creating this place of worship chimed with the prince's wish to reflect the world in miniature in the Wörlitz garden. The idea of various cultures and religions was just as much a part of this as the presentation of different architectural styles.

Jews had been allowed to settle permanently in Anhalt-Dessau since Prince Johann Georg II's Edict of Tolerance of 17 February, 1672, and they enjoyed greater freedom here than in other German territories. In the mid 18th century, about 15 per cent of the population of Anhalt-Dessau were of the Jewish faith; Prince Franz tried to tie them into cultural life as part of his enlightened policy for the principality.

The *mikwe* is to be found in the mound under the synagogue, built by Erdmannsdorff in 1789/90. It was used by Jewish women for ritual purification, and had a separate entrance.

Friedrich Wilhelm von Erdmannsdorff was commissioned to build a new synagogue when the market-place was redesigned in 1788, the new Wörlitz town hall constructed and the old prayer room pulled down. His chosen architectural model was the marble structure in Rome, then known as the Temple of Vesta, built around 100 BC in honour of Hercules Victor, and later turned into a church. Erdmannsdorff got to know it when it still had medieval masonry between the columns, which is why the Wörlitz rotunda, standing on an artificial mound, has masonry with a round window between the pilasters below the roof. This building deviated from the rectangular ground plan otherwise used for synagogues. So architecturally, Erdmannsdorff's solution remained an exception for 18th century synagogue construction.

In the middle of the room was the *bima* – the lectern – surrounded by the men's small prayer desks. The *tora* shrine, which carries a strutted gable supported by two columns, was placed in front of the *tora* niche opposite the men's entrance. The niche itself was covered by a richly ornamented curtain. Opposite it, above the separate entrances for men and women, was the women's gallery, supported by several columns. More candelabras, including two donated by Princess Luise in 1790, completed the furnishings.

The Association of Anhalt Israelite Congregations held regular services in the synagogue until the National Socialists compelled it to give up the building in summer 1937. Two SA men tried to set the synagogue on fire on 10 November, 1938, even though it was no longer in use. Fortunately, this was prevented by a courageous intervention on the part of the garden director, Hans Hallervorden (1873-1971). He was forced to retire shortly afterwards, however! The steps were removed, the view of the town blocked by planting. The name Jewish Temple also disappeared from the park plans, to be replaced by Temple of Vesta.

Even though the exterior was restored shortly after the war, the historical designation is only slowly becoming re-established.

The Wörlitz synagogue was Erdmannsdorff's only non-secular building. Its historical interior was destroyed by the National Socialists after 1938, but the building itself could be saved. It now houses an exhibition on the history of the Jews in Anhalt.

The Ensemble
by the Churchyard

Reinhard Alex

Near Schloss Wörlitz, but hidden from view at first by the kitchen building, is Kirchplatz, a particularly graceful ensemble of neo-Gothic architecture. An impressive view over the complex and its adjacent buildings opens up from a mound by the shore of the lake, the Zedernberg: to the east are the Grey House and the Gallery, on the other side the kitchen building and the princely stables, and straight ahead the town church. The mound, which is supported on the side facing the square by a large wall for growing espalier fruit or vines, used to contain an ice cellar.

The kitchen building, constructed between 1770 and 1772, was the first new building in Kirchplatz. Its façade faces the palace, and matches it with its rich neo-classical half-columns, statue niches, cornice and attic. As was so often the case, Erdmannsdorff, the architect, was inspired by works of the past, in this case the Palazzo Farnese in Rome, designed

The Grey House. It is to be assumed that this house for Princess Luise was built at her request, as the rooms in the palace were open to the public from the outset, and she had to put up with the stream of visitors for over 17 years.

View from Schoch's Garden of the town church, St. Petri, and the palace.

from 1514 by Antonio da Sangallo (1485-1546). Behind the façade is a large room whose niche articulation reflects the exterior to a certain extent. Even though the ceiling vaults were removed in the course of later repairs, and various other interventions took place, the essential elements of the decoration, the casts of ancient statues, have survived. The princely company used to dine here occasionally on hot days, and in winter the room was used for the temporary storage of plants in tubs. Food was then carried into the palace via an underground passage. The kitchen building is now open to visitors as a service centre, after standing empty for a long time; restoration work was completed in the year 2000.

Unlike the façade, the wings of the building on Kirchplatz are articulated with Gothic blind windows, harmonizing stylistically with the nearby buildings. "All the buildings are adorned in the Gothic taste, because of proximity to the old church," August Rode noted in his 1798 description.

For reasons of hygiene, Prince Franz established a new cemetery on the eastern periphery of the town, and Erdmannsdorff provided an architectural setting for it in 1795. The graves by the old churchyard had been levelled ten years earlier, and curved paths laid, further enlivened by planting. In the middle of the lawn sloping up to the church is a monument reminiscent of an ancient sarcophagus, at the point where the recovered remains are interred. Reliefs of winged genii, similarly to those on the entrance gate of the Dessau cemetery, invoke the twin brothers Hypnos and Thanatos, Sleep and Death. Alongside lines by Klopstock, an inscription written by the prince himself reminds us of the place's significance: "Filled with remains of the bones of those who died before us, who afforded us room for our habitation/ As we will make room for others in our turn."

The princely stables, have stood between the kitchen building and Kirchgasse since 1775/76, creating a link with the town buildings. It still contains the original stalls for the horses, solidly designed in all their functional simplicity. The coachmen's accommodation survived as well, along with a masonry dung-trough, with small toilet buildings at its corners. A coach house was to be found at the front on the town side. More careful examination of the sandstone decoration on this gable façade reveals a typical feature of Erdmannsdorff's design approach: neo-classical articulation combined with Gothic motifs, here indicating the closely linked development of the two styles, as it were. But the elaborately decorated gable side opposite is clearly neo-Gothic in manner, given its relationship with Kirchplatz. White, blind pointed arches on the long walls form a lively contrast with the areas of brick, enlivening them sculpturally.

Erdmannsdorff's intention to create links between façade designs for spatial ensembles can also be seen in the buildings in Kirchplatz. So the paint on the gables of the kitchen building, identified in a source as "grey-reddish", originally corresponded with the Grey House opposite, where Princess Luise lived. When Friedrich Wilhelm von Erdmannsdorff built this in 1789/90, he modelled it on Sheffield Place in Sussex, England. First extending over five window axes, the Grey House was not extended until much later, by moving the turreted end walls. Inside, the storeys are connected by an elegantly curving staircase.

The Gallery was then added in the same building line in the early 19th century. Its vaulted hall is particularly impressive because of its neo-Gothic design. Parts of the princely collections are housed in lavishly decorated, glazed cabinets. There was access to this art gallery from the Grey House, and the entrance to the prince's pew in the choir of the church was opposite the outside door.

Inside the town church, St. Petri. The interior of this neo-classical building is characterized by lucid spatial articulation in the nave and transept, galleries on all sides and the gracefulness of the decorative details.

Finally, the new provost's house directly on Kirchgasse is worthy of mention. This two-storey building, painted brickred, was built in 1796, after an earlier building had to make way for the Grey House. Provost Friedrich Christian Gottlieb Reil (1772-1849), author of a biography of Prince Franz, lived here for ten years.

Like a wide bolt, the town church of St. Petri, still Romanesque in its core, closes the boundary of the former churchyard. It is set back from the line of buildings in the street, thus giving a clear impression on this side of the power of the house of God, towering over the surrounding buildings. Its tall tower, articulated and accentuated by corner buttresses, turrets and a slender spire, offers visitors surprising views of the gardens and the areas beyond. From the very outset it has shown countless visitors the way to their famous destination.

The tower is based on an architectural work in Bruges, the Church of Our Lady. Prince Franz himself was considerably involved when the medieval building was extended and redesigned between 1805 and 1809 under his building director, Georg Christoph Hesekiel. Some of the masonry was included in the new building, and the Romanesque recessed portal on the south side, in particular, is evidence of the church's origins; it was consecrated in 1201.

Upon looking at the exterior, what is immediately striking is the huge variety of articulating and decorative elements, as well as the structure of the building: the aisle-less nave and the wide eastern transept, with choir adjacent. Here one finds the prince's pew, in a two-storey gallery. Similar galleries run round all the walls of the vaulted interior. Imaginative ornaments adorn the parts of the building as well as the pulpit, Adolph Zuberbier's organ and the altar. Two paintings donated by Prince Franz hang high in the transept, the *Last Supper* and the *Baptism of Christ*, early works by Heinrich and Ferdinand Olivier, brothers and painters from Dessau. So, there will be scarcely a visitor to the town church in Wörlitz, who will leave unimpressed by this highlight of neo-Gothic ecclesiastical architecture in Anhalt-Dessau.

The churchyard was created after 1770 to replace the old Wörlitz cemetery. It is framed by neo-Gothic buildings and the town church, St. Petri, the largest and most important church in this style in the Garden Realm.

Ludwig Trauzettel

The Wörlitz Gardens – "Pride and Epitome of the 18th Century"

Christoph Martin Wieland

The princely summer residence and hunting lodge at Wörlitz developed from the 18th century as a principal destination for Dessau tourists, visited all the year round. August Rode, the Anhalt-Dessau councillor, still also known today as a writer and translator of Vitruvius and Apuleius, is a born guide to the Garden Realm. In his description of the Wörlitz garden, which remains unsurpassed, he offers the following introductory explanation to visitors: "The garden is on a plain near extensive wooded areas. It is possibly to walk right round it in about one and a half hours; but in order to walk only fleetingly through the internal scenes at least three hours are needed. It is not enclosed by a wall or even a fence. The borders are partly defined naturally by the lake; partly artificially hidden by canals, earthworks, avenues, hedges; also partly left indeterminate. And so strangers consider the surrounding beautiful commons, fields, woods and meadows to be part of it, and are deceived in their idea of its scope." The five individual gardens in Wörlitz are arranged around the four arms of the Wörlitzer See, a dead arm of the Elbe

and, according to Rode, the chief adornment of the garden. To the south, somewhat raised on a sand dune, are the Schloss Garden, dating from 1764 onwards, the little town of Wörlitz and Neumark's Garden on an artificial island. North of the water and extending eastwards, Schoch's Garden and the Weidenheger were established one after the other, followed by the Neue Anlagen (New Gardens) in the late 18th century.

Two other stretches of water south of the dike, linked to the lake by canals, the large and the small Wallloch (literally: earthwork hole), resulted from breaks in the dike. The lakes and waterways are accessible not just by foot; it is also possible to visit the gardens by boat.

The gardens are linked by paths, ferries and sightlines, and some of the gardens run into each other. They make up a uniform *Gesamtkunstwerk (complete work of art)*, with horticulture as the key element combining with architecture and fine art. The initiators' intention was to use ideas gleaned on visits to England and Italy to shape the work of art. Their appearance was to be a re-creation of nature and economically useful, and the new architecture was also to be realized, in the form of almost 60 neo-classical and neo-Gothic buildings and minor architectural items.

The gardens, composed of all nature's components, also included arable areas, orchards and pasture. Working with and tending these areas were also instructive processes, contributing to the education of interested observers. They were to feel transported into the ideal landscapes of antiquity, re-created vividly and shaped by fine architecture and wild nature. Nature acquired this character both from indigenous timber and kitchen garden plants, and also from Mediterranean plants. Lombardy poplars and conifers, sometimes trimmed into shape, were used to look like the stone pines and cypresses of southern climes.

Charte von der Wörlitzer Feldmarcke by Friedrich Coeler. This coloured drawing originated as part of the 1789-91 land survey, and is seen as the earliest plan showing the layout of the Wörlitz gardens; it shows them to their full extent, with their surroundings. The garden design work is not yet complete, particularly in the eastern areas by the "Stein" and the "Grosses Wallloch", but the essential structures, spatial sequences and sight lines can already be made out.

161

"The gardens around Wörlitz surpass all that I have ever seen ... Here, beautified nature opens up in all her manifold works, for all who consider her worthy of loving. The most beautiful things are not the statues, busts, temples, the garden is the most beautiful thing."

Johann Friedrich Abegg, 1798

The Palace Garden

Ludwig Trauzettel

The "garden on this side of the lake" is now called the Schloss or Palace Garden, though this was originally not the case. It is surrounded to the north and west by the lake, the Wörlitzer See, and to the south and east by the town of Wörlitz, which at the designers' behest is masked by planting and cannot be seen. The residence, called a country seat, was to be set in a natural-looking landscape. Access is principally from the south, into the garden from the south embankment or from the market, but it can also be entered from the churchyard, from Amtsgasse, or along the lakeside path from the east. The garden contains all the buildings required to meet the prince's needs for maintaining his court and for the site to function as a temporary official residence: a domestic building with accommodation and the kitchen, stables with coach houses and coachmen's lodgings, and also the princess's private home right by the church. Prince Franz

The atmospheric image of the shell nymph, framed by Lombardy poplars and urns, on the shores of the Wörlitzer See is the starting and finishing point for numerous linked sight lines between the formal Schloss Gardens and the land "on the other side of the lake".

163

The English Seat in the Schloss Garden. Erdmannsdorff built this Palladian garden seat in Wörlitz immediately after the first visit to England, where he had seen the original in Stourhead. The round façade openings are decorated with a bust of the Apollo Belvedere and a Madonna, and a mask of Jupiter Ammon tops the keystone of the basket arch.

himself set up a private refuge in the Gothic House, which was turned into a second palace as the gardener's home was gradually extended.

The country seat in Wörlitz is surrounded by lawns with lime trees planted at regular intervals, arranged as they were at the time of the previous building. West of this area, a small piece of woodland completely encircles the princess's former flower garden, which originally included a greenhouse, a pheasant farm and the gondolier's house. The tea arbour that has occupied the site of these buildings since 1830 faces the new gondola mooring on the lake shore. This public mooring became necessary when visitor numbers increased once the town was attached to the rail network in the late 19th century. Travelling by boat through the waters of the Wörlitz lakes and canals is still one of the most attractive features of a visit to Wörlitz, "without which one cannot boast of having got to know the beauty of these grounds. The prince has made the very best of the Wörlitzer See. The distribution of the great expanses of water, the canals, island groups and grottoes are the triumph of this park ... If one has already covered the most excellent parts on foot in the morning, then in the afternoon one can take a journey on the water, rest on the seat of a gondola and once more, lazily turn over the once-read book of beautified nature page by page ..." The famous Weimar archaeologist Carl August Boettiger wrote these lines in his diary when visiting Wörlitz in 1797.

East of the palace, by the kitchen building with its four Ionic columns decorating the façade, is a summer dining room. Sculptures by the Dresden sculptor Gottfried Knöffler adorn the niches on either side of the room, an Apollo on the left and a satyr on the right. The kitchen building is linked to the palace by an underground passage, originally used for access and for transporting food. North of this domestic building is the garden by the Swan Pool, and at the end of this, by the synagogue, the waterside path leads into the Neue Anlagen. The Swan Pool, and artificial branch of the lake, was also used as a harbour for the prince's gondola in the early years; it could be closed off by a drawbridge. East of the kitchen building, the garden runs into the churchyard. At the opposite end of this was the princess's private garden, almost the only part of the Wörlitz gardens that was closed to visitors by a wall and gate.

From the Schloss Garden it is possible to cross the lake by the official ferry near the synagogue to get to the Weidenheger

Garden on the opposite shore, and Neumark's Garden by the tea arbour ferry. The ferry mooring has remained in the same place since the gardens were created, but at that time visitors were able to work the little wooden ferries attached to ropes themselves.

The prince picked up essential ideas for his Wörlitz gardens in England, but it was above all Italy that served as a model here. The plants used were intended to reinforce the southern character conveyed by the neo-classical buildings. So from about 1770, laurel and other Mediterranean species were grown in 19 antique-style cast iron urns around the palace. They could be wintered in the summer room in the nearby kitchen building. The gardener lived in this building at first as well. There were also wells on both sides of the kitchen building: a sandstone one in the form of an ancient altar, modelled on the Luna altar in Winckelmann's *Monumenti antici inediti*, in front of the neo-classical façade, and another sandstone well, dating from 1787, was given a neo-Gothic design like the other buildings in the churchyard ensemble.

The many Lombardy poplars were also reminiscent of Italy, planted in picturesque groups near the water in particular. These trees, which originated in the Mediterranean themselves, were intended to identify key design points, as they grew like cypresses. It was more difficult to find a substitute for the Italian stone pines and cedars. The poet Friedrich Matthisson, who lived at the Dessau court, reports on vain attempts to cultivate the stone pine: "It remains ... an unutterable loss for Germany's gardens that this royal plant cannot be wintered in our climate ... Several attempts to this fine end in Potsdam and Wörlitz have gone awry." So the

The Nymphaeum, seen from the Schloss Garden. The Nymphaeum is built into terrain modelled for a former ice pit, and was created in 1767/68 as a vantage point "on the other side of the lake". It was used as a garden seat on the opposite bank and as a raised vantage point at the top of the adjacent vineyard mound.

In 1787, the neo-Gothic well by the princely stables was matched in form to the surrounding churchyard buildings. It was originally as refreshment for visitors, as drinking water for animals, and for the gardener to water the nearby plants. The neo-Gothic stables were built in 1775, and also contained the coachman's lodgings.

The Rousseau island in Wörlitz. Of symbolic significance in terms of access to the gardens, but also part of the allegorical labyrinth programme, this copy of Jean-Jacques Rousseau's tomb in the Ermenoville Park professes faith in the Enlightenment. The honorific inscription on the base of the plinth beneath the urn, formulated by Prince Franz himself, is decorated with Rousseau's portrait, a lyre and an oak garland. Here, Franz was particularly acknowledging Rousseau's poetic talents and bourgeois virtues.

gardeners used other trees instead: Austrian pines, Weymouth pines, western red cedars and other conifers. They tried to achieve the umbrella-like crown in a similar way to fruit trees using pruning knife, scissors and twine. Boettiger noted with amazement on this head: "... the prince knows how to make even rebellious northern nature more compliant by artful little tricks. Whether I count the trick, used at many points here, of giving lopped pines crowns that make them in some respects the equal of the fair stone pine, the slender tree of Italian villas, as one such, or whether it should count among the dangerous experiments where the art of beautification comes very close to figured tree-pruning ... I should not like to decide myself."

The Schloss Garden was laid out at an early stage of the prince's efforts to implement the ideas of the Enlightenment so that he could distance himself from baroque approaches in the sphere of horticulture as well. The freedom that the young prince had fought for and won, at a heavy price, for himself and his little state of Anhalt-Dessau, was to be expressed symbolically through the design of his environment. He first looked for a suitable place to do this, planning to realize the project in the extreme west, in Grosskühnau.

When he came back from his first visit to England, plans for the landscape by the Wörlitzer See, where there was still a baroque hunting lodge, became concrete. He used the empty space by the lake shore to the north-east of the palace for his own landscape design experiments, adding a little garden in the English style to the existing palace garden the following winter. This garden related to the English Seat, which was first described as a pleasure house. Erdmannsdorff had constructed this from an idea he had seen in Stourhead, in Wiltshire, southern England. This early neo-classical garden building in Anhalt-Dessau with its façade facing the lake and articulated with four tapering Ionic pilasters takes up the familiar, loggia-like Palladian motif that was used again in a number of creative variations all over the Garden Realm. The fact that the structure, surrounded by plants at the back, has no other decoration on its façade, can be seen as proof that the original intention was not to eliminate the baroque palace and garden situation. The drawings for the first changes to the garden were made by the gardener Johann Friedrich Eyserbeck, who otherwise worked in the Luisium, in Dessau and elsewhere in the Garden Realm. Prince Franz had taken him with him to England in 1763, and sent him there to train for another six months in 1766. These early

The summer dining room, facing the palace, by the kitchen building, created by Erdmannsdorff in 1771. This provides an enchanting view of the garden landscape through the lime-trees retained from the earlier baroque gardens.

baroque garden with formal basin and central drive was removed, along with the rows of buildings opposite. Only planting and landscape arrangements from the previous period became part of the growing new design concept. In the case of the lime boskets from the baroque Schloss complex, it was sufficient to cease lopping them to achieve a natural character and free up views of the "open" landscape. The central drive and the parterre were replaced with an area of grass that increased in size as work proceeded. The town, which was originally encroaching on the banks of the Wörlitzer See, was demolished to a considerable extent. The changed urban periphery was masked with massive planting to give the English country seat the illusion of natural rural surroundings. The curate's and the provost's accommodation were also in the way of Erdmannsdorff's spatial planning and the intended open landscape solution. The cemetery that used to be by the church was redesigned as a garden, after a new burial place had been created south of the town for reasons of hygiene.

Without all this demolition and removal of the original town structures, it would not have been possible to develop a landscape garden between the edge of the town and the shores of the Wörlitzer See. The intended changes had to look like a natural, open landscape by the water. Probably, English models gave Franz and Erdmannsdorff the idea of creating the required distance for their intended garden. Stourhead, for example, which provided many of the ideas for Wörlitz, also planned the inclusion of the former village and church within the landscape garden as part of the creative concept. And a similarly grand approach was also taken in Milton Abbas (Dorset), the only gardens where rivals William Chambers and Lancelot Brown worked together. As in Wörlitz, an entire little town was demolished, and re-accommodated a short distance away; and there too, the abbey that used to stand in the town centre became a set-piece in the garden created for the country seat.

But in Wörlitz, the churchyard was not redesigned as a garden until a while after the palace was built, after a private home was created for Princess Luise in the form of the Grey House. The palace had been open to the public from the outset, and constant disturbances had persuaded the prince to meet the often sickly Luise's desire for seclusion and a private atmosphere. The princess was looking for nature, silence and solitude, and had little sympathy for the earthy festivities and intrigues of the Dessau court. She was often troubled by

efforts resulted in a style, whose character appeared contrary to the baroque view of gardens. The concept seems to be searching for, without really displaying any new qualities in landscape design. The lines of the paths and the edges of the banks and timber seem fussy, and to curve without reason. The intricate new garden areas had deliberately shaken off their symmetry, but they looked all too simple as they were attempting to avoid baroque rigour and geometry without being able to dispense with its formal language. The Swan Pool is even more like a formal basin, even though the line of its banks is curved and it is placed asymmetrically in front of the English Seat. After its beginnings on the shores of the Wörlitzer See, this design approach, adopted in the early Wörlitz phase, soon dominated the whole of the Schloss Garden, and around 1770, it was also applied to work in the areas "on the other side of the lake". There had been similar design experiments in the early stages in England as well, for example by Joseph Switzer or William Kent. Similar spatial approaches can still be found in Chiswick (London) or Rousham (Oxfordshire).

The baroque hunting lodge, not built until 1698, was pulled down in 1768 to make room for Erdmannsdorff's neo-classical country seat on approximately the same site. The existing

Paintings like this ideal landscape by J.F. Bloemen from Schloss Wörlitz gave ideas for early English landscape gardens.

Das Wirthshauß zum fürstl: Garten in Wörlitz | L'auberge du Jardin de Wörlitz

the constant presence of interested visitors. The neo-Gothic house with its gallery extension, used as a winter residence, formed the eastern boundary of the urban space by the churchyard, and had formerly been occupied by the provost's accommodation. It was built in 1789/90, based on ideas drawn from Sheffield Place (southern England), with only five window axes at first. It was not until 1850 and later, in two separate building phases, that it was extended by two times two axes, to look as it does today; the addition of the gallery to the Grey House from 1804 served Princess Luise as "the way to church". East of the Grey House was a small garden, not open to the public at first, to which the princess could retire. The provost's residence, erected south of the gallery in 1796 as a two-storey neo-Gothic brick structure, presumably to designs by Erdmannsdorff, is now the Protestant parsonage for the church of St. Petri. The originally Romanesque church, consecrated as early as 1201, was rebuilt in the neo-Gothic style and considerably enlarged by building director, Georg Christoph Hesekiel, in 1804 and 1809. The churchyard garden was bordered by a fruit-growing wall that also served to support the masses of soil of the Zedernberg, which had seats on top offering views in all directions. The soil came from the original excavations for the Swan Pool. It had not been possible at the time to spread it over the graves in the cemetery that still surrounded the church or for some lively modelling. When the cemetery was moved, the remains had been interred in a sarcophagus designed by Erdmannsdorff. This was set up in the churchyard between 1785 and 1787, and decorated with textual inscriptions based on lines by Klopstock and depictions of genii.

The neo-Gothic decorative façade of the princely stable, dating from as early as 1775, forms the western border of the

Gasthof zum Eichenkranz and Friederikenbrücke. Coloured etching by Johann Friedrich Nagel (1765-1825), dating from 1794. Erdmannsdorff's inn, erected as a neo-Gothic town gate in 1785, alluded to the medieval German building tradition. Those arriving, for whom the little town was hidden from a distance by the plantation around it, were welcomed by this building.

The English Landscape Garden

Ludwig Trauzettel

The gardens in Wörlitz, established from 1764 onwards, are now acknowledged as the earliest surviving examples of the landscape gardening style in continental Europe. This excluded England, which can be seen as a crucial stimulus and source for what was created in Wörlitz, and for landscape gardens in general. This is why landscape gardening is often referred to as the English garden style, even though this developed very differently in Europe from its land of origin.

The revolutionary innovations in horticulture in the early 18th century were the result of social conflicts between the commercial and financial bourgeoisie, the Whigs, and the British feudal aristocracy, the Tories. For the Whigs, who were committed to the ideas of the Enlightenment, free nature expressed liberated thoughts. Hence, a completely new sense of nature developed as a result of rejecting the baroque architecture and horticulture, which were subject to strict rules. At first, gardens inspired by nature came into being in London and its environs and then all over the country, with buildings using clear, simple architecture following ancient and Renaissance models. The green island created by centuries of sheep grazing and deforestation in favour of solitaire trees offered ideal conditions for the new landscape gardens with stately homes apparently embedded in them. 17th century landscape painting also provided models for this, with ideal Arcadian landscape by painters like Claude Lorrain, Gaspard Poussin or Salvatore Rosa. They were turned into three-dimensional garden images, like theatrical settings for the country seats. In his didactic poem, *Der englische Garten*, William Mason issued the following instructions: "Look at such glowing scenes as once taught Claude to adorn the canvas with a southern brush! Take such scenes, engraved in memory, and bring them home to England. There endow the motifs with the forms of home, in order to create, if nature has the means, many a new Tivoli for cataract, rocks and shady zones." The mature Renaissance gardens of Mediterranean and Chinese garden design offered further stimuli. Among the first gardens to meet the Whigs' requirements were those in Twickenham and Chiswick. The way they developed, and also the plans and descriptions that survived, may seem more like rococo gardens from today's point of view, but the natural character subsequently showed through more markedly in each successive garden. New design approaches were added. Programmatic statements soon started to determine the character of the garden pictures that were staged along the paths and in the various garden areas. Viewers were to be led purposefully through artfully composed landscapes, linked to each other by sight lines. The early gardens had been initiated by poets, painters, philosophers and the rural gentry themselves, but now the profession of landscape gardener started to emerge. William Kent (1684-1748) and Lancelot "Capability" Brown (1716-1783) were among the outstanding practitioners. As a counter-movement to Brown's very freely designed landscapes, William Chambers (1723-1796) argued for a sublime garden, turning against landscapes alleged to have developed naturally, that "differ very little from common fields" and speaking up for a rapid sequence of contrasting atmospheric pictures, with his myth of Chinese garden art. He described Chinese design intentions as follows: "Nature is their pattern, and their aim is to imitate her in all her beautiful irregularities."

So the new landscape garden developed in many different directions in England. Erdmannsdorff and Prince Franz studied the various tendencies in English design and brought them together in Anhalt-Dessau to create a new quality of garden: the garden as a universal work of art. They brought the impressions they had gained on the Grand Tour back to Central Europe, translating their enthusiasm for antiquity into reality and drawing their southern European experiences into their creative solutions. Today, English academics visiting the Dessau-Wörlitz Garden Realm point out that it is easier to gain an impression of and understand the English design approach in these gardens than in the British Isles: this identifies the empathy shown by the initiators when the gardens were created. Boettiger tried to explain this in his diary in 1797: "Perhaps there is now no landscape gardener in England itself with such a masterly understanding as Franz of the art of nuancing by mixing green a hundredfold, and painting green in green. This and his associated skill of grouping the clusters and clumps of bushes pleasantly and strewing the grass mat with them is a highlight that one should focus on from the so many hundreds of views afforded."

churchyard and concealed the remaining local buildings that still extended into the Schloss Garden at the time. It was Duke Leopold Friedrich, the grandson and successor of Prince Franz, who finally assigned a newly designed garden area to the entrance façade of the stable building and coach house, which was less elaborately decorated, by pulling down more town houses when he divided the garden from the town in the 1820s. As a border, he used the rocks from the market that had previously surrounded the poplar-fringed square as a local meeting-place, like a Roman circus.

Neumark's Garden

Ludwig Trauzettel

In Neumark's Garden, like the Schloss Garden, part of the early phase of the Wörlitz designs, the intricate and regular spatial structures of the 1760s, have survived despite modernization in the 19th century. There were structures of this kind at first in the parts of the garden "on the other side of the lake" as well, but they fell victim to the floods of 1770 and 1771, and were then worked over more lavishly and more meaningfully. Anything that was considered complete was retained in Neumark's Garden, and with some exceptions was scarcely changed as the the periphery of the gardens moved outwards. Carl August Boettiger criticized this approach, pointing out in 1797 when describing the parts that had been created first that this "must be one of the prince's earliest, and ... could be considered as psychological evidence of how the prince was thinking at the time. Now much would turn out completely differently ... The great

Left-hand page ‹ It was possible to eat close to nature in the English way in the summer dining room in the kitchen building. In the cold season, the room was used to accommodate plants in tubs from the palace garden.

Neumark's Garden was a working garden that had been beautified. Fruit-growing areas, where modern fruit cultivation was tried out and demonstrated to visitors in an exemplary fashion, were established in the 18th century, along with tree nurseries and vegetable patches.

The Eisenhart in Neumark's Garden. This bridge, named after the building material (Eisenhart = iron-hard), and the pavilions served as an entrance to the former domestic garden. The right-hand pavilion, the Otahaitisches Kabinett, used to contain an ethnological collection, and the other was a public garden library until 1818.

The Praying Boy at the end of the Eisenhart pergola. This plaster cast of the ancient 1st century BC copy of a figure known as Ganymede has stood on a plinth in the rendered niche, framed in bog iron ore, since about 1780. The statue was based on a model at Sanssouci.

177

error is that the prince always extended the park by small sections, always adding something, thus losing the unity of plan and composition, also ... does not have the heart to change ... an early area, and adapt it to the whole." Today we are thankful for this approach by the prince, who always undertook changes in the garden himself, without a preparatory sketch; it ensured that this horticultural development has remained comprehensible. Unfortunately, Prince Franz had all the written notes about the genesis of the gardens destroyed in 1810.

Neumark's Garden, which was named after the gardener responsible from 1771 to 1783, Johann Christian Neumark (1741-1811), was used as a domestic garden until he fell ill and was later moved to Oranienbaum. The buildings were not added to the gardens, which were established in the 1770s, until the 1780s. The princely kitchen's fruit and vegetable requirements were met here after Prince Franz had acquired the land formerly occupied by citizens' gardens. The area on the western shore of the lake, which was higher and protected from flooding, also accommodated tree nurseries and fruit plantations. In 1771, retreating floodwater had eroded a gully to the north-west. The peninsula this produced was separated by a canal from the meadowland beyond Coswiger Weg, and so the new island was protected from uncontrolled access and intervention. This meant that two essentially English ideas were incorporated into the basic concept of the garden, the beltwalk and the ha-ha: the path running all round the garden allowed visitors to experience the inside and outside areas, and the canal designed as a ha-ha does not obtrude from any direction as a visual border. The horse-drawn carts needed for the work were brought to the island via a ford, and pedestrians reached it, as today, only via ferries or the "Eisenhart", which serves as a bridge. This is named after the material it is built from, bog iron ore, which was used for building the romantic rocky areas because of its volcanic appearance. The rooms in the building for the gardeners and the fruit cellar were also part of the maze created in 1783/84, an allegorical part of the garden. It adjoined the Eisenhart on the north-western side. As August Rode tells us as a contemporary witness, it was not intended to be a baroque maze, but was supposed to represent the course of human existence, the path the prince's life had followed, shaped by parents, teachers and companions. As in reality, visitors must first take various erroneous paths, overcome obstacles in winding curves or straight lines, in order to arrive finally in Elysium, after many situations from which there seems to be no escape. Even in ancient days, Elysium embodied the "dwelling-place of the blessed", and was a frequently used design motif in English gardens. From here it was supposed to be possible to see the princely tomb on the Drehberg, 2300 metres away through the arches of the Eisenhart wall. Inscriptions along the way, like "Wanderer, choose your path with reason", suggest sense and intellect, and enable visitors to find their bearings. The Rousseau island that precedes Neumark's Garden is part of the programme presented by the labyrinth, but at the same time symbolic: an enlightened greeting for travellers arriving from Dessau.

Neumark's Garden was remodelled and modernized in the 19th century, but its original basic structure remained unchanged. The tree nursery existed until 1914, but the fruit trees had already been replaced with decorative shrubs. The restoration work, started in 1984, is intended to make clear to visitors the original thinking behind the design. As soon as the clumps of fruit trees planted in recent years articulate the spatial structure of the gardens once again, the original spatial relationships will regain their effect when later, fashionable trees and bushes have been removed.

Fruit growing and agriculture: beautiful and useful

Ludwig Trauzettel

An idealized image of antiquity making comprehensive use of a world made beautiful had already found favour as an idea behind the newly emerging free and natural garden art. The motto, coined by Horace (65-8 BC) in the *Ars poetica*: "He who mixes the useful with the beautiful will gain every applause", was also used as a maxim for life and creativity for Prince Franz and Erdmannsdorff in the Garden Realm. The useful element of the new (English) economy formed a harmonious unity with the beautified park landscape. There was nothing that did not have a function, everything was intended to be understood as an instructive programme according to its creator's intentions, and it was also to be taken up and imitated by the local people and visitors. Right into the very heart of the gardens, pasture and arable land, orchards and flocks of animals, as well as the agricultural work, contributed to the effect made by the artfully constructed garden images.

In the early stages, fruit cultivation and modern English agriculture were only practised as models in Neumark's Garden and later, in the area around the Grey House in Schoch's Garden. In the Gothic House, the prince had a pomological cabinet with a collection of wax copies of the latest fruit varieties and literature on fruit cultivation. The varieties were tried out in the adjacent gardens and the best ones planted all over the Garden Realm. In the late 1780s, Prince Franz drew a 13th part of his entire income from leasing fruit-growing land. In about 1800, the high-yielding avenues of fruit trees, some of them with several rows, had spread along roads, dikes and ditches throughout the principality. In Wörlitz, as a result of the demesne directed by Georg Karl von Raumer, a model commercial farm was established, a temple to Ceres, the goddess of fertility, which delighted architects with its Palladian buildings, matching functional and social aspects, and which was able to serve as a model to farmers from other countries

Schoch's Garden

Ludwig Trauzettel

Schoch's Island ▸ The garden north-west of the Wörlitzer See, bounded by the Coswiger Chaussee, the Elbe dike and the Weidenheger, is named after the man who planted it and first tended it, Johann Leopold Ludwig Schoch the Elder. The area is divided into two by the Wolfskanal. Schoch's Island, the eastern part, includes the area around the Gothic House with the orchard, and the Grove of Diana and the Nymphaeum on the other side of the large meadow. West of the island, next to arable land and domestic gardens, are the Flora Garden, full of flowers, and the Romantische Partie, which leads to the area on the Elbe dike. The Weidenheger, which is adjacent to Schoch's Island to the east, came into being at almost the same time, and was designed in the same way. Design ability had advanced here since Neumark's Garden and the Schloss Garden were created, but is different again from the Neue Anlagen (New Gardens), which were

View over the Golden Urn to the synagogue and the church. In the same way as the equality of all religions is addressed in a literary fashion in Lessing's Parable of the Rings, the atmospheric picture created around the Golden Urn lends form to Prince Franz's tolerant approach as a garden art motif: this is his way of stating his view on the equality of all religions. The urn marks the last resting-place of the princely couple's first-born daughter, who died in 1769.

established later, where the landscape approach of Johann Georg, the younger Schoch, is in evidence.

When working on Neumark's Garden and the Schloss Garden, a personal formal language still had to be found, but the people responsible for Schoch's Garden had already mastered the art of handling English landscape design. Grohmann's analysis in his 1795 *Taschenbuch für Gartenfreunde* fits this garden particularly well: "The law of nature is also the law of the garden artist, purposefulness without purpose, regularity without [recognizable] regulation. His art is to conceal what art did, and to form and show all as nature; he does not want to reveal the cost of his effort; he does not preen with splendour and precious outward show; the most natural stone that nature will give up to him is the one he loves most ... If English garden is the model of all, then the Princely Garden in Wörlitz may and can be a model of this latter ..."

Schoch's garden as it looks today is the result of 20 years of restoration work. This means that it is again possible to see the new quality of garden design that Prince Franz was able to achieve in the second phase of laying out the Wörlitz gardens between 1771 and 1790, with advice and architectural planning from Erdmannsdorff and help from Johann

Leopold Schoch the Elder's experienced gardener's hands. This part of the gardens may be considered as the heart of the Wörlitz Park, as it presents the clearest image of the intellectual drive, ideal world and aims of the people who created it. Prince Franz lived in this private garden that was open to the public quite uninhibitedly for a long time, without the usual court business. Here he built his own private refuge in the form of the Gothic House, his own museum and his own happiness. Surrounded by model agricultural and fruit-growing enterprises, he lived out his unfulfilled youthful dreams of a free life in the country that he had first wanted to spend in England. "Since the separation from the princess ... this Gothic House became the centre of all his pleasures, even in love, and his permanent home," Boettiger noted in his diary in 1797. And August Rode added in 1817: "He built the Gothic House and collected everything around himself there that could help to set his mind in the world that had come before." Here Rode was drawing attention to symbolic intentions and to the prince's pride in taking private and usable buildings in the neo-Gothic style as a means of indication of his own tradition and history, and his striving for independence. This had shaped the youthful prince as he came to terms with Prussia, and motivated his move to free garden art.

Floodwater at the Temple of Venus. The dike's design is enhanced by planting and buildings, and forms a transition from the northern edge of the garden to the open landscape of the water meadows. The dike has withstood the regular Elbe floods for over two centuries.

The iconographic programme realized as a universal work of garden art, the convoluted tissue of educational ideas, was supposed to make an aesthetic impact, to appeal to the visitor's mind and trigger continuing thought patterns. Interested parties were not just supposed to experience and enjoy nature, they were to feel joy, terror and awe, contemplate moral matters and concern themselves with the gods of antiquity; they were to taste the shiver of the past and of transience, of life and of death. Apparently unmotivated and random as in nature, where nothing is without meaning, contrasts are built up in the garden scenery, which create the tension in the effect made by the gardens. Neo-classicism alternates with neo-Gothic, distant views with design highlights close by, dark areas with light gardens. Places for pious contemplation follow those associated with sensual delight; a peaceful idyll takes over from garden images full of conflict and confusion.

The work, started in Schoch's Garden in 1766, was already fairly advanced when the terrain, which was only just above water-level, was submerged in the floods of 1770 and 1771. The garden was subsequently created a second time, in even greater quality. These gardens represent a second stylistic phase for Wörlitz, and are to be understood as a sequence of garden pictures staged in three dimensions. The pictures open up along a guiding pathway that changes direction to show viewers ever-changing impressions and experiences. They experience the garden as a *Gesamtkunstwerk* (a complete work of art) only by moving, by looking *and* walking. The variety of park architecture, buildings and sculptures within the garden's sophisticated sight line network does mean that not all the objects can be seen at all times and from any viewpoint. So, groups of trees and bushes hide the view and change the spatial effect for visitors as they move along. Backdrop plantations are intended to deceive the eye and act as a framework for the three-dimensional garden images. The viewers' movement creates an effect like that of a revolving stage in a theatre. The actual size of the whole complex and the relationships within it are concealed from the viewers at first. Distractions, perspectives and pictorial details deceive and surprise the wanderers. They are intended to surrender to the moods that the garden pictures evoke in all their manifold variety. Park architecture or unassuming sculptures, scarcely discernible in the distance, direct their eyes in all directions. Sudden or unexpected impressions keep their interest alive, and they are stimulated to see and to think.

The White Bridge, built in 1772, is one part of the instructive bridge programme in the gardens. An important architectural treatise by A. Palladio was also behind the bridge in London's Kew Gardens, on which this one was modelled.

The Temple of Flora, built in 1797/98, is the architectural highlight,
dedicated to the goddess of flowers, youth and beauty, of a part of the
garden that is particularly richly endowed with flowers.

The Temple of Flora, originally used as a music pavilion, is decorated
with an ancient statue of Flora; the walls carry flowers copied by the
Berlin painter J. Fischer in 1797 from the at that time recently published
book on flowers by the Jena professor Batsch.

Top ▴ The gardener's house in the Hofgärtnerei. The garden inspector's neo-Gothic home and workplace was built in 1798/99 and based on an English country house. The Hofgärtnerei developed into a plant and seed business in the 19th century.

Bottom ▾ The Luisenklippe, built on the Elbe dike by Erdmannsdorff, was named after Princess Louise Charlotte of Saxony-Gotha, who was the first to ascend it.

Top ⁃ Benches and garden seats draw visitors' attention to the gardens' visual links and particularly attractive garden scenes.

Bottom ⁃ The warning altar, decorated with Apollo and the Muses, is probably the earliest monument to nature conservation and monument preservation in Germany. It carries the inscription "Wanderer, heed nature and art and spare their works".

Wörlitz

Top ‣ The Wolfsbrücke, here seen from the gondola landing-stage in the Schloss Garden, stands at the mouth of a canal that divides Schoch's Island from the vegetable and flower gardens in the western part of the park.

Bottom ‣ Working animals and cultivation are part of the "living garden images" all over the Wörlitz Park, here seen against the background of the stone Wolfsbrücke, built in 1811.

Top ‣ Nocturnal work by an Elbe beaver, near the Mittelhölzer guard-house, has felled a poplar. Almost eradicated fifty years ago, and then made a protected species, the population of this shy rodent has risen considerably.

Bottom ‣ The peacocks, related to the princess as a symbol of Juno, originally enlivened all the prestigious areas of the Schloss Garden, but are now to be found only in the orchard by the Gothic House.

Palm House, Hofgärtnerei and Temple of Flora, seen from the Gothic House. A neo-Gothic plant house was built near the gardener's house in 1799. It was used to accommodate the tender plants intended to emphasize the southern character of the areas around the neo-classical build-

ings; before it was completed, they were wintered in the summer room of the Gothic House. The building on the left did not become a palm house until the 19th century, when cultivating this plant family became fashionable.

Particularly attractive scenes in the gardens were marked with seats. Here, strollers can linger, look at architecture and works of art nearby or in the distance, or succumb to the staged moods presented by the garden images. Boettiger was impressed by this in 1797, and confided in his diary: "It is a rule of landscape gardening, followed very conscientiously in these gardens, that no restful seat should ever be placed without a purpose. An expert assures me that there are up to 150 seats and benches in the park and gardens as a whole, and in every case, if the question : why here? is asked, it is possible to give a satisfactory answer oneself after some thought and looking around. Some benches open up quite surprisingly beautiful views, as though things that seemed to have been muddled together had suddenly shot apart as if at the stroke of a magic wand, and had now lined up on both sides as if on parade ..."

The gardens on Schoch's Island around the Gothic House and in the raised orchard, which was protected from flooding by a surrounding dike, were designed first. As Rode explained, "its actual purpose, if ever ... the Elbe should ever again break through the outermost embankment, then at least this part of the garden would be protected from the fury of the waves." The orchard was planted with fruit trees. A vault was built for the gardener Schoch on the Great Meadow side. He is interred here in a sandstone sarcophagus. This attracted much attention at that time, as until then only mock tombs were customary, to stimulate ideas and atmospheres. Thus Boettiger noted in his diary: "It is always a fine thought, and the prince has done himself honour by putting it into practice, that he interred the mortal remains of his landscape gardener Schoch here, in a mound surrounded by dense foliage, quite close to his favourite dwelling, and had the inscription placed on a tablet: the work of his hands beautified these lands. May his spirit surge and sway like these bushes here."

Visitors usually reach Schoch's Island via the Wolfsbrücke, which was built over the Wolfskanal in 1811, replacing a wooden bridge from the time the estate came into being. The sandstone bridge, decorated with urns and iron railings, is named after the peasant Wolf, who had originally had his field here. It is an important starting and ending point for many visual links within the garden. The path over the bridge leads past the Gothic House into the Neue Anlagen (New Gardens). As well as the Wolfsbrücke, five other bridges lead on to this island, which was formed artificially by canal construction: the Hornzackenbrücke, an early bridge form

In the Grove of Diana. This sculpture of the Roman goddess of hunting with dog, completed c. 1780 by Johann Christian Ehrlich, is part of the gardens' mythological and educational programme. Diana referred the educated visitor to Ovid's *Metamorphoses*.

intended to look like a fallen, "split oak tree", was put in place in 1774 to connect the Gothic House and the domestic garden on the other side of the canal. The White Bridge, south of the Kleines Wallloch, was built in 1772 after the Wolfskanal was completed and is modelled on William Chambers's timber arch construction in London's Kew Gardens, a self-reinforcing structure by the architect Palladio. A wooden pivot bridge led north to the Elbe dike, preceding the present Agnesbrücke, built in 1958, and the sandstone New Bridge led over to the Weidenheger. This last bridge was built in 1910, to succeed the 1772 wooden bridge, and is decorated with reliefs of the gods Venus and Cupid surrounded by tritons.

Other key design features on Schoch's Island, which is framed by the Wörlitzer See and canals, were the Nymphaeum near the New Bridge and the Grove of Diana on the bank of the Small Wallloch. The little wood dedicated to the goddess contains poplars, planes, rowans, elms and yew-trees, and has been planted with rhododendrons since about 1930. The stone Diana, with a hound at her side, is placed on a slight eminence in her grove, which is decorated with a round bench. The Nymphaeum, open to the Schloss Garden and originally providing garden seating, is built into the mound of what used to be an ice cellar. A sculpture of a miner has stood in front of its original access shaft since 1780. Walkers experience this surprising scene when climbing up to the hidden vantage point of the hill in the vineyard, which affords a fantastic view of the lake and the Schloss Garden.

It was only after Erdmannsdorff's death that the warning altar, decorated with Apollo and the Muses, was built in the north-eastern part of Schoch's Island in 1801. With this, probably the earliest monument to nature conservation and monument preservation in Germany, Prince Franz erected a memorial to his friend, advisor and co-designer. It carries the inscription "Wanderer, heed nature and art and spare their works".

The western areas of Schoch's Garden ‣ After work on Schoch's Island was complete, the areas to the west of the Wolfskanal, largely used for agricultural purposes, were included in the aesthetic design of this part of the garden. The gardener responsible lived in the Gothic House, but as this was increasingly being equipped and extended to meet the prince's needs, its kitchen garden expanded westwards, towards the Coswiger Chaussee. This was where Prince Franz performed his fruit cultivation experiments; the

The "Boy with a Thorn" on the Weidenheger, carved in sandstone c. 1782 by the Dresden sculptor Pfeiffer, is one of the larger-than-life sculptures, intended to make an effect from a distance, that together form a series of visual links.

View from the Luisenklippe to the Temple of Venus. What according to Boettiger (1797) is the "most beautiful and regular building in the entire park" is raised on a small rocky massif at the end of the Elysian valley.

Erdmannsdorff's ten-column Doric sandstone monopteral temple, built in 1794, forms the end of many visual axes in Wörlitz Park.

highest-yielding varieties were later to be used all over the Garden Realm. As well as this, he planted mulberries in the immediate vicinity of the Gothic House, as he was also experimenting with silkworm breeding. Trees and bushes discovered on his travels were cultivated in the tree nursery, which was walled, because of the risk of theft and vandalism that was already setting in. Boettiger reported on the prince's walled orchard, which he found locked: "... This used to be open to all. But because of the most wanton destruction of the valuable foreign plants, the prince felt himself compelled to close this nursery ... Within this little space ... the prince has his treasury ... and the strength of his Garden Realm ... depends on its tending and survival. Here one has to be guided around by the prince himself, and have him convey his experiences and observations on the culture and picturesque landscape use of every bush and every kind of timber."

New aesthetic ideas became increasingly important. So a flower garden was established alongside the tree nursery. This was a new high point for horticultural endeavours, and it acquired a temple to the goddess of flowers, the Temple of Flora. William Chambers had built a temple like this in the form of the Casino in Wilton (Wiltshire) in southern England, which also relates back to the Temple of Clitumnus in the Italian town of Spoleto. The nearby nursery developed into a horticultural base: by the turn of the century, there was also a garden inspector's dwelling with a house for wintering tender plants. Further houses for special crops, pineapples and melons, for example, were also built here.

The Hofgärtnerei, the focus for horticultural and fruit-growing experiments, and for plant care, is now on the edge of the gardens. The neighbouring citizens' gardens and arable areas were originally part of the gardens, which blended seamlessly into the surrounding countryside, finally concluding with the Elbe dike. Observation buildings to check on flooding at this dike were conceived as visual links from the gardens, just as they were intended to show the way to Wörlitz from a distance. The Arcadian landscape east of Wörlitz with the Bertingwachhaus and the Mittelhölzer Wachhaus (observation buildings) was also included, so that visually the gardens covered considerably more than their actual area. The scale of the main and ancillary buildings in relation to each other and the design elements of the façade of the Mittelhäuser Wachhaus were also intended to give the impression that a country seat with three wings could be made out in the far distance.

At the same time as the extensions to the Hofgärtnerei, a canal was dug north-west of the Kleines Wallloch, thus opening up this part of the gardens to boat traffic and extending the transport facilities up to the Hofgärtnerei. It drains water from the Wörlitz estate off to the north-west. The Romantische Partie came into being north of this canal, presenting the sensitive and sublime garden ideas of that period. It was entered from the south over the Chain Bridge. Its chains were hung between two artificial cliffs in 1781; this swaying suspension bridge was intended to confuse and frighten visitors, following an idea by William Chambers. From a distance, the wooden planks attached to the chains looked like a rope with people balancing on it. Like the supposed hermit's home in a grotto under the chain bridge, the bridge itself is committed to the aesthetic of the sublime. Visitors reach the cell of the mystagogue, the "initiator into the sacred secrets", via the prayer precinct by the altar,

This cast of a Medici Venus stands in the open rotunda of the Temple of Venus, which concludes an area in the Romantic style.

decorated with sayings by the prince and Lavater. August Rode identifies the two paths that continue from here, "the mindless, weary ascent of man without knowledge and spiritual culture" to the right and to the left, the underground "mysterious path of the mystics, of the apprentices of sublime wisdom, who convey ... secret revelations ... to their adherents". The section following the Freemasons' testing path leads through underground passages and ends under the Temple of Venus, in the Grotto of Vulcan. The Luisenklippe, constructed in 1798 , is also part of this programme. Opposite this artificial rock structure with a neo-Gothic bay extension is the Temple of Venus, built to Erdmannsdorff's design in 1794. This is modelled on the ruins of the Temple of Venus in Hadrian's villa in Tivoli. In Wörlitz, the Grotto of Vulcan is immediately underneath the statue of Venus inside the Elbe dike, which has been extended here; the grottoes of Aeolus and Neptune are adjacent. So the underground buildings are dedicated to the four elements earth, fire, air and water, and they conclude the allegorical path of insight that started in the mystagogue's cell. North-west of the Romantische Partie, on the dike by the Coswiger Fahrt, is the skaldic tomb dedicated to the Nordic poetic tradition. It could be seen from the Gothic House before the dike was raised in 1773.

Walking through the underground passages of the Romantische Partie brings visitors to the Elbe dike almost without their noticing. It borders the garden on the north side and offers sweeping views, both of the Elbe water meadows, which used to be adorned with numerous old oaks, and also of the various different gardens in the grounds. There is seating of different kinds along the path running along the dike and past the Neue Anlagen, to alert walkers to the best visual links and garden scenes from this raised position.

The garden on the Weidenheger ‣ The garden on the Weidenheger borders Schoch's Garden to the east, and came into being immediately after the great floods of 1770 and 1771. As August Rode reveals in his description, "this garden ... with its open and closed areas ... has an entirely clandestine character." The first designs had been destroyed by the water

as far as the Golden Urn and the Wachhaus zu Pferde. The Wachhaus, which serves as a flood lookout post, is still the only building to dress the set in this part of the garden, on what was temporarily the north-eastern periphery of the park. The stone façade, articulated like an Ionic temple, is decorated by a relief of a youth with laurel wreath, leading a horse. It is based on an ancient tomb relief in Tivoli.

The floods had even obliterated the canals that had already been dug, and destroyed all but the abutments of a completed wooden bridge; the topography of the whole area had been changed, because the masses of water pouring into the area of what is now the Grosses Wallloch had taken considerable quantities of soil with them, which were deposited as a tongue of land around the present Weidenheger, but also near the Schloss Garden. This had created a new landscape, which had to be taken into consideration in future designs. The most effective way of enclosing and stabilizing this newly washed up, infertile land, was by planting. Fast-growing poplars and willows were chosen as the first to inhabit this sandy terrain. The name "Weidenheger" (willow enclosure) was given to this new area that had been reclaimed and enclosed on what was then the edge of the garden. Two long sight axes cut through its northern section, one leading from the "Boy with a Thorn" to the shell nymph in the Schloss Garden, and originally bordered by Lombardy poplars. The other axis points to the distant Temple of Venus.

On the south side, the Floating Bridge provides a link with the tongue of land that is the "Kleiner Heger". This bridge, constructed as a pontoon and attached to chains, could be pushed aside to allow boats to pass through the Sonnenkanal. In addition, by removing this floating bridge, unwanted observers could be kept away from the Bath of Venus on the so-called "horseshoe", if one intended to make use of the little expanse of water by the Romantic bark house, built in 1785, in order to bathe in natural seclusion. This practical purpose is also symbolized by the sculptor Pfeiffer's neoclassical sandstone copy of an ancient Venus bathing. Like all the garden sculpture, this larger-than-life statue is intended to make an impact from a distance, and can be seen along many of the garden's sight lines.

The Neue Anlagen

Ludwig Trauzettel

The last of the five individual gardens at Wörlitz is on the eastern side, and was not established until the 1790s, after the other sections were already present in terms of basic structure and design. The Neue Anlagen – New Gardens –, the name that was also used at the time, are now counted as part of the so-called third Wörlitz design phase. The previous gardens were characterized by a particularly dense iconographic and architectural programme that made an impression through garden pictures, but the Neue Anlagen derive their impact through the generosity of their designed landscapes, their areas of water, meadows or arable land. These are framed by gallery planting, with the few architectural highlights also setting an accent in the new spatial structure. The canals and paths also take second place within the spatial situations formed by the planting. Even though the artistic design is restricted to these areas, it sets the tone for the whole area of

The Amalieninsel (Amalie's Island) in the Grosses Wallloch. The Amaliengrotte (Amalie's Grotto), named after the crown princess and topped by a vine arbour, was built in 1793 by building director Georg Christoph Hesekiel.

the Neue Anlagen. August Rode describes this area in 1798, which "is a garden, but also beautified landscape; as most of the land ... is field. The strangeness of these gardens lies mainly in the way that taste and art were able to use these very bounds, and to give an all-enlivening charm to the main objects of the whole at the two opposite ends – to the Pantheon with the stretches of water beneath it and to the volcano and the tip of the lake -, and to link them to each other and to the lake."

In this last phase of creating the Wörlitz gardens, the prince as a dilettante designer was already able to rely on Johann George Schoch, the gardener's son trained in France and England, who was able to deal with the new sections. Until then, his father Johann Leopold Schoch (1728-1793) and the other gardeners had simply had to realize the spatial conceptions devised by the prince and Erdmannsdorff within the terrain. The changes the younger Schoch made by the Schmaler See and the Grosses Wallloch were influenced by the first English landscape gardener Lancelot "Capability" Brown (1716-1783), who beautified over 2000 country seats in the British Isles. Schoch had been able to study his brilliant use of the available "capabilities" for the garden art-work that was to be designed

in numerous English gardens. The art lay in not showing that the garden had been created artificially. Everything had to look as though nature had created this landscape by chance. The younger Schoch also seems to have learned how to take the particular qualities of a landscape and remodel and enhance them artistically as a work of garden art. As well as his work in Anhalt-Dessau, he was employed to create gardens in Braunschweig, Halle, Dieskau and Hohenpriessnitz.

The creative highlights of the Neue Anlagen are the landscapes by the Grosses Wallloch and around the artificial rocky island, the "Stein" Island. The Grosses Wallloch itself, as the peak of landscape design in the Wörlitz area, anticipates later developments in the classical German landscape garden. The Pantheon, the Rotes Wallwachhaus and the Piedmontese farmhouse are architectural accents around the expanses of water, which the younger Schoch had designed and replanted in a masterly fashion when laying out his shorelines. The effect was further enhanced in terms of richness of experience by artistic land-modelling on the Amalieninsel (Amalie's Island) and the Island of Remembrance. The islands served as destinations for the gondola trips that were already popular in the 18th century, undertaken "in order to better observe the

The Iron Bridge over the Georgenkanal was copied in a ratio of 1:4 from Wilkinson's bridge in Coalbrookdale, which was much admired in Europe. This bridge form was considered revolutionary; in Wörlitz it was juxtaposed with a ford, the earliest way of crossing a water-course.

mutual relation of parts of the garden to each other, and the effect of the whole" (Rode 1798). Visually, the islands conceal actual size, distort perception and thus enhance the experience of the landscape. The water flowing into the Wallloch from the east, then drains westwards into the Sonnenkanal. The Sonnenbrücke over this canal leads south to the rocky "Stein" island, the second highlight of the Neue Anlagen. The Sonnenbrücke (Sun Bridge), with its originally gilded iron bars, was intended to be reminiscent of Inca culture, and look like the radiant beams around the full disc of the sun when reflected in the water as the boats glided through.

The Italian landscape and the Georgental (George's Valley) on the canal of the same name link the two main points of the Neue Anlagen, the Pantheon and the "Stein". Prince Franz dedicated this lightly modelled landscape to his brother Johann Georg, and named it after him. The material excavated from the canal was used to create small mounds on which

seats were placed to give a better view over the distant areas of Schoch's Garden and the Schloss Garden. A ford, halfway along the canal, allowed agricultural vehicles to cross to the fields on the other side. The path by the canal shifts east on to the other bank over the Iron Bridge at this point, leading on to the rocky "Stein" island, the culmination of the Italian section that started at the Pantheon on the Grosses Wallloch. This artificial island was created between 1788 and 1794 in the eastern part of the Wörlitz Park. It is a brick structure of several storeys, clad in natural stone. Its architectural programme derives from the environs of Naples, and is supposed to be set in a landscape design that looks as natural as possible. The poplars and figs surrounding the island also indicate an Italian influence, and make a transition to the open landscape to the east. The second feeder stream for the Wörlitz waterways is marked symbolically here, near the artificial rock structure, by a grotto dedicated to Egeria, the Roman nymph of springs.

The Rotes Wallwachhaus was built to designs by Erdmannsdorff soon after the early flood disaster in 1770/71. It stands by the Grosses Wall-loch, not far from the breach point, as a lookout post for flooding.

The Art of Bridge-building

One typical feature of the Dessau-Wörlitz Garden Realm is its instructive educational programme, intended to contribute to the enlightened humanistic education of the visitors. As D. Sturm said in 1806, in Friedrich Justin Bertuch's *Allgemeines Deutsches Gartenmagazin*, the garden functioned as a vivid example of art history: "Perhaps there is no English garden of even the slightest significance that would not contain a temple ... here we are dealing with garden art that is permitted to draw from the very sources of art ... It can and is allowed to be a living history of art." The educational architecture programme here also includes the history of bridge-building, with all its technical possibilities – unique in European garden art in this level of completeness. Prince Franz may have got the idea of bringing the elements of bridge-building history together in a garden, and demonstrating all its forms, from Sir Francis Dashwood's West Wycombe in Buckinghamshire, England, a garden ensemble that indubitably inspired the prince. Like scarcely any other, it is composed with an educational architectural background, whose programme made use of a whole variety of bridge forms, among other elements. Dashwood did not, however, achieve as much variety as Wörlitz.

There are over 50 technically and stylistically different bridges within the Garden Realm, showing visitors a range of possibilities in the development of bridge-building, vividly and in beautifully designed surroundings. 19 of these bridges are to be found in the Wörlitz gardens alone. The variety in the Wörlitz garden experience derives from the large number of different water-crossings, from the ford via the tree-trunk laid across the water to a reduced copy of what was then the most modern iron bridge (Ironbridge, Coalbrookdale). The originally gilded Sonnenbrücke over the Sonnenkanal was inspired by Inca culture, the wooden pivot bridge on the Agneskanal suggested a Dutch model. The drawbridge in the Schloss Gardens took up a homegrown German structural tradition, while the swaying chain suspension bridge goes back to Chinese ideas, though the model was discovered in Switzerland. Chambers's realization of Palladio's design in London's Kew Gardens of a self-reinforcing timber strut frame led to the form of the White Bridge over the northern mouth of the Wolfskanal. In the Chinese garden in Oranienbaum, wrought iron structures were mainly used in the attempt to recreate the diversity of Chinese bar construction. The movable bridges, none of which have survived in their original form, also include three floating bridges. Of the three structures, presumed to have been in the form of small boats made of wood, and fastened between the banks on chains and hasps so that they could be pushed aside to allow boatmen to pass, only an iron pontoon bridge between the two parts of the Weidenheger remains. Following the principle of always combining the "beautiful with the useful", the bridges for access traffic and load transports were made of solid stone, but the pedestrian bridges were of lighter materials.

Overall, the wooden, stone and iron structures, drawbridges, chain, pivot and floating bridges in the Garden Realm demonstrate a variety of technical means by which walkers can overcome obstacles on a more or less steady footing. Grohmann wrote as early as 1795 in his observations on the Wörlitz bridges: "In respect of the bridges executed over the canals here and there, some wider and some narrower, this garden is certainly incomparable. They seem to have wanted to exhaust the art here. With every bridge the structure and the type of form changes, and each is so close to nature, executed in the most natural of resources, that one does not even see that they were trying to fulfil a purpose, just as nature does ..."

By setting up the sophisticated Wörlitz waterway system, Prince Franz at the same time made it possible for visitors to gain access to the gardens on foot and to experience the artificially designed landscape and its bridges by boat. When travelling through the gardens by boat, something that people have been keen to do ever since they came into being, the bridges form a frame for designed pictures. But for pedestrians, the bridges themselves are part of a system of paths that serves as a "silent guide" through the gardens. In this way, viewers always reach a particular design highlight at the bridges, and are thus made aware of it subconsciously.

The Town of Wörlitz

Ludwig Trauzettel

The little town of Wörlitz is north of the Wörlitz estate, on a raised sand dune. It was first mentioned in the year 904, and so this former farming community can look back on a thousand years of history. We have scarcely any records of the early centuries; the original fortifications and older buildings were destroyed by fires. The town's present appearance dates from the 18th century. Under Prince Leopold, the town was extended westwards as the dike was built, and his grandson Franz continued the work after 1768. He shifted the line of the dike further northwards, where it still runs today. Substantial buildings, giving the town its character, were erected in the course of the urban changes necessary for the beautification of the area and to accommodate the Schloss Garden. Erdmannsdorff erected the key buildings in the town of Wörlitz, as he had in the gardens. Town and garden related to each other spatially and through visual links, but

With his town hall, built between 1792 and 1795, Erdmannsdorff also shaped the new urban image of the farmers' town of Wörlitz, now a thousand years old.

planting between the two screened the urban development from the natural scenery and the countryside. Erdmannsdorff paid particular attention to the situation at the town's entrance points. He wanted travellers to be received symbolically by architecture that was modern and trend-setting.

The Jewish cemetery with the House of Ceremonies at the south end of Wörlitz were built in 1790, followed in 1795 by the overseer's house with volute gables and the mortuary for the Christian cemetery at the south-eastern entrance to the town. The latter still contains the burial places of the poet Friedrich von Matthisson, the gardener Eyserbeck and members of the Schoch family. The demesne, a model farm with stable, land-workers' accommodation and a three-storey house, based on Palladio's Villa Emo in Fanzolo, was built at the east end of the town in 1783-87. The Wörlitzer Ökonomie (economy) and its outlying farms had been turned into a trust in 1776 and handed over to Georg Friedrich Raumer, who had just returned from England. It developed into a widely-known model business under his direction, with 825 hectares of arable land and 210 hectares of meadowland. 49 families of threshers worked on the farms, complemented by day labourers at peak times. Even the Old School in Griesen, a tripartite Palladian brick building built to Erdmannsdorff's design in 1788, with teacher accommodation and stables, was intended to put travellers in the right mood for Wörlitz aesthetically. Visitors coming from the west were received at the "Zum Eichenkranz" inn, designed by Erdmannsdorff as a neo-Gothic town gate, which accommodated most visitors to Wörlitz in the early days.

Notable buildings in the town include the brewery, built in 1790 and the town hall, 1792-1795, a two-storey rendered brick building topped by a little tower from a model in James Lewis's *Designs in Architecture* (1780). The church, the provost's residence and the synagogue face both the town and the gardens. The long, narrow market place – a meeting-place and a playground at the same time – between the Schloss Garden and the town hall, forms the core of Wörlitz. Until the prince died, it was like a "Roman circus", surrounded by a sandstone-covered brick wall with openings. The fruit trees and Lombardy poplars planted around it linked the town to the Schloss Garden. These were removed in 1830 by Leopold Friedrich, the prince's heir.

Like the tower of the neo-Gothic Wörlitz church here, the churches in
the Garden Realm were useful to travellers, even from a great distance,
as orientation points and signposts through the area's beautified nature.

IV

LUISIUM

Uwe Quilitzsch

An Arcadia
for the Princess

"Luisium, near to Dessau, is a small area, I would like to say a grove, forming this garden full of simplicity, full of the most simple nature." *Johann Gottfried Grohmann, 1796*

Even as crown prince, Leopold Friedrich Franz of Anhalt-Dessau took pleasure in the little park only a few hundred metres north-east of Dessau, and known as "Vogelheerd". Here, where birds (Vogel = bird) used to be caught with nets, his uncle and guardian, Prince Dietrich, created a place for his ward that offered prestige as well as recreation appropriate to his age and standing. Surviving garden designs refer to grottoes typical of the period, artificial ruins and cliffs, and even a skittle alley is mentioned. And, of course, there was a little castle. As a young regent, Prince Franz made his first experiments with modern English landscape design here, even before the famous Wörlitz gardens. He had a

route laid out in the "English manner" from Dessau to the Vogelherd that still exists, running past the Jonitz mill. This path was no longer oriented axially, but given the S curve so admired by William Hogarth. Thus, the new ideal of beauty in garden design took shape for the first time in Anhalt-Dessau. It was an ideal expressing a longing for harmony and peace, for which modern contemporaries were striving. Influenced by the teaching of Rousseau, they sought refuge in nature, even though it seemed rough and threatening to them. The ordered nature of modern architecture and garden design in England seemed appropriate to their needs.

The Luisium neo-classical country seat and the garden reflect the impressions the prince gained on his visits to England. After the Grand Tour, which took him and his advisors to Italy, France and England, and the completion of his country seat in Wörlitz, he turned his attention to the Vogelherd in about 1774. He had the antiquated buildings of his youth pulled down one after the other, and redesigned the park in stages as an English landscape garden. A modest estate emerged subsequently, embedded in natural river-valley woodland, and with the intended intimate character. Even though the 14 hectare site had to be protected from flooding by dikes, the garden designers managed to create a fluent transition to the surrounding countryside. Similarly to the Wörlitz system, the dikes were built into the system of paths, opening up views of the garden from slightly raised positions. Ideas and suggestions by Princess Luise of Anhalt-Dessau were probably included in the work as well: the prince had dedicated the house and park to his young wife from the outset. The estate was called "Luisium" after its owner from 1780.

Schloss Luisium with the White Bridge. Friedrich Wilhelm von Erdmannsdorff drew up the designs for an elegant country seat in the style of a neo-classical villa, which fits harmoniously into the surrounding nature.

Some elements of the old park were retained for the new gardens, including an avenue running from north to south that splits the gardens into an eastern and a western area. Other avenues and axes were redesigned as visual links – in English garden design, "the eye had separated itself from the foot". Walkers have to follow the silent guides – the paths in the gardens – if they are to experience the meticulously planned garden pictures properly.

The gardens ▸ The Luisium garden realm is entered via three differently designed gateways. The eastern section originally had a regular ground plan. The prince used it as a domestic garden and organized appropriate beds and planting. The largest building, the neo-classical Orange House, is part of a domestic yard with four wings. A local stock of citrus shrubs will be built up here in future, and will decorate the garden in the summer months. The neo-Gothic Schlangenhaus was built on an artificial mounds not far from the orange house. But the little pavilion had nothing to do with snakes – "Schlangen". It was given this name popularly because of a gargoyle in the shape of a crowned dragon's head – the building is now an idyllic holiday home. An artificial ruin based on

a model at Painshill near London and a sculpture of a veiled female figure, said to have been inspired by a Hölderlin poem, complete the design of the domestic garden. A sight axis draws the eye towards the palace, along a line of ancient sweet chestnut trees. In the 1930s, the eastern garden was turned into a landscape garden with completely different features. The domestic yard is still a reminder of the former commercial use, along with some old fruit trees and an old mulberry bush.

The western part of the gardens was a present to the princess. In comparison with Wörlitz, the programme for its layout is smaller, and underlines the intimate quality of the artwork. It is designed around a pond, a dead arm of the Mulde. The largest building in the garden, to which a number of sight axes lead, was built here on a mound from 1774 to 1778.

The neo-classical building, built to plans by the architect von Erdmannsdorff, is more reminiscent of a country seat than a palace, appropriately to the character of the surrounding garden. The charm of the setting and its exquisite decoration and furnishings are well-nigh unsurpassable.

The basement accommodated the servants' quarters and the kitchen. Above this is the main floor, which was used for

A long sight axis leads from the south portal of the palace to the church in Jonitz (now Waldersee), whose tower serves as a tomb for Princess Luise and Prince Franz. The neo-classical Pegasus well can be seen in the foreground.

public functions. The rooms on the second floor were the princess's private quarters, and the mezzanine could house guests and servants. The belvedere on the pyramid roof offered views of the surrounding area. The wooden White Bridge below the house makes a very picturesque impression. It crosses a narrow arm of the pond. A grotto and a neo-classical summerhouse were built in the eastern part of the gardens. This section is sparingly furnished with sculptures. Two small sandstone urns are placed near the pavilion. Water for the flowerbeds came from an elaborately designed well very close by. The princess loved flowers, and had magnificent hyacinth beds planted here. Several sight lines lead to the neo-Gothic buildings on the Fohlenweide. These were built as backdrop architecture, and are no longer part of the Luisium as such. They were built on a slight eminence that offered protection from floods.

The key design features in these gardens were the trees and shrubs. The stock has changed in parts over the years, but the basic structures have survived, thanks to constant tending. Anyone walking through the Luisium with their wits about them will notice the astonishing variety of indigenous species. There are admirable old specimens of old trees such as oak, beech, chestnut, tulip tree, larch, pine and yew – the indispensable treasure of historic gardens. But in the Luisium it is above all the amazing wild herbaceous plants that deserve special attention in any season. Where else would one find anything like as many Listera ovata, twayblade (an indigenous orchid)? And countless Lilium martagon, turk's-cap lilies, or Anemone nemorosa, the unassuming wood anemone, grow on the unfertilized meadows. In spring, the meadows are covered with countless fragrant violets like a gigantic, overwhelming carpet. In summer, they give way to delicate Campanula patula, the bellflower, shimmering in delicate blue, and the white contrast of Leucanthemum vulgare, the ox-eye daisy.

The animal world has just as much variety to offer: maybugs, butterflies, red-bellied toads, tree frogs, nightingales, owls, foxes, wild boar and deer feel at home in this refuge – an atmosphere that has a very special effect on visitors to the Luisium today, as it did 200 years ago. A contemporary wrote enthusiastically as early as 1829: "What would I give for my home town to have a garden like this, such a friendly haven, nearby! ... one would like to build oneself a hut here and, leaving behind everything that presses and pains and tor-

The neo-Gothic Schlangenhaus once served as a garden pavilion. The unique atmosphere of the garden can be enjoyed here today – the house is let as a holiday home throughout the year.

ments, begin a new and more beautiful life amidst the song of nightingales." *Johann Anton Ludwig Richter, 1829*

The country seat in the Luisium ‣ The Dorpat university professor, Karl Morgenstern, noted in his notebook in 1801: "As the princess's country seat is on so small a scale that even a private man of average means could have something similar built, I noted down the elevation in a few rough lines."

The plain and yet elegant outline of the building harmonizes impressively with the garden landscape around it. Luise, who was very interested in literature, music and the sciences, wanted to gather like-minded friends around her here, and thus make the house into a place of intellectual exchange and inspiration. Friedrich Wilhelm von Erdmannsdorff, who had to take these ideas of his client's into consideration, delivered the designs for the ambitious building in 1774, and construction work was in full swing from 1775. The architect modelled the exterior on the famous villas of the Veneto and their neo-Palladian copies in Great Britain. It is evidence of his intensive study of architectural works from his own library. Publications by master builders from ancient times

to his own day, by Vitruvius, Palladio, Serlio, Scamozzi, Alberti, Blondel, Perrault and Adam, provided him with ideas. The Luisium makes it clear that Erdmannsdorff had paid particular attention to Nikolaus Goldmann's work, *Vollständige Anweisung Zu der Zivil-Bau=Kunst*, first published in 1696. Goldmann writes that "... building-art ... [can] be treated as a science and also as an art". This science was based above all on mathematics, he says, and must therefore be built on logical laws, and these in their turn can be applied to architecture. Goldmann introduced the detatched house in his publication. Erdmannsdorff gave the baroque building type a modern look. The modular scheme of building sections he developed was first applied to a "rural" building at the Luisium: two storeys of apparently the same height rise above the basement, topped by a mezzanine floor. The roof is topped by a belvedere. The façade is articulated with simple windows and continuous cornice bands. No sculptural decoration was used here.

The plain exterior met neo-classicism's demand for "noble simplicity and quiet greatness", based on ancient art, but also matched the prince's modern intellectual approach. The Luisium can rightly be called an example of "built Enlight-

Morning atmosphere by the artificial ruined arch. Such structures, reminiscent of ancient Roman triumphal arches, provide accents in the landscape at several points in the Garden Realm. Beyond the ruined arch is a mysterious sculpture of a veiled woman on a high plinth.

enment", as it combines the most modern architecture, an enlightened intellectual attitude and scientific insights.

Even in the building period, from July to October 1775, the prince and his wife travelled to England, with the architect among their companions. One of the things they were looking for on this visit was inspiration for the gardens of Schloss Luisium. There was no other building in the Garden Realm where so many freshly acquired ideas and experiences were included as the building work proceeded. This was Luise's only visit to the country her husband admired so much. She made the acquaintance of the internationally celebrated painter Angelica Kauffmann in London, and in northern France she met the American-English artist, Benjamin West. She later acquired graphic reproductions of works by both artists for the Luisium.

The Schloss was dedicated on the princess's birthday in 1778. A visitors' book was kept from 1780, which could be an indication that the house was able to be shown to the public from then on. The princess or the prince conducted their visitors through the magnificent rooms personally, and when they were away, a chatelaine instructed by Erdmannsdorff took over this role.

Erdmannsdorff developed an interior design of elegant poise and balance. The décor adopted what was then the most modern formal language, and helped to create a style in its turn.

The main floor can be entered via either the north or the south façade, through a main portal placed on the axis. As in Wörlitz, the approach ramp for carriages is on the north side of the building. It describes a semi-circle, thus setting the building off effectively. Servants entered the basement through a plain side entrance on the east side. Despite the modest dimensions of the 144 square metre square ground plan, Erdmannsdorff created rooms that were imposing and elegant at the same time.

The two doors in the north portal give access to the cross-vaulted vestibule on the main floor. Its green walls are decorated with ornamental and figure paintings in co-ordinated colours. The architect and his clients found models for this in the diverse art literature, inspired by antiquity, of the 17th and 18th centuries, including the publications of Johann Joachim Winckelmann. Figure depictions make rich allusion to the lady of the house's interests and inclinations: Flora suggest flowers, Apollo the sciences and a bacchante cheerful

The eastern entrance to the garden is marked by two pavilions built in 1815/16 from examples in the pattern book, *Designs for rural retreats as Villas ...*, which James Malton had published in London in 1802.

Luisium

festivities. Motifs like a wedding, Cupid and Psyche and bacchanalian scenes invoke the private sphere and the house's atmosphere of cheerful celebration. The ceiling painting shows the grotesques that Erdmannsdorff was so fond of. The architect had a rich stock of motifs to hand in the form of the drawings he had made himself in Italy, or he used the above-mentioned pattern books.

A double door, topped with lunettes, takes the visitor from the vestibule and into the Great Hall. This transversely placed room takes up the full width and half the depth of the ground plan.

The walls of the room are articulated with 22 white-green pilasters in marble stucco, imitating Verde antico. Their colour and mass give the room a weight that is not quite appropriate. This was criticized even by contemporaries. Even such a committed admirer of Erdmannsdorff as the reticent August Rode remarked: "The main feature is the hall ... And yet I dare not give the word to the coupled pilasters." The impression is ameliorated by the abundant incident light admitted by the four English sash windows. Even this structural detail shows how closely the prince and princess and their architect drew on English models.

The south portal is part of this room. Its glazing makes it like an additional window, attracting attention to the garden landscape. The walls between the pilasters are decorated with wax tempera paintings and stucco reliefs. The wall paintings are by the Berlin painter Johann Fischer, who had been employed earlier in Wörlitz. Ancient deities appear in the rectangular fields, along with the famous Borghese dancers that Winckelmann praised so highly. The graceful round dancers may have been inspired by the figures in Botticelli's *La primavera* or by Neopolitan tarantella dancers.

The square fields by the doors contain allegorical depictions of painting, poetry, reading and music, variations on Michelangelo's sibyls in the Sistine Chapel. Bourgeois motifs of ideal female occupations replaced glorification of the princess's person. At the ends of the room are striking painted garlands of fruit recalling motifs in Raphael's Vatican Loggie. In contrast with decorative baroque painting, which helped to demonstrate magnificence and affluence through opulence, the fruit here is handled very naturalistically. The most delicious products of the garden and of the greenhouses are reproduced in this way: oranges, white grapes, white currants, apples, plums, red grapes, pears, peaches,

Previous page ‹ The faun fountain imitates an ancient spring enclosure. The herm of a faun, the god of woodlands, cattle-breeding and corn-fields, living in Arcady, is placed on top of a round-arched substructure. The sculpture is flanked by two sacrificial altars.

Atmospheric pictures of Schloss Luisium, which stands on a little eminence, emerge at all seasons. The little pond in front is a dead arm of the Mulde, whose present bed is about 800 metres to the west.

cherries, pineapples, pumpkins, red currants, melons, figs, oranges, strawberries, hazelnuts, artichokes, Seville oranges, pomegranates, gooseberries, limes, lemons, black cherries, peppers, white cherries, pea-pods, blackberries, blackcurrants and maize. But the ceiling paintings in the Great Hall occupy the central place in the Schloss decoration programme.

Contemporaries described this modern house as a "temple of the female virtues", referring mainly to the pictorial figure motifs on the hall ceiling. August Rode also saw it in this way, remarking in 1801: "The main item is the hall. Allegorical presentations of the female virtues, devised and drawn by Herr Friedrich Wilhelm von Erdmannsdorff, and painted by Fischer, stand forth as adornment in medallions between the pilasters ... and in the manifold fields of the ceiling. Delectation for the mind and eye." Professor Karl Morgenstern quoted the chatelaine instructed by Erdmannsdorff, who also tells in full what is happening here: "Ceiling: the circle in the middle: religion, with a torch in her right hand, embraces, with love, virtue. Both are flying on a rainbow, the sign of grace, heavenwards. A wreath of amaranth, the flower of constancy, surrounds the whole.

First small oval: Love, a female figure with a winged child, embracing each other and kissing, in the clouds.

Second. Innocence, a girl with the lamb under her arm, under a thatched roof; nearby sits a child weaving roses.

Third: Gentleness: the lion humbling himself before the beautiful woman, who fetters him with bonds of roses.

Fourth: The purity of the soul: a girl rests her left hand on a unicorn that is standing amiably by; with her right hand she collects a bowl of water that flows from the nearby rock.

First octagon: Taming the desires, and moderation; the former with the whinnying, rearing horse, the other at the water urn, offering his fodder to the other horse who is passing by.

Second. Honour, in the form of a female figure sitting in a white dress, with a long staff in its hand. Good reputation (also a female figure) is placing a laurel wreath on its head.

Third. Faithfulness, accompanied by a dog, is getting into a departing bark, where she is received by friendship. They extend their hand to each other, so that they may not be parted, even in storms.

Fourth: Humility, with the sheep at her side; modesty in the middle; patience, carrying a cross. They are all holding hands and walking so calmly towards the Temple of Immortality."

The choice of the virtues was made with educational intentions, as well as relating to the princess personally. Viewers were to be instructed morally and taught in the spirit of education for good.

It is well known that marital affection between the prince and the princess waned increasingly in the mid 1780s. The Luisium became the princess's preferred refuge. She did receive friends and relatives here, but there were also lonely days for which she herself longed to an extent, achieving what she called the "blissful relief of solitude". But sometimes she found this solitude oppressive, as she confided to her diary: "After table, as it was the day when the people are all allowed to visit my garden, I stayed in my room and worked at the table there ... But at 8, when the people had left the garden, I still could not go down again because the dew was already falling and the air was very cold. And so I ate downstairs in the hall in the moonlight – o God, what I felt like then!"

A door led from the hall into a small separate room, offering the lady of the house the opportunity to withdraw with selected people during social events in the reception room.

The central ceiling painting depicts the battle between the Lapiths and the Centaurs. Greek aristocrats like to relate to the Lapiths as victors over the uncouth Centaurs. As Prince Franz emphatically alluded to his family's links with Ascanius, the founder of Rome, in the Wörlitz dining room, it seems reasonable to assume that here, too, the prince and princess were indicating their line's claim to power and prestige. Prince Franz and Erdmannsdorff were familiar with the motif from their visit to the Baths of Titus in Rome in 1766. Also, Ludovico Mirri published his *Pitture delle Terme di Tito* in 1776, near the time the house was being furnished and decorated.

The architect deployed his profound knowledge of ancient mythology with almost effortless ease in his designs for stucco and painting. Because viewers are placed at such a distance, it is often not possible to distinguish between sculptural and painted décor with any certainty. The central ceiling painting is surrounded by swans and peacocks. The swan is a reference to Venus. As so often in the very special iconography of the Garden Realm, the architect was alluding to Princess Luise's royal blood: Hera or Juno is the divine consort of Zeus or Jupiter. The peacock is one of her insignia of power. The delicate reliefs articulating the walls also repeat the peacock motif.

The banqueting hall in the Luisium, the largest room in the house. It is decorated with high quality murals and stucco work. Elegant furniture and sculptures complete the neo-classical interior. Music was played in this room, and the princess often sat at the fortepiano herself. The open door of the hall affords a splendid view down to the church in Waldersee.

The Graphic Art Cabinet. This room comes as a surprise. Even the ceiling and the door leaves were used to accommodate the graphic sheets.

Highly individual spatial compositions of this kind are signs of Erdmannsdorff's creative mastery.

217

Two walls are covered with strawberry-coloured silk wall hangings. Paintings hang against this fabric background, positioned by the princess in a highly individual arrangement. Lack of source material means that it is no longer possible to reconstruct the reasons for this hanging or for the categorization intended.

By the door is a contemporary, sensitively painted copy by Anton Maron of Raphael's *Madonna della Sedia*. Two mountain landscapes by the Weimar painter Maria Dorothea Wagner attempt to harmonize with a copy of Caravaggio's *Card-players*, also by Maron. Princess Luise made a particular protégé of the Stuttgart painter Ferdinand Hartmann. The large-format painting, *Hebe Gives Water to the Eagle*, is by him; the princess used to lovingly call it "my Hebe". The composition of the picture and the warm colour tones lend the painting a sensual quality. The small-format picture, *Eros and Anteros* (Love and Love Requited), in a fine neo-classical frame, is also by Hartmann. It was particularly highly esteemed by contemporaries because of its innovative presentation: there had been no pictorial form of requited love in the history of art

until that time. The large-format portrait of Elisa von der Recke, a copy based on the original by Anton Graff, deserves particular attention. The subject was one of the Dessau princess's closest confidantes. The two women met in Dessau in 1784. Often Elisa was the only person Luise could talk to, a real "soul-mate", as the princess said herself. Elisa, née von Medem, was a self-confident, independent woman. Her diaries report many meetings between the two friends in the country house outside the gates of Dessau.

The simply designed staircase in the Luisium is a remarkable feature, used by the gentry and the servants alike. This almost bourgeois simplicity, which had already been suggested in Wörlitz, ended a centuries-old tradition of imposing staircases. This can definitely be seen as a proof of genuine enlightenment, even though there were separate entrances to the house. The oak staircase, rising very comfortably, leads to the second floor of the house. On the first floor, the princess first entered the cabinet of mirrors by the staircase. This little room is given over almost entirely to mirrors, a design device that had already been used in the

The cabinet of mirrors or the princess's dressing-room seems to be flooded with light and almost transparent because of the mirrors. The walls and ceiling are decorated with realistic paintings of plants and animals.

baroque and rococo periods. The Luisium mirrors also add uncertainty to the spatial situation, and create an airy atmosphere; however, the austere lines of the room are free of illusionistic principles, aimed more at linking the interior with the surrounding landscape garden. This room, flooded with light, gives the impression of an open garden arbour, an effect further reinforced by the naturalistic wall and ceiling paintings. Fruit garlands enliven the surfaces, and the decorations are complemented by sacrificial scenes with figures and bacchanals. Wall cupboards were installed behind the mirrors in the corners of the room. Some naturalistic bird images attract attention in the upper areas of the walls. Recent research has established that these were species that could be seen in the Luisium at the time. An eagle was presumably included as the Prussian heraldic beast, but also featured in the Ascanian arms, and next to it are painted songbirds like warblers, great tits and crested tits. A particular ornithological feature is the painted rare white-spotted blue-throat on the southern wall cupboard, which only frequents this area every 40 to 60 years as a rule. This suggests that the residents of the day must have seen one. Clearly, the

cabinet of mirrors was the princess's dressing room. It is the only room with a fireplace; it is of artificial porphyry, and placed in a corner of the room, offering few possibilities for impressive decoration of the kind to be found in Wörlitz at that time.

The library is in the room next door. With only ten square metres to play with, Erdmannsdorff managed to create a pleasant place here, in which to spend time. He accommodated the princess's reference library in four corner bookcases, and covered the whole room with a ceiling whose lightness derives from its umbrella-like structure. Outside, a tribute to Minerva is depicted in a circular frieze, painted in the grisaille style. The arts and sciences were entrusted to her as goddess of wisdom and understanding. This quite clearly identified the princess's role as mother of her country and protectress of the sciences. Erdmannsdorff turned to Pietro Santo Bartoli's antiquities publication, *Admiranda Romanarum antiquitatum ac veteris sculpturae vestigia*, which appeared in 1693, for his model for this frieze. Working towards the inside, zoomorphic hybrid creatures – griffins – are painted on a sky-blue ground in seven ellipses; perhaps this is an allusion

Portrait of Princess Luise of Anhalt-Dessau by Angelica Kauffmann. The painter, who enjoyed a considerable reputation even in the 18th century, painted the picture when the Dessau princess visited Rome in 1796. Her brother-in-law, Prince Hans Jürge, had acquired it for the Georgium.

The Pompeian cabinet. The name of the room is a reminder of the sensational excavations near Naples. The remains of ancient art that came to light influenced European neo-classicism considerably.

219

to the companions of Apollo. The other seven segments illustrate 35 different kinds of butterfly. Presumably this is a reference to the goddess Psyche. Most of the specimens can be found in the insect book by the famous Maria Sybilla Merian, *Metamorphosis Insectorum Surinamensium*, dating from 1705, which deals with exotic specimens from South America. The publication must therefore have been known in Dessau.

The seven segments, running in towards the middle, show personifications in round medallions of the Seven Liberal Arts: grammar, rhetoric, mathematics, arithmetic, geometry, music and astronomy. The allegories are framed by three spandrels each, with painted bird motifs. These are species indigenous to the Garden Realm, painted naturalistically: bullfinch, nuthatch, chaffinch, hawfinch and blue tit appear, along with house sparrow, bunting, goldfinch, fieldfare and kingfisher. With a bit of luck, the last can still be seen over the Luisium pond.

The blue-washed walls of the room provide an effective background for the red chalk engravings based on paintings or graphics, mainly on works by Angelica Kauffmann. The wallpaper door should also be mentioned: regardless of the graphic art attached to it, it led into the princess's dressing and washroom.

The room adjacent to the library is hung in red silk damask. It is possible that the princess used it as a bedroom. A figure that can be interpreted as Charity is to be seen in the middle of the finely stuccoed ceiling. Again this suggest the princess's quality as mother of her country. The most famous art object in the house, a monumental painting by Angelica Kauffmann, *Cupid Dries Psyche's Tears*, was in the Red Cabinet until the 1930s. It was put on the market in 1987, and is now in the Kunsthaus Zürich. The Dessau princess acquired this magnificent composition on her visit to Italy, on 22 March, 1796, directly from the artist in Rome. Johann Wolfgang von Goethe came from Weimar specially to see the picture in 1797. He was most impressed, and wrote to Kauffmann, whom he admired: "A few days ago I experienced very great joy through you in Dessau, where I contemplated the excellent picture of Cupid and Psyche with the greatest interest ..." The picture later became available to a wider audience through an engraved copy by the Dessau Chalkographische Gesellschaft.

Of course, the Dessau princess sat for this major portrait artist in Rome as well. The result is a remarkable likeness, and now adorns the "Red Cabinet".

The princess had the room at the north-west corner of the house arranged as a painting gallery. The ceiling painting is based on Guido Reni's missing painting, *Bacchus and Ariadne*. The walls are in a delicate shade of green and decorated with Erdmannsdorff's favourite motifs, grotesque paintings based on those of Raphael in the Vatican Loggie. The vertical articulation is in the form of narrow fields in which tendril growths like scarlet runner beans, nasturtium, hops and reed mace can be made out. Here, Erdmannsdorff was repeating the motif of the arbour, which was still a symbol for emotional fraternity and marital connections in the 18th century. And indeed, the sensitive princess did receive a select circle of friends at the house, including Elisa von der Recke, Frederike Brun, Friedrich Mathisson and Alexander von Humboldt.

The areas intended for hanging paintings were left plain. There used to be 22 paintings here, including six views of the Rhine by the artist Christian Georg Schütz the Elder, who was very highly thought of by the prince.

Erdmannsdorff offered a very surprising and unusual solution for the decoration of the graphic art cabinet, which follows the painting cabinet. The artist used all the available wall surfaces, including the ceiling and the door, to accommodate 119 graphic sheets. Despite the fact that the little room is decorated with an abundance of motifs that were new at the time and despite the different dimensions of the works of art, the room does not seem at all cluttered and restless. Reproductions of paintings, views of London, Italian, French and Dresden landscapes, ancient scenes with gods and genre scenes, are all brought together here.

The portraits of English people, who were important to the Dessau prince, deserve mention: they included the famous minister, William Pitt the Younger, and Sir Joseph Banks, who sailed around the world. Sir William Temple, owner of the famous gardens in Stowe, Buckinghamshire, which provided models for much of the Dessau Garden Realm design, is also represented.

The colour scheme in this room seems particularly sophisticated. The light, white stucco stands out particularly well against the delicate blue, strong blue and lilac backgrounds. Here, the influence of neo-Palladian interiors by Robert Adams and William Chambers is particularly apparent. At the same time, in Staffordshire in the English Midlands, the potter Josiah Wedgwood had developed his famous Jasper Ware, using the same range of colours.

Erdmannsdorff skilfully placed the bookcases in the corners of the little room in the library. This left him room for the densely hung graphic art.

Luisium

An indigenous orchid in the Luisium. Many specimens of the unassuming twayblade (Listera ovata), which has blue flowers in the spring, are to be found in the grass under the sweet chestnut trees near the house.

Tree frogs warming themselves in the sun on a blackberry bush. There are many of these amphibians in the Luisium; they can be recognized by their striking croak, though they rarely show themselves.

The smallest room in the house is in the north-east corner, and Erdmannsdorff designed it as a Pompeian room. The central ceiling painting shows ancient female genii. They are surrounded by four vedutas of the area around Naples. He had four views of Vesuvius erupting painted in a frieze under the ceiling. These are evidence of a particular interest in geology and a personal connection with Sir William Hamilton. The Vesuvius pictures and two wall paintings are based on his publications of ancient vase pictures.

The princess met the diplomat on her visit to Italy in 1796. However, she consistently avoided Lady Emma Hamilton, the diplomat's second wife, who had since become famous. Even so, she allowed two allegorical etchings by Gavin Hamilton showing Lady Emma as "Poetry" and "Painting" to be hung in the Pompeian room in the Luisium. Most of the paintings in the room have religious connections.

The built-in wall cupboard around the window on the east wall of the room is an interesting feature. The unusual neo-classical frames and furniture in the house, of which those in the Pompeian room are particularly fine specimens, were made by local craftsmen.

Princess Luise loved her refuge. The estate as a whole was only open to the public for two days per week. The relative seclusion of her country seat afforded her sensitive soul the peace that it enjoyed all too infrequently.

It is the extremely happy combination of nature and art that gives the Luisium its unique charm. Wide areas of gentle meadow alternate with patches of open woodland. Buildings and sculptures, whose proportions are consistent with their natural surroundings, are fitted in harmoniously.

It almost seems that the Luisium was designed to fulfil the ideal formulated by the Italian poet Torquato Tasso as early as 1575: "Pleasing to the eye, the beautiful garden opened up: it offered standing waters, moving crystals, abundant flowers, plants and herbs, sunny hills, shady valleys, woods and caves at a single glance; and – this further enhanced the work's beauty and worth – the art that created all this is nowhere visible." (*Gerusalemme liberata*)

Left-hand page, top ‹ The former Fohlenweide. The stud's grazing area, with its grazing sheep, goats and horses, looks like an Arcadian landscape.

V

GEORGIUM

Edeltraut Dettmar

A "truly charming" garden

Johann Georg Prince of Anhalt Dessau, who created it ‣ "The final crown was set upon my journey when I had the honour to make the acquaintance of Prince Hans Jürge of Dessau, a quite excellent gentleman, who steals the heart of everyone who has seen him." The literary critic and sometime friend of Goethe, Johann Heinrich Merck (1741-1791) was full of praise for Prince Johann Georg of Anhalt-Dessau (1748-1811), the brother of the reigning Prince Franz. And he was not alone in this. Excerpts from letters and diary entries by third parties give a picture of a highly educated, open-minded, likeable and intelligent man. The prince was only fourteen when Frederick II of Prussia tried to recruit him to serve in his army. This was not because the prince was particularly suitable. It was a demonstration of power by the great king, who was looking for a substitute for his vassal Franz, who had resigned. Prince Dietrich of Anhalt-Dessau (1702-1769),

uncle and guardian, skilfully held back his permission for years. So Hans Jürge, as he was generally known, was able to join the Grand Tour that Prince Franz and his companions were undertaking in England, France and Italy from 1765 to 1767. He was a young man who was eager to learn, and he knew how to make the best of the opportunity he had been offered. However, on his return the prince did bow to political and also financial necessity and embarked upon a career as officer in the Prussian army. He did not gain high military honours. It is, however, worth mentioning that the Roman sculptor and antiquities dealer Bartolomeo Cavaceppi spent some time with him in Potsdam in 1768 and made several clay copies from ancient models for his "most devoted benefactor". Johann Wolfgang Goethe also enjoyed Hans Jürge's company when he spent a week in Berlin in 1778 as companion to Duke Carl August of Saxony-Weimar and Eisenach.

To the annoyance of Frederick II, Prince Hans Jürge tendered his resignation in 1779, when he had advanced to the post of commandant of Stettin.

After returning to Anhalt, he associated closely with the reforming circle around the reigning prince again. He enriched the intellectually open-minded atmosphere of the Dessau court by opening up his own house to scholars and artists and conducting a lively exchange of ideas with princely houses who supported the Dessauers' enlightened and humanistic ambitions. His marriage to Caroline von Hill (1748-1822), the daughter of a war and demesne councillor, was not officially recognized. Hans Jürge lived in Vienna from 1804 until his death in 1811, officially because he suffered severely from gout, but probably also to attend to the Anhalt princely house's diplomatic interests at the imperial court. His grave in Vienna has not so far been found. After

Georgium

The Georgenhaus – Schloss Georgium as seen from the south, with the side wings, which were added in 1893. Even the first, still careful design for the park shows the country seat set to one side of the entrance avenue. It thus gives up its position as a fixed point in the complex and becomes a component in the universal work of art comprising Schloss Georgium and its park.

Johann Friedrich August Tischbein (1750-1812), Christiane Amalie, Hereditary Princess of Anhalt-Dessau with her children, 1797. Tischbein worked as court painter at the princely court of Anhalt-Dessau from 1795-1800. The stimulating cultural atmosphere here took him to the apogee of his portrait art, and he achieved a sensitive neo-classicism. Christiane Amalie of Hessen-Homburg, who is portrayed here, married Friedrich, Hereditary Prince of Anhalt-Dessau in 1792.

Caroline's death the prince's estate was auctioned and thus dispersed to the four winds. The Georgengarten and the country seat had already passed to the hereditary princess, Christiane Amalie (1774-1846), the widow of hereditary Prince Friedrich of Anhalt-Dessau (1769-1814), by order of Franz, now Duke Franz.

As very little source material is available, many questions about Prince Johann Georg's personality and life remain open. He would perhaps have been forgotten entirely if he had not created his own memorial in the Georgium, which also explains much about his intellectual world.

The park in its historical dimension ▸ Immediately after his return to civilian life, the 31-year-old Prince Hans Jürge looked for a peaceful and satisfying field in which he could work. What could be more obvious than to involve himself in something that was going on all around him, the cultivation and enhancement of the countryside. In the spirit of the maxim that the useful should be combined with the beautiful, hence the unity of park and land used for agriculture should be particularly emphasized, he decided in spring 1780 to develop a site north-west of the town of Dessau. The chief characteristics of this area were clayey soil, poorly yielding sandy stretches, and remains of river-valley woodland that were marshy, boggy and prone to frequent flooding.

Three people from the prince's circle were available to Hans Jürge for his ambitious project: Friedrich Wilhelm von Erdmannsdorff, who was sympathetic to his intellectual and artistic tendency of preferring ancient forms to sentimental architecture, and two gardeners of quite different character for planning and executing the horticultural schemes. The first plans for the garden, with numerous corrections, were received from Johann George Schoch (1758-1826), who was only 22 years old. Johann Friedrich Eyserbeck (1734-1818), who was a generation older, was involved in the further development of the ideas from as early as summer 1780. Hans Jürge felt that working with the two of them would meet his requirements for combining tradition and a modern approach to create a harmonious whole. The front part of the park in particular takes intentions of this kind into account. The fact was that the great educational journey he had undertaken in his youth was also a journey through the history of the European garden – from the Italian Renaissance, where elements of the ancient Roman villa garden persisted,

via French baroque gardens to the most recent creations based on the English model.

A general plan, dating from 1796, shows the Georgium's generous dimensions at this stage. The intensively designed, highly cultivated garden areas hug the avenue linking the nearby town and the Elbe loop to the north. This avenue, known as the Georgenallee, was also included directly in the park design as a key sight line. The southern end was marked inside the town of Dessau by the Eugen Pyramid, which was pulled down in 1952, and at the northern end the view extended to the Elbe pavilion on the Streitwerder.

One crucial facet of the complex as a whole was that the park sections, seemingly complete in themselves, were embedded in open agricultural land extending along the flood protection rampart on the Elbe, erected by Prince Franz, to the eastern tip of Lake Kühnau. There the park border was marked by the surviving obelisk. Avenues fringed with fruit trees, or alternatively with poplars, ran through and structured the Ziebigker Feldmark. This offered the eye a welcome break from the cultivated fields; from an economic point of view, the fruit trees fitted in harmoniously with the field and meadow landscape, as they provided a useful crop. The individual garden sections were connected within themselves and also to each other by a dense network of visual links; extensive views of Dessau also opened up from time to time.

The park was not contained by any walls; ditches, hedges and game enclosures kept the view of the surrounding

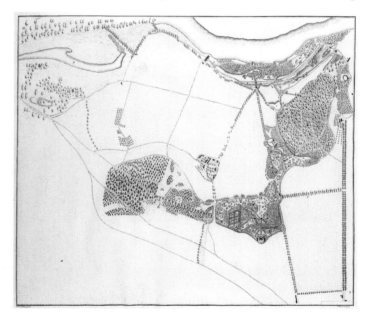

Overall plan of Prince Johann Georg's estate, drawn in 1796 to accompany August Rode's description of the Georgengarten. It impressively supports Rode's introductory remark: "But in the wider significance, the Georgenhaus is also understood to be all the landed property transformed, as it were, into a garden."

countryside open. Constantly changing moods and ideas were evoked by a dense sequence of garden images in the highly stylized southern section. A varied composition of coniferous and deciduous trees with their different shades of green created dark, secluded areas contrasting with open areas, flooded with light; particularly striking is the way a wide area of meadowland complements a large piece of woodland. Buildings and seats, but also curving paths and picturesque groups of trees, formed the starting point or the end of surprising visual links. Often, paths led into the dense planting alongside the visual axes, a special feature of the Georgium. Unexpected openings opened up views of the adjacent gardens.

The areas of countryside to the north-east, the Beckerbruch and the Streitwerder with its link to the Elbe, and the sandy Kienheide to the west, were not subject to such a thorough design approach, but it is precisely this "closeness to nature" that made them very popular with contemporary visitors. August Rode published a description of the Georgengarten and the house in 1796; it is the only comprehensive primary literature.

Work in the park was seen as essentially complete when Hans Jürge moved to Vienna in 1804. The area included in the overall concept covered two square kilometres, and was a creation much admired by contemporaries. Visitors often judged it similarly to the archaeologist Carl August Boettiger (1760-1835), feeling: "that in Prince Hans Görge's truly charming gardens ... one often feels more drawn by true nature than in the Wörlitz artistic creations."

Decline and return to historical values ▸ The chequered fate of the Georgengarten started as early as the mid 19th century. It was first cut into when the Berlin-Köthen railway line was built. In 1893, a complete new Jugendstil (Art Nouveau) park, the centre-piece of which was the mausoleum, came into being opposite the main entrance to the Georgium. In the early 20th century, increasing industrialization in the town of Dessau caused it to sprawl across the fields and the Kienheide, to the very edge of the garden's heart. No one was really aware of its historical importance any longer. The curved lines of the paths were changed in part. Sight lines and broad areas of the park became overgrown; ageing tree-stock, both indigenous and, in particular, foreign stock, was not replaced by replanting at all, or if it was, it was in line with design ideas from the late 19th and early 20th centuries.

Top ▴ The triumphal arch. The architectural model in Rome is named after the Roman commander Drusus, but it was in fact part of a water supply system for the most famous popular baths in Rome.

Bottom ▾ The Blumengartenhaus. Flowerbeds featured in the Georgen-garten as well. This is the flower garden, reconstructed in 1985/86 from historical sources, between the palace and the neo-classical garden pavilion, with the "wilderness" behind it.

Many architectural items were irretrievably lost and cannot be reconstructed as there are no precise descriptions available.

The political situation after the Second World War threatened the existence of the Georgium at first. It was not until 1961 that reconstruction and cultivation measures were launched that again took account of the park's historical value. One success arising from these continuing efforts was its recognition by the European Union in 1994 as one of the 66 European gardens most worthy of funding. As part of the Dessau-Wörlitz cultural landscape, the park has been part of the Central Elbe River Landscape biosphere reserve, and was designated a World Heritage site by UNESCO in the year 2000.

From country house to Schloss Georgium. The Anhaltische Gemäldegalerie ▸ Like the Luisium before it, Erdmannsdorff also conceived the Georgenhaus in 1780 as a free-standing pavilion, borrowing from Nicolaus Goldmann's (1611-1665) *Vollständige Anweisung zu der Civil-Bau-Kunst*. A pavilion-like, two-storey building stands on a well-proportioned rectangular ground plan. The long sides are articulated by six Tuscan pilasters. The mezzanine, intended to accommodate visitors and servants at the time, is concealed behind the frieze-like entablature. The central protruding section, articulated above the pilasters by triglyphs, with a pediment on top, emphasizes the vertical and carries the eye up to the crowning, belvedere-like structure on the roof, which affords a magnificent panorama of the Elbe and the countryside around Dessau.

Entirely in the educational spirit of its owner, the Georgenhaus was not open only to friends and invited guests. Strangers could go round it as well, accompanied by a castellan specially trained by Erdmannsdorff. This was not always entirely to the taste of the mistress of the house. The original art inventory is for the most part no longer documented, but August Rode describes it. The reliefs in the stucco work, which is kept relatively plain, contain richly allusive indications of the atmosphere the prince wanted for his house: the ballroom is dominated by a cheerful bustle among the retinue of Bacchus, the god of fertility and wine; a continuous band of oak leaves accentuated the frequently recurring motif of the lily in its life-giving symbolism. In one reception room, three Graces remind us of the virtues a woman should strive for – grace, combined with chastity and true love –, but in another, Venus brings the erotic element to mind with Cupid's arrows. In Caroline's drawing room, Hermes, the messenger of the gods and of peace, but also of dreams, adorns the ceiling medallion.

The Georgenhaus went through two building phases, but this is only discernible at first glance to the attentive observer. The most visible result of the extensive architectural changes in 1893 are the two side wings, which changed the simple neo-classical country seat into a horseshoe-shaped palace.

The Georgium has housed the collections from the Gemäldegalerie since 1959. The Anhaltische Gemäldegalerie (Anhalt Art Gallery) was established in 1927 and used to be accommodated in the late neo-classical Palais Reina in central Dessau, which was destroyed by air raids in 1944/45. The art treasures themselves were moved out before the war, but taken to the Soviet Union as spoils of war in 1946. They came back to Dessau via Berlin in 1958/59, as part of the Soviet action to return cultural treasures.

The Anhaltische Gemäldegalerie holds 2000 paintings, and is now the largest collection of old paintings in Saxony-Anhalt. The main body of the collection consisted of works of art from Anhalt princely collections, which were enriched by major works from the 16th to the 20th century. The gallery has Princess Henriette Amalie of Anhalt-Dessau (1720-1793), the youngest daughter of the Prussian field-marshal Leopold I Prince of Anhalt-Dessau (1676-1747), to thank for extensive holdings of Old Netherlandish, Flemish and Dutch paintings, with works by Roelant Savery, Jan Brueghel the Elder, Hendrik Avercamp, Balthasar van der Ast, Adriaen van Ostade and others. The selection of Frankfurt painters at the time of Goethe, unique outside Frankfurt, is from the same source. The princess's collection also included a number of Old German paintings.

Works by Lucas Cranach the Elder, Hans Baldung and Bartholomäus Bruyn speak for the high quality of Old German art in the collection. Important artists like Adám Mányoki, members of the Tischbein family of painters and Wilhelm Schadow are represented by outstanding portraits. Joseph Anton Koch, the Olivier brothers, Anselm Feuerbach, Franz Lenbach, Wilhelm Trübner and Hans Thoma represent the 19th century. And finally, familiar artists like Max Klinger, Max Slevogt and Fritz Winter stand for the 20th century.

Hans Baldung, called Grien (1484/85-1545), *Adoration of the Three Kings*, 1510. This painting is the inside of the right-hand wing of a Marian altar. Its counterpart with the *Birth of Christ* is in the Öffentliche Kunst-sammlung in Basel. The panel with the Adoration was split after 1926; the back, supporting a workshop piece, was destroyed while the paintings were in storage during the war.

known to have been in Dessau from 1775-1795, and created most of the sculpture for the Georgium, using one of Cavaceppi's terracotta models from the Blumengartenhaus as a model for this sandstone figure.

A long lawn bordered with trees extends north of the palace. Their massive crowns mask the side wings of the palace when viewed from the park boundary, thus giving a rough impression of how the house must have looked originally. Gleaming through the western plantation is the guest house, which was intended to provide a secluded stay for the prince's guests. The interior was kept correspondingly simple.

Its four outer façades were each designed differently, thus providing, at the same time, the culture and education that were always desired. The east side demonstrates the Gothic, and the west side, a simple, classical-Dutch version of the baroque style. Both these façades are very reticent in their design, but mark the prince's awareness of tradition. On the north side is an entirely personal design by Erdmannsdorff, with cool, austere components anticipating Berlin and Weimar classicism. Erdmannsdorff carefully chose rustic elements in the Italian manner for the south façade, but adds a separate little garden here, enclosed by dense planting. After intensive horticultural work, the building is now visible from a greater distance in a manner appropriate to its historical worth, and has thus become an attractive starting and end point for visual links within the park.

Extensive gardens run along the road that forms the northern boundary, enlivened and articulated by tree and shrub planting. Gently curving paths lead through grass or wind behind the scenes along the sight lines. Motifs reminiscent of the great educational journey give this spacious garden scenery its concrete intellectual content: the Ionic temple is a reminder of the visit to Tivoli, but also of the monopteral temple in Stowe Park in England, which the prince had also seen. This round temple is close to the park boundary, and occupied a key visual position within the gardens as a whole. It was the point at which many viewing axes met from all over the park, and also led out from here into the park and far into the countryside. The most striking views from the temple across the park today include, once again, those of the palace, the friends' guest-house, the statue of Diana and the Roman ruins.

These Roman ruins, the concluding feature on the west side of the park, cite the magnificent columned portico of the Temple of Saturn in the Forum Romanum. In the 18th century, however, the columned porch was erroneously identified as the Temple of Concordia. Like its model in Rome, the portico is usually seen obliquely from the side, which means that the eighth column is invisible, hence the popular name "The Seven Columns". Very little remains of the dark green, slender pines that used to tower over the temple outside the gardens, forming a lively contrast with the lighter green of the deciduous trees inside the park. But it is still worth looking out of the park through the columns, as the Roman ruins are linked visually by a straight avenue to the Amaliensitz, whose brightness catches the eye about four hundred metres away. This is the only surviving scenic building on the Kienheide, named after the Hereditary Princess Christiane Amalie of Anhalt-Dessau. Further motifs used to link up with the Kühnau Park from here. The Amaliensitz was influenced by the gardens in Stourhead. It is a little roofed seat, and its façade is a variation on the Serlio-Palladio motif.

A long narrow sight axis runs eastwards from the Ionic Temple out of the park and into the adjacent, so-called transverse avenue, ending at the railway line. Originally, an avenue of fruit trees and poplars led to the White Pyramid, otherwise known as the Gänsewall Pyramid, a dike observation building that is visible from some distance. This setpiece building was partly used to store flood protection equipment, but it also created a visual link between the Georgium and the Luisium.

Shortly before this east-west axis meets the Georgenallee on its way from Dessau to the Elbe, the latter departs from its straight course and describes a semicircle that takes it through the partially destroyed "built-over arch", also called the Dutch or Red Arch. It originally supported a small room whose windows faced north-west and drew the eye to the obelisk by the Kühnauer Wall. A fictitious extension of this access lead to Holland, to the bourgeois culture that served as a model for the princely house of Dessau. Hans Jürge's great-grandmother, Henriette Catharina of Orange-Nassau (1637-1708), also came from Holland. The back wall of the room was decorated with copperplate engravings after paintings by the famous Flemish artist Peter Paul Rubens from the Palais Luxembourg in Paris. The arch is set in an artificial mound that it is possible to climb, to give access to the pavilion. At the foot of the mound, an erratic rock with a cast copy of the bronze medallion created in 1904 by

Emanuel Semper has, since 2004, once more served as a memorial to the founder of the gardens, Johann Georg.

The actual point where the axes meet is reserved for a unique motif in the Dessau-Wörlitz Garden Realm, the "Sunken Seat". Modest and yet striking, the place was characterized by fruit trees. Walkers get an entirely new view of the surrounding area from a round excavation about one-and-a-half metres deep with stone benches, into which steps lead down. Everything seems more sublime and expressive. Particular motifs drew attention all around: to the east, the above-mentioned pyramid glowed on the Gänsewall. If you looked south, there was a view towards Dessau over the Eugen Pyramid, erected in 1781 and demolished in 1952 (tomb of Prince Eugen of Anhalt-Dessau, 1705-1781), to the tower of the Georgenkirche. The picturesque view of the Ionic Temple can still be enjoyed. Finally, to the north, the Triumphal Arch, also known as the White Arch, spans the Georgenallee, now back on its axis. The mounds of excavated soil on both sides were intended to create the impression that the ancient ruin had been covered with earth for millennia and only recently dug out. At the same time – the travellers from Dessau had experienced this in English gardens –

flocks of sheep could use the arch to cross the road without dirtying it. But above all, the arch was to provide a stylistically correct frame in the ancient manner for the monument to Prince Franz that was visible in the background.

The memorial to the prince itself is to be seen as a respectful bow from the younger to the elder brother. It was important that, in this park intended to stimulate the mind and the spirit, Prince Franz did not appear in triumph on horseback, as his rank and tradition would suggest. Instead, he was presented as a Roman scholar – with clear borrowings from the statue of the Emperor Augustus. The monument used to stand in the middle of a square, surrounded by tall hedges, whose design as a "little philosophers' garden" was supposed to encourage meditation in the spirit of antiquity. But only the pedestal with the affectionate inscription still indicates where the statue once stood; the statue itself was destroyed in the Second World War, and its remains have disappeared. On passing through the Roman Triumphal Arch and walking past the memorial site, the transition from the mainly classical Georgengarten to the very sensitive areas in front of the Beckerbruch has occurred almost imperceptibly. A wide range of emotionally charged elements unfolds in several

The Fremdenhaus – a guest-house for friends – is a little ABC of architectural styles: it has one (neo-)Gothic, one Palladian, one baroque and one neo-classical façade. After years of falling into disrepair, the building was reconstructed in 1992-1994 and has since housed the Anhaltische Gemäldegalerie's important graphic art collection.

The round Ionic Temple. Like its predecessors in Italy and England, the monopteral temple stands gleaming white on its eminence. Walkers standing on the central round slab in the temple were afforded an impressive panorama with views over the park boundaries into the open countryside, and narrow sight axes within the garden.

237

small garden spaces. First of all, a triangular altar with rams' head on the corner of the slab is hidden away under slender beech trees (a roundel of Lombardy poplars used to provide the ancient atmosphere). Round about are strewn remains of neo-classical stone benches, already offering a reminder of the notion of vanity, which will subsequently occur many times. Two of these benches used to stand on a long mound and were dedicated to some of the prince's learned friends, as were the two arbours nearby.

A long, irregular stretch of water conveys delicately Romantic moods. The ruined bridge, which was conceived as such, and the round arch are picturesquely reflected in the lake. The latter is associated with entering a time long past, a theatrically-placed memento mori.
Continuing the idea of a "melancholy contemplation of the tides of human things", visitors find the so-called stone circle of old German tombs amid the dense bushes. Reflections echo here, both of the sublime *Weltschmerz* of the Scot, James Macpherson's (1736-1796), depictions of nature in the Ossian poems that he dreamed up, and also of Friedrich Gottlieb Klopstock's (1724-1803) national poetry, which sometimes includes sensitive nature lyrics.

Driving away all that was melancholy, Erdmannsdorff once more invoked the charm of neo-classical light-heartedness with the delicate Vasenhaus, built on a slight eminence. This little set-piece building significantly completes the circle, from European cultural roots via traditions north of the Alps to the prince's own present day. Inside it is "decorated with

cheerful copperplate engravings, showing customs from Paris's formerly frivolous great world," and the view over the broad fields and meadows to Dessau proclaimed the new delight in life and nature, taken by the age of sensibility. Honouring both the living and the dead is taken for granted in this life-affirming atmosphere. The memorial urn to Duke August Wilhelm of Braunschweig-Lüneburg-Bevern (1715-1781), a long-standing friend of Hans Jürge's during the latter's ten years of military service in Szczecin, acquires entirely aesthetic significance.

The copperplate engravings have disappeared, the open space is considerably cramped as a result of tree-planting for a pheasant farm in 1887, and in the 1920s, a natural stretch of water was transformed into a regular basin with Jugendstil access points. Despite this, the graceful charm of this garden image has been retained to the present day, in a way that is entirely its own.

A simple bridge of planks and stripped trunks now leads from the sensitive part of the garden into the park areas adjacent to the north-east, which have been left largely in their natural state. Huge oaks, some dating from the time the park came into being, have had conservation orders placed on them, and wild fruit trees provide welcome food for game living in the wild. Contained expanses of water still form regularly in spring in this wild and natural marsh-and-meadow woodland with its own informal system of paths and canals. On the embankment bordering the Beckerbruch, the path leads through the side arches of the Vorderer Sitz, or Foremost Seat.
The dike then leads on to the Fürstensitz (Prince's Seat). A variant on the Palladian motif that seems almost archaic dominates both the façade and the rear of this set-piece building. A sweep of meadowland used to stretch out below the seat, whilst a dead arm of the Elbe, with three suggested islands, meandered at its side. This natural experience has changed radically. Years of gravel mining during the time of the GDR created a considerable area of water, something hitherto lacking in the park as a whole. The Wallwitzsee now creates a new and atmospheric picture. It is significant that Hans Jürge chose this idyllic woodland park for roofed seats or mounds dedicated to particularly close family members, including his sister Henriette Katharina Agnese (1744-1799) and close friends from the Dessau reformist circle.

The Amaliensitz. August Rode wrote about the many roofed seats of this kind that are to be found in the park: "They are intended as pleasant refuges in case of sudden rain, as resting-places, where one can enjoy excellent views and, at the same time, one's company or one's solitude with pleasure, but are also intended to beautify the prospects. Every seat carries the name of a person whom the prince remembers with affection."

The ruined bridge was meant to provide a picturesque garden backdrop, but also to be a reminder of the inexorable march of time. Erdmanns-dorff provided a design for this atmospheric garden motif, dating from 1785. A very similar situation is illustrated in Christian Cay Lorenz

Hirschfeld's (1742-1792) *Theorie der Gartenkunst*, which was published at about the same time. Hirschfeld was the most famous German author of books on garden art.

239

The area around the Vasenhaus and the memorial urn to the Duke of Braunschweig-Lüneburg-Bevern. This garden picture originally made its impact because of the large open space that opened up in front of the little set-piece building. Solitaire trees planted some distance apart drew the eye down the gently contoured mound to the water – now in a rectangular basin.

When the lake was finally landscaped in the early 1990s, the three historical islands were specially remodelled, and a fourth island was added. Roughly assembled erratic blocks on the shore and on the southernmost historical island invite visitors to rest and look around. The path along the shore winds its way to the Agnesenhügel, offering varied views of the lake. From the top of this hill, an elegantly curved nude of a hermaphrodite, seen from the rear, can be made out on the middle island. This mythical hybrid creature, created by forsaken love, gives a sense of longing for Italy and for the magical poems about gods and men in the ancient poet Ovid's *Metamorphoses*.

The path through a gently rising chain of hills, the remains of a terminal moraine from the Ice Age, finally leads to the Wallwitzberg, at the eastern end of the park. A magnificent view of the River Elbe opens up unexpectedly at the side of the path from a simple brick bench known as Fleschens Sitz

(Fleschen's Seat). An ancient square altar and a large sandstone urn, which, at the time of writing, are slowly sinking into the earth at the foot of a mound, along with its pedestal, were intended to invoke memories of Arcadia. Today, they simply provide food for thought.

By building the medieval and Romantic Wallwitzburg above the Elbe, Hans Jürge was taking up a historical epoch long past, in which it was thought long-lost virtues could be rediscovered. The symbol of the newly awoken urge for freedom, which called upon the "spirit of faithfulness and forbearance" of the ancient German forefathers, was the Gothic architecture that was already seen as the national architecture in England. The castle takes its name from the aristocratic Wallwitz line that lived in Dessau in the 16th century and owned lands in this area. A spiral staircase in the tower led to a platform offering an extensive view towards Dessau and over the Elbe to the Zerbster Land. The castle greeted travellers to Dessau from afar. Today nothing but a few ruins remain.

A magnificent natural space opens up on the way back via the Streitwerder Elbe embankment: on one side there is an open view of the river, and on the other side, restricted by the hills and the dense trees and bushes of the Beckerbruch, the eye ranges over a meadow landscape, structured by nothing but a few groups of trees and solitary oaks. In these water meadows, flooded annually by the river, the figure of the "Sleeping Shepherdess" lies on a sarcophagus. It is a copy of an ancient Roman sarcophagus lid, known as the "Dying Cleopatra". Surrounded by silver poplars, this motif is once again intended to make the wanderer reflect in sensitive melancholy on the natural cycle that grants only a certain time to any earthly existence.

Erdmannsdorff created another architectural highlight in the park in the form of the nearby Elbe Pavilion, whose white paint constantly attracts walkers' attention as they move northwards along the Georgenallee. The tower thrusts upwards on a small, square ground plan. It invited walkers to linger a little, offered the distant views that people so loved and was at the same time part of the flood protection system. Used for years by the water protection police, it is now available as an exclusive holiday home for visitors to the Dessau-Wörlitz Garden Realm. Finally, the gardens conclude with a large, simple sandstone urn on the embankment by the so-called Leopoldshafen, in memory of Hereditary Aunt Anna Wilhelmine, Princess of Anhalt-Dessau (1715-1780), the mis-

The Vorderer Sitz – Foremost Seat –, completely reconstructed in 1988/89 based on drawings by Erdmannsdorff and historical photographs. A long meadow opens up in front of it, bordered by a dense backdrop of woodland.

tress of Schloss Mosigkau. The flood protection dike itself was planted with several rows of fruit trees, and catches the eye from far over the fields on the landward side.

So, it is not in all parts of the gardens that today's visitors are able to experience the world of emotions from the age of sensibility of two hundred years ago. The changes brought about by time and the natural cycle of growth and decay are too great. But anyone passing through the park with an attentive eye is still captivated by this wonderful creation of nature and art.

Wallwitzberg zu den Anlagen vom Georgen Garten gehörig, aquatint by Christian Haldenwang (1770-1831), based on original by Heinrich Theodor Wehle (1778-1805), Chalcographische Gesellschaft Dessau, 1800. The sheet shows the original condition of a part of the Georgengarten that has now run completely wild and gone to rack and ruin.

VI

THE
GARDEN
REALM

Uwe Quilitzsch

A Residence for the Enlightenment

A Residence for the Enlightenment ‣ "But I intended to advise you to travel to Dessau ... You need four to five days for this tour if you want to see everything and enjoy it at your leisure ...". These are Johann Wolfgang von Goethe's words in a letter to his life's companion, Christiane Vulpius, in Weimar. She did not take his advice until a few years later.

The Weimar poet, who passed this recommendation on to his companion, had an eye for the comprehensive reforms that were being carried out by Prince Franz of Anhalt-Dessau. He commended his efforts towards "greatness and completeness" on a number of occasions. Many projects of this kind in Germany, aiming at intellectual and economic renewal, were ahead of their time historically, and fell on stony ground. Sometimes they lasted for a few years, and were then forgotten again. Only progressive contemporaries still remembered them respectfully decades later.

The following is intended to provide a brief outline of how Dessau affected the whole of Germany in the second half of the 18th century. Prince Franz's country was seen as a synonym for progress, and so it is not surprising that major intellectual figures and rulers alike had to come to terms with these things.

The general situation ‣ As hereditary prince, Franz resigned from Prussian military service in 1757. The princes of Anhalt had traditionally served Prussia since Johann Georg II. Shortly after the outbreak of the Seven Years War, the young Dessau prince had to choose between a threatened imperial ban to be imposed on the imperial princes operating against the Habsburgs and the anger of Frederick the Great. He chose the latter evil. The hereditary prince now had to declare his country neutral as well, which inevitably brought

down concealed hostility from Prussia. Anhalt was not formally occupied, but Frederick systematically bled the little agricultural land dry by marching through it and demanding forage and forced contributions. The country had no military significance, and was practically helpless in the face of this. The population suffered dire hardship. In order to be able to meet some of Prussia's demands, the Dessau prince pawned his table silver rather than raising duties, which was the usual practice. It was popular gestures of this kind that subsequently impressed upon the Dessau prince's subjects the sense of the aura that surrounded him.

Dessau must have been greatly relieved when the Peace of Hubertusburg was proclaimed in 1763, as the country was on the verge of financial collapse. What happened now on the basis of internal policies influenced by the spirit of the European Enlightenment was unique in Germany. The ruler low-

Das Herzogliche Schloss in Dessau. Nach der Natur gez. von Leopold Ahrendts 1830,
oil painting on tinplate.

ered taxes, declared relief from duties and abolished forced imposts. He wanted to reformulate the principles by which he ruled his country, so he and a chosen team of advisors travelled through Germany to Holland, France and England from 14 July, 1763 to 2 July, 1764, so that he could inform himself about new developments. As a scion of the House of Orange and grandson of the Old Dessauer, he was welcome everywhere. One of the great English war heroes, Sir John Clavering, offered to accompany the Dessau prince, and in London he attended the baptism of the later Duke of York, Prince Frederik August, in Kensington Palace. The young Dessau prince particularly hoped that in England he would find a model for his future reform-oriented government policies. On his return, he went about his work with great concentration. He and his advisors developed a balanced programme of reforms intended to address socio-economic matters first, then public education and training, and finally the spheres of life affected by art and creativity.

He worked out very precisely that there were two problems in the country that had to be solved first: provision for the poor and raising educational standards. His initiative met with little positive response at first among the affected parties, as traditionally, beggars all over Europe were organized in guilds with their own hierarchies, and the Anhalt population was not very interested in education because of centuries-old structures and customs. But the prince pursued his aims doggedly, and brooked no contradiction to his absolutist legislation. The government pursued infringements of his decrees with the same severity invested in them. From 1784, Prince Franz had his collected legislation published to make it generally binding; the local authorities' duty of supervision was expressly emphasized.

The prince had building plans for a workhouse and poorhouse drawn up at an early stage – even before commissioning state buildings. The building dedicated to *Miseris et Malis*, mainly intended for law-breakers and beggars, was erected from 1766 to 1770. Begging became a punishable offence in Dessau. Incidentally, fines were very often assigned to the benefit of the poorhouse.

Economics ▸ Anhalt-Dessau was very much an agricultural country, and thus essentially dependent on income from the

As a result of the Second World War and the post-war period, only the walls enclosing the west wing of the residential palace of the princes of Anhalt-Dessau, the so-called "Johannbau", dating from the 16th century, survived. The staircase tower housing the spiral staircase, which is important in German architectural history, was erected according to plans by the Zerbst master builder, Ludwig Binder.

land. The Old Dessauer had created clear conditions relating to land ownership. He had compelled the local nobility to sell their estates and had restructured the country. He had taken almost all the land into princely ownership and acquired additional external territories. For example, he had purchased large estates in the area of Bubainen/Norkitten in East Prussia at a reasonable price, supported by his royal friend, Friedrich Wilhelm I of Prussia.

Prince Franz was able to use this basis created by the Old Dessauer to implement his reforms comprehensively, without the agreement of the landed nobility. He abolished the three-field system of agriculture that had been used since the Middle Ages, and introduced clover cultivation, the keeping of stabled cattle, fertilization and other innovations in its stead. He made Anhalt-Dessau's hop harvest famous. Farmers performed outstandingly in the field of cattle-breeding. All this put the royal town in a highly favourable light; it was surrounded by a belt of fertile community farmland, enhanced in its turn by the gardens scattered around it. This juxtaposition of the beautiful and the useful that was practised so often in the Garden Realm particularly impressed visitors from elsewhere.

Trades in Anhalt-Dessau were organized in guilds that had existed since the Middle Ages. Profound changes were in the air in 1796: Erdmannsdorff drew up his forward-looking paper, *Thoughts on a general preparatory teaching institute for mechanical trades and fine art.* He appealed for a "close co-operation between craft and art", on the basis of his experiences in England, for example in Josiah Wedgwood's successful manufactory. In quite practical terms, it was possible to point out the well-nigh incredible triumphs being achieved at the time by the Weimar entrepreneur, Friedrich Justin Bertuch, who was on excellent terms with Dessau. He developed a small artificial flower workshop into a flourishing production plant for fashionable goods of all kinds, founded publishing houses and ran mines. He advertised his wares skilfully in the then famous *Journal des Luxus und der Moden.*

Tolerance ‣ Contemporaries were full of praise for the degree of religious tolerance in Dessau, something not customary in most other states. The Köthen theologian Lebrecht Ludwig Baentsch noted in his *Handbuch der Geographie und Geschichte des gesammten Fürstenthums Anhalt,* dating from 1801: "Tolerance is quite at home in Dessau, and this is why Protestants, Catholics and Jews live mingled together in peace and harmony, doing their business, with none dis-

turbing the other in his religious customs and divine worship."

The reformed, Calvinist faith was predominant in Anhalt-Dessau, emanating from the prince's household. The prince granted the Lutheran and Catholic confessions, which were also represented in the country, the right to practise their religion freely, and this also applied to the Jewish congregations. As far as the tolerance of the Jews was concerned, this certainly also derived from financial considerations. At first, the government provided almost all Jews with the obligatory letter of protection, but later the wealthier brethren were singled out.

Anhalt-Dessau developed as a place where the Jews were emancipated. Despite the humiliating restrictions and resentments that still prevailed, honest efforts were made to integrate this race into the enlightened state. It must have been unique in Europe at the time that in Wörlitz, for example, the Jew Hirsch could acquire land and the Jewish secondary school, the Franzschule, bore the name of the ruler of the country. In Dessau from 1806, David Fraenkel published the *Sulamith, a magazine promoting culture and humanity among the Jewish nation.*

Attitudes were by no means as liberal in the friendly royal residences of Berlin and Weimar, so for the Jews, Dessau seemed to be the "... land rediscovered for the nation..."

The School of Philanthropists – the Dessau Philanthropin ‣ "Here, those famous philanthropies came into being that aimed for natural popular education, equal training for mind and body, making men not solely scholars, but vigorous men, for the world and for life. The name of a man like

The portrait of Johann Bernhard Basedow in the library of the palace in Wörlitz. Wall painting before 1783.

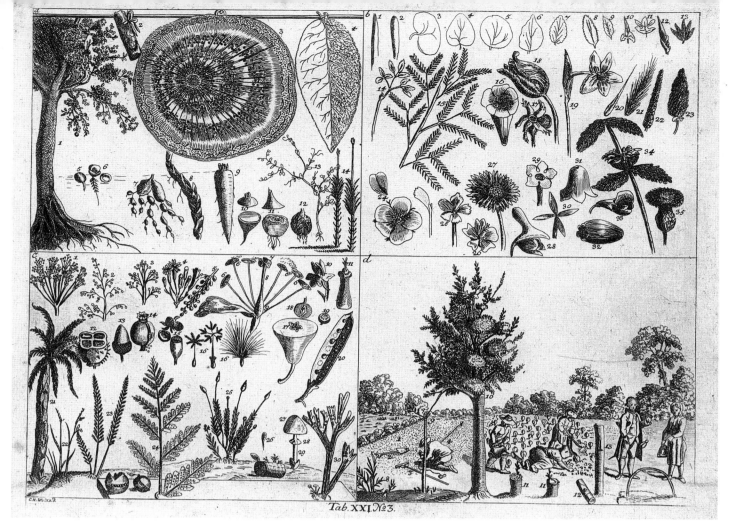

Tab. XXI. No 3.

Basedow lives blessedly on in the most recent times," was how a certain Dr. D. remembered one of Germany's most important schools in a "Contribution to the topography of the Leipzig-Berlin railway" in 1841.

Fundamental promotion of the Enlightenment in terms of education was put into practice in Dessau. In 1774, Prince Franz founded the Philanthropisches Institut in Dessau. This made the little residence town on the Elbe and the Mulde richer through an institution that caused a considerable stir. The man the Dessau ruler chose for the office of director was one of the most controversial 18th century educationalists: Johann Bernhard Basedow of Altona, which was Danish at the time. He appointed a choice selection of teachers to the institution. Questions of religious freedom had to be addressed, along with education according to nature, physical fitness and practical activities. Continuing conflict among the teachers meant that complicated opinion-forming processes took place in the school, but ultimately also led to the failure of the enterprise. So the Philanthropin was

granted only a short life, like so much that was founded in Dessau. It had to close as early as the 1790s – the time was obviously not ripe for it.

The Chalkographische Gesellschaft zu Dessau 1796-1803 (Chalkographic Institute of Dessau) ‣ The Dessau prince and his allies von Erdmannsdorff, von Waldersee and the Weimar entrepreneur Bertuch decided to found a forward-looking enterprise in 1796. The budget was secured with the aid of a joint stock company; the prince himself was the principal shareholder. An independent association of artists was established. It added to the royal town's cultural diversity and also pursued enlightened educational aims. It was intended to make the production of modern graphic art into a new source of employment. It was also hoped that targeted distribution of works of art would lead to an improvement in general taste. The actual initiative came from the Hildesheim and Paderborn canon, Baron Friedrich Moritz von Brabeck. The priest was an art-lover and had built up a hand-

Botany. Copper plate from Basedow's Elementarwerk. Ein geordneter Vorrath aller nöthigen Erkenntniß. Zum Unterricht der Jugend ..., Dessau, 1774.

Tab. XIX.

some collection of paintings at his Söder estate near Hildesheim. He employed copperplate engravers to make reproductions of his pictures, until he became aware of his financial limitations.

He therefore turned to the Dessau prince with his project, publishing in 1796 a memorandum to this end entitled: *Vues sur l'Etat des Arts en Allemagne, et sur l'Institut de Gravure établi à Dessau.*

At the same time, Erdmannsdorff wrote his *Entwurf einiger Gedanken über die Führung des artistischen Theils unserer chalcographischen Arbeiten*, about the artistic management of the engraving institution. This programmatic essay contained the artistic director of the society's principles relating to artistic education and the neo-classical view of art.

The Dessau society's declared intention at its foundation on 1 October, 1796, was to measure up to the best of the English and French copperplate engravers. The director was Graf von Waldersee, with von Erdmannsdorff as artistic director, and commercial management entrusted to the skills of the Weimar entrepreneur Bertuch. The enterprise was not primarily interested in profit, but in artistic aspirations, the desire to shape taste. Erdmannsdorff came up with themes for the graphic artists, and chose the paintings to be reproduced; here too public taste was not the driving force, the sole criterion was quality, guaranteed by the great names of art history. A large number of highly qualified young artists, familiar with the latest graphic techniques – largely developed in France and England – like aquatint and scraperboard engraving followed the call to Dessau.

A total of 169 titles on the following subjects are listed in the society's list of publications: Bible stories, mythology and history, imaginative compositions, portraits, ideal landscapes, Italian landscapes, Swiss views, views of the Dessau-Wörlitz Garden Realm and of Silesia, and academic pieces.

These relatively rare sheets are now sought-after collectors' pieces. Shortly after the death of Erdmannsdorff in 1800, and despite tremendous efforts by Bertuch, who had built up an intelligent and wide-ranging sales network, the

Some professions depicted in Basedow's *Elementarwerk*, Dessau, 1774.

society started to decline because of financial problems. The Chalkographische Gesellschaft Dessau had to give up seven years after it was founded.

Independent publishing, the dream of the "Scholars' Republic" ‣ Scholars and writers had started discussing their ideas for a "Scholars' Republic" even in the early 18th century. One important aspect of these theoretical statements was the relative independence of authors from publishers. The latter exploited the authors' intellectual products ruthlessly, often fobbing them off with the most meagre fees.

Carl Christoph Reiche was born in Havelberg in Prussia, and was later to emigrate to America. He felt himself called to found the "Buchhandlung der Gelehrten" (Scholars' Bookshop) in Dessau in 1781, followed a little later by the "Verlagskasse" adjacent to it. In his first publication, *Nachricht und Fundations=Gesetze von der Buchhandlung der Gelehrten, die in der Fürstl. Anhalt. Residenzstadt Dessau errichtet ist*, about the principles on which his bookshop worked, he was full of praise for the princely privileges he had been granted and his freedom from censorship: "... and where because of you the scholar can be certain that his writing, so long as it is an honestly intended piece of instruction or defence of a person or thing, but not a wanton mockery of man, of religion and of good morals, will certainly be printed, will never be made confiscate ..." and precisely that "... will merit the scholars' applause."

The league of publishers and booksellers, who were challenged by this, understandably mistrusted the enterprise from the outset. Competitors were in a state of constant alertness, massing around the Leipzig publisher Erasmus Reich, owner of the Weidmanns Erben publishing house, and the Berlin bookseller August Mylius; they made every effort to resist the young Dessau enterprise. But there was determination on both sides. The "Buchhandlung der Gelehrten" was popular with an enormous number of eminent authors: Bahrdt, Basedow, Bernoulli, Bertuch, Büsching, Chodowiecki, Claudius, Campe, Forster, Gleim, Goethe, Herder, Hirschfeld, Lichtenberg, Matthisson, Rochow, Salzmann, Schröckh, Sophie La Roche, Sprickmann, Voss, Wieland and Zollikofer had their work published here, along with Pestalozzi and Lavater. The Dessau publisher Reiche worked hard – but none too skilfully in entrepreneurial terms – to achieve the dreamed-of ideal: he allowed his authors to enjoy the benefits of having, so to speak, their own publishing house, but his "Buchhandlung der Gelehrten" carried all the economic risks.

In the year the publishing house was founded, the "Verlagskasse", a kind of joint stock company, was also established. It was intended above all to help young and unknown authors to make a breakthrough. The printing costs for the publication were advanced, and, at the same time, the author was paid up to 50 per cent of the retail price as profit. The shareholders included the prince and Basedow, and also Christoph Martin Wieland of Weimar.

Even though, according to its own records, the "Buchhandlung der Gelehrten" employed over 200 authors in 1783, and its aims were based only on noble motives, the enterprise was finally doomed to failure because of flagrant errors in financial procedure.

The Dessau Philanthropic Institute

Uwe Quilitzsch

Prince Franz brought Johann Bernhard Basedow to Dessau and charged him with the founding of a modern educational institution. The ruler bore all the expenses generated. It opened at Christmas, 1774, on the birthday of Hereditary Prince Friedrich of Dessau. The educationalists' declared intention was an allround education, free of class constraints. Basedow's four-volume *Elementarwerk* was used as the basis for teaching, a work that had been promoted by the Russian Tsarina Catherine the Great and the Dessau prince. It is seen as the most important 18th century German work on education.

Physics, geometry, mechanics, anatomy, horticulture, crafts and sport were taught, as well as the "classical" subjects such as fencing, dance and foreign languages. The prince had Carl Gottfried Neuendorf implement a comprehensive national school reform in 1786/87. The best-known teachers included Carl Friedrich Bahrdt, Johann Heinrich Campe (who wrote his *Robinson* in Dessau), Johann Schweighäuser, Christian Hinrich Wolke (who was later called to St. Petersburg), Zacharias Becker, Johann Christoph Friedrich Guts-Muths, Friedrich Matthisson and Ulrich Anton Vieth. The Dessauers undertook fruitful exchanges with similar German educational establishments like Johann Gotthilf Salzmann's Schnepfenthaler Institut and Friedrich Eberhard von Rochow's school in Reckhan, near Potsdam. The Dessauer Pädagogisches Institut closed down in the early '90s as a result of financial difficulties, quarrels among teachers and the intrigues of the Dessau clergy. But the Educational Institute's progressive ideas spread all over Germany, thanks to the Dessau teachers.

The following quotation dates from as late as 1808: "It can be said with pride – what an important share of the happiness of so many generations does Dessau not have, where a man like Basedow – a bright sun in the firmament of pedagogy – worked tirelessly to prepare thousands upon thousands for their great purpose." (From: *Herzoglich Fürstliche Regierungs=Jubelfeier zu Dessau im Monat Oktober 1808. Umständlich beschrieben von einem fremden Augenzeugen* (Ducal and princely celebrations in Dessau in October 1808, described in detail by an outside eyewitness).

LEOPOLD FRIEDRICH FRANZ   FÜRST ZU ANHALT DESSAU.
Seiner Durchl. dem regierenden Marggrafen   Carl Friedrich zu Baden und Hochberg &c &c

Equestrian portrait of Prince Franz of Anhalt-Dessau. Scraperboard
sheet by J.J. Freidhof, after a painting by Ph. J. Becker. Published by the
Chalkographische Gesellschaft Dessau, 1800.

The Dessau deer park was established as a princely hunting-ground in the 17th century. It was originally fenced, and contains an abundance of old solitaire oaks. Long avenues directed at the Dessau palace facilitated the care and protection of game.

Ludwig Trauzettel

Beautified countryside between Dessau and Wörlitz

Nature in the Garden Realm, carefully designed, beautified and imbued with meaning, always made an overwhelming impact on visitors. The impressions made by art, architecture and vigorous landscape, which today's visitors try to take home with their cameras, was captured with paintbrush, pen or pencil by many travellers at the time it was created. Others wrote down their memories and paeans of praise, and some of this was printed. Sources of this kind can provide important insights for the restoration work in the Garden Realm, which started some 20 years ago. For example, Joseph Röckl (1779-1826), the Dillingen professor of pedagogy and aesthetics, summed it up like this in his essay: "Dessau's charming and paradisiacal area is acknowledged to be one of northern Germany's most beautiful stretches of countryside. Its graceful situation on the river Mulde, from which blessings and fertility seem to pour out over this little

principality in all directions, awakens in the traveller ... new life, and chokes all those bitter sensations that had to develop, in such numbers and with such necessity, in all his long progresses through arid and empty areas! – ... But the gifts of nature delight all the more when art, which reshapes and ennobles everything, lays, as it were, the final hand on the work, in order to show us as much perfection as possible. And truly Dessau distinguishes itself excellently on this head. Whatever direction one proceeds in around the lovely town, everywhere one meets traces of the purest taste, and feeling for beauty and art expresses itself in manifold and numerous ways. – But the princely gardens unveil the greatest charms. Who would not surge with sweetest rapture in the enchanting Luisium? Who does not draw new life from the labyrinth of the Georgian Garden? And then nearby Wörlitz? – If all persons of sensibility agreed to hold a solemn

feast for Flora, based on the Roman custom, they would have to assemble in the magical climes of Wörlitz. How beauty and multiplicity compete here in nature and art is indescribable. While the opulent abundance of blossoming nature seems to breathe the spirit of mirth into all creatures, art is at the same time courting us for countless pleasures. – The great sight of a magnificent palace, the comely form of a well-adorned summer cabinet, the swaying gondola, to travel on a mirror-bright, spreading lake; a statue of lofty vigour – the source of sweet feelings; a darkling grotto, dedicated to the friend of loneliness and noble ideas; everywhere, the most interesting of forms meet the peaceful water."

Of the 600 square kilometres of this area of land that was once redesigned as a gigantic garden, 142 square metres have survived. They are listed, and UNESCO has made them into a

Garden Realm

Hunting has been one of the most highly appreciated pastimes in the Garden Realm since the 17th century, and still attracts a large number of visitors.

257

World Cultural Heritage Site (for this, see the map of Anhalt-Dessau on pp. 288/89). This little country's royal residence was in Dessau. Here, the reforms and work on beautifying the area were planned, prepared and carried out between 1758 and 1830. Pilgrimages were made with guests to Wörlitz with its park and gardens, still the most popular destination for most visitors. This place, 15 kilometres west of the residential palace, was not just a summer seat – the stream of interested people flowed to this "holy of holies" (Wieland) of the Garden Realm throughout the year. The effect the gardens make is unsurpassed, above all when the fruit trees are in bloom, or when the trees are in bud or in their autumn colours. It was just as delightful – and still is – to explore the gardens' visual patterns from the frozen canals.

Travellers were put in the right mood for the highlights to come by the newly designed routes, planted as avenues leading to Wörlitz, and directed from park to park. Design details and architectural works around the gardens attracted attention to the enhanced landscape. And so, visitors arrived at the eagerly anticipated destination of Wörlitz, instructed by the effect of the architectural and pictorial decoration on the way: a school was created using garden art, a museum of education, of the Enlightenment and of art.

The effect of the Wörlitz gardens as the highlight of this complete work of art would not be complete without experiencing the gradual approach via the parks and palaces that are about half an hour apart. The whole diversity of the programme devised by Prince Franz and Erdmannsdorff is staged to make an overall effect, and can be appreciated and understood only as a whole. Dessau-Wörlitz is a UNESCO World Heritage Site today, because of the brilliant and still effective interplay between all the elements of artificially designed nature in a landscape that demonstrates a wealth of ideas, which were extraordinarily progressive and enlightened for their time. The World Heritage committee's assessment when justifying its decision was that the Garden Realm is "an outstanding example of the philosophical principles of the Enlightenment, implemented in a landscape design combining art, education and commerce".

Beautifying the whole principality involved the work of many people. Countless assistants were employed on the extensive excavations when building the canals and dikes during the 35 years it took to create the parks and gardens. No one can estimate today how many plants Prince Franz grew and set to realize his design for the whole country. As well as this, over 250 individual buildings of different sizes

The Raues Wachhaus on the Fliederwall. Prince Franz had dike watchtowers built at regular intervals for the protection of the dikes and the Garden Realm. Protective measures were organized and supervised from here when the river was high. Like this neo-Gothic building dating from 1772, also called the Hermit's Chapel, the watchtowers also fulfilled an aesthetic function within the landscape picture.

were erected in this period. So that no one would be able to assess the effort made and the expense at a later stage, the prince had all the documents and accounts for his work on enhancing the countryside destroyed in 1810.

The essential changes were completed around 1800, by the time Erdmannsdorff died; but in individual parts of the country, work on the new designs continued after the prince's death. Here there was no long-term planning – one activity followed the previous one; first the paths were built, then the avenues were planted, seats added and the edges of the woods and plantations decorated with fruit trees and flowering shrubs. Provost Friedrich Reil wrote in retrospect in his biography of the prince in 1843: "If one can call him (Franz) the mind in which everything fermented and from which everything was born, then Erdmannsdorff was the trusted and initiated companion, the soul of all the movements throughout the building programme, of the indoor and outdoor beautification and decoration. Under him and the prince was Hesekiel, as director of building. Herr von Raumer dealt with earth culture and everything associated with it; the forester Wöpke dealt with dike and bank construction; the parks and gardens were managed by Schoch, ... Eyserbeck, Obereit, Neumark and Klewitz, the father, each in his own place. Most of them had been with the prince in Holland, England and France, and had learned what each could use for his trade."

The Dessau-Wörlitz gardeners Johann Friedrich Eyserbeck (1734-1818), Johann Christian Neumark (1741-1811), Johann Leopold Ludwig Schoch the Elder (1728-1793), Johann George Schoch the Younger (1758-1826) and Dietrich Wilhelm Albert Klewitz (1767-1840) were the planters who, in the real landscape around the Elbe and the Mulde, implemented the ideas, which Erdmannsdorff and his princely friend had gleaned on their travels. Even in the baroque period, a gardener had to use his skills to translate an architect's ideas into reality outdoors, just as masons and carpenters had to implement plans for the building and in the interior. And for a long time this was no different in Dessau-Wörlitz. It was not until the 1790s that the prince and his architect started to place greater trust in the younger Schoch's creative abilities.

The gardeners in their turn had day-labourers, peasants and servants available to them for work such as the extensive earth movements. Together they built canals and dikes, roads, avenues and axes. They created, detail for detail throughout the Garden Realm, green walls, viewpoints, gardens and visual links with their living "vegetation bricks". Prince Franz, who "by setting a glowing example to others, promised servants and subjects a golden age"(Goethe in *Dichtung und Wahrheit*), thus provided work and made the children of his country prosperous.

Wanderers came across impressions, visual sequences and staged garden pictures as they passed through the landscape of the entire Garden Realm. If seeking a way eastwards, they could choose different routes, linked together like a net, via three available bridges. The northern route led from the Jägerbrücke past the Luisium to Wörlitz via the gardens on the Sieglitzer Berg and the Fliederwall. There were two ways from Dessau via the Mulde Bridge: south of the Luisium, the route took visitors via the old main road through the Garden Realm, past the Schwedenhaus and again along the Fliederwall by Vockerode to Wörlitz, or they used the south road through the deer park via Mildensee and from there via the Kapenmühle or Oranienbaum to the Wörlitz gardens. But the routes through the Garden Realm do not come to an end once Wörlitz is reached. Dikes and paths marked with buildings and planted once more lead through the enhanced landscape on the Schönitzer See or the little towns of Riesigk and Rehsen, visible from afar because of their churches, to the eastern border, first with Electoral Saxony, then with Prussia.

The roads that still lead through the Garden Realm have mainly survived as elements of the original infrastructure. They are crucially important if the *Gesamtkunstwerk* is to be experienced as a whole. Even though the original structure of made and unmade roads and paths is lost, they have survived in their original width, along with the trees edging the road, mixed with fruit trees, the ditch and the "gate trees" at junctions, gaps and bridges. As in the parks, the curves in the roads were managed so that viewers experienced varied and diverse views of the countryside. Travellers were surprised by a new landscape scene at many corners, and new landmarks appeared on the horizon as the journey proceeded. Even from a distance, visitors were put in the right mood for the coming experience, but then distracted again by small buildings, planting or visual links.

The northern route from Dessau to Wörlitz ran mainly along the old Elbe dike, and was also one of the main roads at the time. When using it, it is still possible at times when the rivers are high to gain a sense of the destructive and unpredictable power of the water, which the designers had to contend with when the gardens were first created. Generations

before, Prince Franz had already built a considerable number of dikes parallel to the Elbe to reduce the annual flooding from its waters and thus make it possible to use the area for agriculture all the year round, regardless of the river levels. The dikes had fallen into disrepair with time, and had already been renovated and improved by Leopold I between 1735 and 1738. He established a second main line of dikes behind the summer dikes, and protected these with plantations, solitary timber and flood-prevention modelling against wear and tear from flotsam and ice in particular when the water was dangerously high in winter. Thus Leopold provided lasting protection for the dike system, which after being extended and raised by his grandson Franz, proved adequate and withstood the power of the masses of water right up until the early 21st century. The Old Dessauer did not take the dikes through the countryside in a straight line, as this would have offered the water too many points at which to attack, but took existing currents, flood gullies and original water-courses into account. He created bulwarks, dike reinforcements and raised sections in high-risk areas, and also placed ice deflectors at points where movements were dangerous, all of which he had learned to do as an experienced Prussian commander when constructing defensive bastions. Prince Franz continued his grandfather's work, especially after the disastrous floods of 1770 and 1771, while at the same time enhancing his Garden Realm. The flood dikes extending throughout the country became roads and orchards at the same time, for everything was used for a purpose and thought through in terms of both functional and aesthetic aspects. Prince Franz tried to learn from his experience of the floods and the damage they caused. He had the

weak points where there were strong currents or where the dikes changed direction, reinforced again, and installed an observation and warning system. "Hereupon an expedient embankment order was published, in which the senior and junior officials, manual labourers and parishes were advised of the posts they had to man at high water, and everyone was told precisely and in great detail what he had to attend to and what he had to do" (Reil). The Wallwachhäuser – embankment lookout buildings – erected along the Elbe dike were there to provide better surveillance and contained "the utensils necessary for building and protecting earthworks, like carts, faggots, poles and the like ..., which were always sound and available, and were not to be used for other works" (Reil). "The stranger believes at first that these buildings are there only for embellishment, but is most pleasantly surprised when he discovers that nothing is here in vain, and everything must adorn and be useful at the same time," Boettiger explained. The chief forester Leopold Wöpke (1738-1809), who was responsible for flood protection and the dikes, and who was most familiar with the currents at high water, directed the practical work of construction, maintenance and protection. If the threat was acute, the prince himself hurried to the danger points to supervise and lead the deployment of the day labourers and helpers who had been summoned. It is reported that the ruler showed equal commitment in the event of major fires.

Winter floods were seen as particularly dangerous as the dikes could very quickly be damaged by ice pressure and drifting floes, and the danger that the dike turf, which did not take root sufficiently in the early stages, might be washed away and thus cause a breach. The oaks already planted in front of the dike by Leopold I were intended to hold the ice floes back, and absorb some of the pressure from them. Unfortunately, large numbers of these oaks were felled after the floods in 2002, so that dikes conforming to German industrial standards could be built. This means that a crucial part of the original effect made by the landscape has been lost. Prince Franz had nine mounds, secured with paving stones, constructed on the side of the Schönitzer See where the current flows. They were intended to break the ice and keep flotsam, ice floes and the current well away from the Wörlitz dikes. On one of these mounds is the Proteus Rock, dedicated to Neptune's servant. The inscription was prepared by the prince's own hands, and still reminds us today: "Hear, you who come after, a voice that warns you. Careful industry created this mound and these bushes, in order to

The Limes Tower near the Schönitzer See. This timber-frame tower was also part of the flood defence system of dike watchtowers, planned by

Erdmannsdorff. The combination of oak trees, ditches and dikes was intended to represent the *limes*, the fortified Roman border.

protect the field-saving earthworks from the destructive ice. Do all you can to maintain them."

During his long reign, Prince Franz paid close attention to maintaining the aesthetic and economic changes in the landscape, and in the reign of his successor, Leopold Friedrich, the designed landscape with its world of plants and animals was under the same strict protection, anticipating present-day efforts relating to monument conservation and environment protection. Legislation in force at the time makes it clear that the ruler tried to educate his subjects and visitors, and threatened severe punishments for the destruction of roads, plantations and dike installations. For example, the prince proclaimed "that no one should dare criminally to knock over or to damage a planted fruit tree or other tree, to whomsoever it may belong … and that" anyone contravening this "was to be punished with one year's cart-drawing" (Order no. 175 dated 19.4.1791). It was also forbidden, under threat of arrest and fine, "to travel on the paths and roads with unduly heavy loads in wet weather, and to damage the trees planted by the wayside." The rules and regulations from the prince's day may surprise readers today, but they were intended to secure the constructed routes, dike installations and ditches. They also dealt with the care and protection of game, bird protection and fishing, tree and shrub conservation and the planting of living fences. The prince obliged those living near the dikes to combat voles, to protect the dikes from damage. Owners of orchards were legally required to eliminate caterpillars and other pests.

When designing his Garden Realm, the ruler was able to have recourse to the water-meadows created by his grandfather,

Leopold I, and largely taken into his possession. As well as renewing the dikes, the prince had also drained the marshy land by digging ditches and diverting the water that flowed off them into the Mulde via the Kapengraben. Now, water-meadows with solitaire oaks defined the sweeping character of the landscape, an effect that is still wonderfully preserved in part today. These solitaire meadows came into being because of the grazing practice of previous centuries. As the pigs and cattle that were kept in this part of the country scarcely allowed any young timber to grow, the remaining shady oaks developed into mighty, picturesque solitaire trees. Prince Franz used their aesthetic effect when designing his Garden Realm. The "sacred tree", appreciated since the days of the Germanic peoples, had always been particularly important to Prince Franz. From the late 18th century, the common oak acquired a new meaning as a nationally charged metaphor – to be found, amongst other places, in the works of famous poets like Klopstock and Goethe. Like the neo-Gothic style in architecture, this beautiful and powerful tree in its natural surroundings symbolically invoked our own traditions and history, and was considered a symbol of national independence and freedom. Prince Franz supported this idea by using its fruit, the acorn, as decoration on the New Tower of his Gothic House. Erdmannsdorff chose "Eichenkranz" (garland of oak leaves), a symbol of bourgeois virtue, as the name for the inn he built for interested visitors to Wörlitz at the time the gardens were created. The Dessau artist Carl Wilhelm Kolbe (1757-1835), known as "Eichen-kolbe" (Oak Kolbe), produced numerous engravings that have preserved, for our times, the charming character of this water-meadow landscape, enlivened by herds and flocks.

The water-meadows north of the Elbe dikes can still only be used as pasture or to grow fodder because of the constant risk of flooding. This maintains their character and enlivens the landscape.

The large amphibian population on the wet water-meadows in the area flooded by the Elbe and the Mulde still provides a natural feeding-ground for the stork, which has otherwise become rarer as a summer guest in Central Europe.

Many fruit trees, wonderfully coloured in spring and autumn, grew in these meadows as well as the oaks. The old wild pear and cherry-trees, in particular, were used and treasured as fine wood for furniture-making.

Conveying enlightened ideas as a motif in designed gardens was not restricted to the highly stylized parkland. Town planning, architecture and fine art all over the country were an open book for those interested, showing the new thinking of that period, and this symbolism, despite developments in subsequent centuries, is still to be recognised, chapter by chapter, in the remaining structural and garden art. The buildings erected by Prince Franz attracted attention, regardless of their purpose and size. Junctions, dike crossings or bridges were made to stand out against their surroundings, through their striking architecture and concentrated planting, and could be seen from a distance. Travellers used the church towers in particular as signposts, to get their bearings even from some way away. The churches in Mosigkau (1780), Riesigk (1800), Pötnitz (1804-06), Wörlitz

(1804-09) and Vockerode (1810/11) are landmarks of early neo-Gothic ecclesiastical architecture in Germany. Travellers were greeted by elements of the new architecture near to the point they entered a town or village. In Wörlitz, for example, when entering the town from the east, they saw the demesne, its design based on Palladio's Villa Emo, whilst at the south entrance was the school building, also influenced by Palladio, followed by the ceremonial building at the Jewish cemetery. Coming from the west, the Rousseau Island underlined the idea of the Enlightenment, before visitors ordered quarters for the night at the "Eichenkranz" inn, built in the style of a neo-Gothic town gate.

The boundaries between the town of Wörlitz, the gardens and the surrounding meadows were not as clear as they are today, where roads now separate the Wörlitz garden area, still extending over 112 hectares, from their surroundings. The original complete work of art, which was, to the largest possible extent, free of fences and open to all, covered a much larger area and began as soon as Wörlitz was visible in the

Fruit trees are characteristic features of planting in the Garden Realm. The roads and dikes were mainly planted with fruit trees – often up to four rows of them – as well as Lombardy poplars. Often species were mixed, and the regular planting broken up by special solitaire trees to create highlights in the design.

distance. The Drehberg, the Berting and the settlements of Münsterberg and Riesigk can be seen as the actual entrances to the Wörlitz gardens. The transition from the gardens to the aesthetically-enhanced surroundings is kept fluid by skilful mingling of plantations and arable land. "Whatever road one chooses, one always sees Wörlitz in a position that is pleasing to the eye. The whole area is a pleasant landscape. As soon as one leaves the woods, a broad greensward stretches before the eye like a green carpet. Here and there, mirror-bright waters gleam, linked to each other by canals that look like natural brooks, and over which bridges pass in a variety of forms ..." wrote August Rode in 1798. His account of the "Arcadian landscape" that precedes the Wörlitz gardens describes the area that starts immediately after the Berting Park and runs along the Krägensee and the Forthgraben to the town boundary. At the point where the path descends the Fliederwall to the foot of the dike, travellers in the prince's time saw their destination for the day presented symbolically in the distance: the neo-classical, neo-Gothic ensemble of palace and church could be seen as a garden image, framed in fruit-trees. Idealized architecture, to which

visitors were now clearly drawn, was presented as a distant goal, picked out from nature that was wild, but cultivated. This was paying tribute to antiquity and a foreign high culture, and also, full of pride, to local history and building traditions. The countryside along the way, following this moment of greeting, represents an open section of the Wörlitz garden masterpiece, with modelled terrain, ditches, avenues, buildings, garden seats and solitaire timber. There is an extensive view over a landscape structured by planted avenues, the poplar field and the surrounding expanses of water. A white wooden bridge focuses the architectural design at the point where the ditch meets the Krägensee. The Schinderberg, a man-made mound next to it, served as a raised garden seat; the prehistoric monument carried a gallows in darker days. From here the route used to lead through an avenue of poplars and on to Wörlitz. The avenue "is here and there cut out for flowered semicircles and seats" (Boettiger). Recognizable bays by the road with a footpath beside it (the original "lower way" for travellers on foot) with conspicuous planting still provide accents along the way and indicate the passing-places for coaches in the avenue, which

Haideburg, on the edge of the Mosigkauer Heide. This neo-Gothic building was created by Erdmannsdorff in 1782-84 as a hunting and forestry lodge, and was intended to symbolically invoke national traditions. The Prussian kings' coronation castle in Königsberg gave the idea for this palatial building with a five-storey tower.

used to be much narrower. These could be identified from some distance by modelling, seating and planting. The seats at the edges of a view of "meadows and greensward interspersed with canals and enlivened by domestic creatures, taking their pleasure and grazing in herds and flocks ..." (Boettiger).

The situation in the area outside the gardens has been recreated in recent years; for decades, rank growth, heaps of rubble and car parks had artificially distanced the garden from the surrounding countryside.

On the route about two kilometres east of Wörlitz, on the southern periphery of the Elbe's original glacial valley, is a natural eminence that may have been a cult place, even in prehistoric times. "The place has been called Drehberg from time immemorial because it is higher than the rest of the terrain, and thus remains dry at time of flood ('treuge' – dry – which people round here pronounce 'drehe')" (Rode, 1798). The prince intended this site to be a last resting-place for his family from 1773. At the same time, he developed the Drehberg as a setting for the public festivals held annually here and attended by the local people and numerous guests in the 18th century to celebrate the princess's birthday on 24 September. In order to combine the gravity of death with the

joy of the living, between 1776 and 1799 the inhabitants of the country competed on the various circular paths and the poplar avenue leading to Wörlitz in sports events like horse-racing and running, following the model of antiquity. The site was about 130 metres in diameter, circular, and originally planted with Lombardy poplars. Marking its centre was a neo-classical pavilion on a conical mound of earth, designed by Erdmannsdorff. It was demolished in 1826 by the prince's grandson and successor, along with the rest of the ancillary buildings. Four sight axes, accompanied by Lombardy poplars and fruit-trees, originated from the central building almost at right angles to each other. These led to Oranienbaum, the Kapenmühle, the Krägengrotte and the Elysium of the allegorical labyrinth in the Wörlitz Park. The prince himself was interred neither here nor in the burial-place Erdmannsdorff built in Dessau. His last resting-place is in a mausoleum by the church in Jonitz, near the Luisium.

Like all his ancestors, Prince Franz was a passionate huntsman. The young prince was strong-willed and eager to learn; he was taught hunting and practised it under the auspices of his educators at the Vogelherd (now Luisium). As well as acquiring knowledge of history and the French language, he also gained "skills in the knightly arts, riding, fencing,

The Riesigk village church, built by Hesekiel from 1797-1800, in which three of the prince's sisters are interred, is a neo-Gothic accent in the designed landscape that can be seen in the east of the Garden Realm from a great distance.

264

dancing and carriage-driving" (Heese). The prince enjoyed hunting and riding throughout his life. He died on the evening before his 77th birthday on 9 August, 1817, as the result of a riding accident. He reported after his first visit to England: "It was mainly hunting, which the English love so passionately and that was my passion too, that carried me away and not infrequently put me in danger of breaking my neck or my leg; far from being an apprentice of the wild huntsmen, I soon became their master" (Reil).

Despite his enlightened views, he did not relinquish the customary feudal privilege of his rank relating to the practice of hunting. For the prince, hunting expressed the traditional freedom and independence, for which he worked throughout his life, from the time he rebelled against Prussian pressure in the early years of his reign. He also pursued this pleasure ostentatiously in deliberate defiance of Frederick the Great's circle, where hunting was rejected. So hunting in Dessau, especially the elaborate sow hunts and hunts on horseback, developed into the famous autumn events that eminent guests attended annually, among them Carl August of Saxony-Weimar, Friedrich Wilhelm II of Prussia and Goethe. The Dessau ruler also used the hunt meetings as an opportunity for political and diplomatic conversations, for

example at the time of negotiations concerning the League of German Princes, and later with Napoleon as well. The Dessau hounds were so excellently trained that the prince even charmed the French emperor, thus preventing major harm to Anhalt-Dessau during his campaigns.

Even though Prince Franz had built the neo-Gothic Haideburg on the edge of the Mosigkauer Heide, where there was a great deal of game, there was no designated hunting territory in the little country. Hunting took place all over the Garden Realm, including the Oranienbaumer Heide, where aisles for hunting had been cut in a star-shaped pattern in the woods since his grandfather's day. Records state that 729 stags were killed between 1781 and 1809 alone. The prince's illegitimate son and head forester Franz, Count of Waldersee

The meadows in the Muldeaue are now typical of this landscape, adorned with fruit-trees. As former grazing land, they are evidence of the natural husbandry practised in and after the 18th century.

Fruit from Prince Franz's "Pomologisches Cabinett". Wax replicas like these, now rare, were made in Friedrich Justin Bertuch's "Landes-Industrie-Comtoir" in Weimar.

Old oaks on the Kupenwiesen. The northernmost route from the residential palace in Dessau to Wörlitz originally ran along the flood dike on the Kupenwiesen, with their covering of trees. The historical character of the Elbaue flood area, structured by old oak and wild fruit trees, has survived successfully here.

(1763-1823), wrote a long poem called *Der Jäger* (The Hunter), which was later published in book form. This contains a great deal of information about the varied details of the hunt, which also included the forester's work in tending the woodland, and the care and protection of game. Waldersee praised hunting among other things in the following lines:

"... When game and hound are forced to seasonal rest
E'n then he's (the hunter) mindful of the careful tending
Of all his woodland, dark and safe retreat
For warmly cradled, fiercely hunted game.
E'en then the forest's clever cultivation
Can fire the muses of his mind and hand."

In the flat countryside north of the Elbe dike, which was regularly subject to flooding, every elevation in the terrain offered shelter to the game during the annual period of high water. The prince had had the area near the Elbe known as "forest solitude on the Sieglitzer Berg" surrounded by a wicker fence, so that roe deer and stags that had got into the woodland garden through the game opening could not get out again when the floods receded. The care and protection of game also influenced the look of the landscape in Anhalt-Dessau. The enhanced meadowland, the planted and designed tracts of woodland with their peripheral areas and clearings offered optimal conditions for wild animals that could be hunted. And apart from the aesthetic effect of the trees' colourful foliage and blossom, the acorns from the oak-trees and the wild and domestic fruit provided important food for these animals.

The little town of Mildensee, east of the Mulde in the south of the Garden Realm, is a design highlight, even though it did not become involved in the enhancement of the Garden Realm until a relatively late stage. The town is now part of Dessau. In the 18th century, it consisted of the market settlement of Pötnitz and the nearby villages of Scholitz and Dellnau. Following the pattern of Wörlitz's approach to economic matters, the demesne leaseholder Christian Gebhard Nordmann (1755-1822) started to implement his new agricultural aims here from 1778. Nordmann, who went down in German agricultural history because of his breeding of Spanish Merino sheep, West Friesian cows and Pötnitz wheat, erected large buildings to accommodate his 4000 sheep. The practical, cost-saving plank truss construction of the buildings is still surprising today. In Mildensee, in a landscape designed like a park around a dead arm of the Mulde (hence the name Mildensee = See (lake) of the Milde (Mulde)), is the Tower of the Eight Winds, built by Pozzi (1766-1842) in 1812. The building is named after the original in Athens, upon which it is modelled, and stands on top of a high lakeside hill that Prince Franz had not had built up until 1810. The neo-classical, yellow-washed brick building, visible from a great distance, is also popularly known as the Napoleon Tower, and served as a dike watchtower. Legend has it that Napoleon, in the company of Prince Franz, punished a soldier here who had looted in Mildensee, even though the emperor had forbidden this.

The dikes extending to the centre of the former villages of Pötnitz and Scholitz divide the landscaped area of the Dessau deer-park from the village development. Not far from this park, the neo-Gothic building for the rural constabulary also stands, another architecturally interesting example of a plank truss roof in the shape of an ogee arch. The formerly Romanesque church in Pötnitz, rebuilt in the neo-Gothic style between 1804 and 1806 to plans by Pozzi, was included in the design as a point-de-vue.

The Sieglitz Park

Uwe Quilitzsch

"I also visited the Silitzerberg, a little palace, or if one prefers, a temple with four columns on the bank of the Elbe, with its salon and chambers in the depths. It is surrounded by oak trees that are several centuries old, and legend claims a thousand years for one of their number. It is the most charming wilderness that I know." *Prince Charles Joseph de Ligne, 1799*

Prince Franz had a secluded landscape garden laid out, halfway between the Luisium and the old fishing village of Vockerode. His choice lighted on a flood-free hill in the middle of the natural water-meadows, and was known at the time as the Silitzer Berg. Lively horticultural and architectural activity commenced here in 1777, but the work was to continue for only three decades, with interruptions. A woodland garden was created over an area of about 23 hectares, seen by contemporaries as an "ordered wilderness". In fact,

Statues of Diana and a faun mark the entrance to this isolated park.

the gardens were developed from the surrounding dense river-valley woodland, and in comparison with Wörlitz, the Georgium and the Luisium, had very little open space available. Today, the open areas are almost completely overgrown. The steep bank of the Elbe formed the northern border of the Sieglitz Park; the river has changed its course since the 18th century, redefining its bed in the course of the annual floods. It used to form a natural boundary, and was part of the garden design. The terrain is surrounded by magnificent solitaire oaks. Sight lines fanned out from the Solitude, the main building in the park, leading to points-de-vue in the landscape: to the statue of a faun, to the Wilhelm urn and to a sculpture of Diana. The faun and Diana make an allegorical statement about the purpose of the park. It was a place of woodland solitude, relaxation and inspiration. Everything was fenced, to ensure a full stock of game.

Access was via three gates, all with different designs. In the Dessau spirit of stylistic pluralism, Erdmannsdorff variously used different architectural forms as a style primer. Coming along the dike from the direction of Dessau, visitors went through a gate in the baroque style. The sandstone piers topped with pine-cones have now been reconstructed, and are accompanied by volutes. The prince had the Vockerode gate designed in simple neo-classical style. Two small gatehouses, topped with triangular pediments, allowed pedestrians to enter, and the road between them was available for coaches. The neo-Gothic, architecturally elaborate Burgtor (Castle Gate) marks the third entrance, when coming from the direction of Wörlitz. This brick structure is reminiscent of the kind of backdrop architecture favoured by the English architect Sanderson Miller in Prior Park near Bath. In keeping with the motif of a medieval castle gate, the so-called castle ruins are to be found in the immediate vicinity – the remains of a collapsed sandstone Renaissance portal. There used to be a small harbour below the castle wall, but it has now silted up.

Various visual links lead to other highlights of the park. The eye is often drawn by sculptures and monuments. A large sandstone urn is a memorial to Wilhelm Count of Anhalt, who fell on the Prussian side at the battle of Torgau. He was a mutual friend of the Prince of Dessau and Georg Heinrich von Berenhorst, former adjutant to Frederick the Great. The monument stands slightly raised on an old flood dike that merges into the terrain here.

The neo-Gothic Burgtor is one of three differently designed entrances to the Sieglitz Park.

Not far from this is a plain memorial stone with inscriptions of a sentimental nature by 18th century poets, who are scarcely known now: by Ernst Wolfgang Behrisch, an educator of Anhalt-Dessau princes, advisor to Prince Franz and friend of Goethe's youth, by Ewald von Kleist and Friedrich von Hagedorn, whose portraits are to be found in the Wörlitz palace library.

At the heart of the park is the so-called Solitude. Erdmannsdorff's noble architecture was still standing as a ruin until about 1970. The building was later pulled down by military units for no known reason. They went about their task thoroughly, so that all that remains of the former splendour are the foundations. Nothing has survived of the formerly lavish interior, which is recorded in photographs.

Historical views existed of the building, like one by the Berlin architect Friedrich Gilly dating from 1797, and numerous photographs from the last century. Erdmannsdorff had designed a long brick building on a high base, covered with rusticated rendering. Four Tuscan columns supported the pediment on the main façade, which faced the Elbe. Erdmannsdorff designed the interior of the house as an elegant refuge, which Prince Franz enjoyed withdrawing to.

He often took the waters here, to ease physical discomfort. The house had a tiled bathroom to this end. The warm water came from the nearby kitchen building through underground pipes. As well as the bathroom, the house accommodated a kitchen, a bedroom with alcoves, a servants' room and finally a large room, elegantly decorated with stucco and painting. The inscription "To Recovery" indicated the purpose of the Solitude. A second inscription above the entrance presented a puzzle for some time: "In memory of the XXVI Septbr. 1783". The mystery has since been solved: the date related to the secret meeting that took place here between the Dessau prince and the Prussian Crown Prince Friedrich Wilhelm at the time of negotiations concerning the League of Princes. At that time, in the course of the War of Bavarian Succession, the rulers of smaller imperial territories were attempting to conspire against the Habsburgs and ensure mutual support.

In recent years, industry, science and monument conservation have worked together to make restoration of the Sieglitz Park area possible. It has therefore been possible to reclaim from nature the historic gardens with their architectural remains.

Only the foundations of the former Solitude have survived.
Reconstruction of the little palace presents a modern day challenge.

Ludwig Trauzettel

Nature and art
on the Kühnauer See

The western park in the Dessau-Wörlitz Garden Realm, which includes Grosskühnau and all the designed landscapes north-west of the Mulde and Dessau, such as the Kienfichten (Kienheide), the Ziebigker Feldflur and the Georgengarten with the Beckerbruch, ends west of the Kühnauer See at the former state boundary of the Principality of Anhalt-Dessau. The former village of Grosskühnau was mentioned as a settlement as early as 945, and has had a chequered history. It is on the edge of the delightful Elbe water-meadows. It was probably in 1316 that the river left behind a powerfully structured dead arm with no feeder stream in the form of the Kühnauer See. It is still fed today by flood water from the Elbe and the Mulde during the annual floods.

This area was initially supposed to be the starting-point for the parks to be created in the Garden Realm. But Prince Franz changed his mind and turned his attention to Wörlitz.

The reason for this is still unknown. Presumably, he was afraid of the floods, and did not want to dispute or redesign the property, recently renovated, of his uncle and former guardian Prince Dietrich, who had inherited the existing manor house and the estate from his mother in 1746. Prince Franz therefore preferred to move the experienced Kühnau palace gardener Johann Leopold Ludwig Schoch the Elder to Wörlitz, where the landscape conditions, inside the dike and protected from floods, were more suitable for a large landscape garden. After the death of Prince Dietrich in 1769, Prince Franz handed over the land around the old Kühnau lease-house, called a Schloss or palace, as a home for his youngest brother, Prince Albert (1750-1811). Years later, Albert had large parts of the house pulled down because of its condition and had a new palace built upon the old foundations between 1779 and 1782, in which Erdmannsdorff

and Pozzi were presumably involved. Here, this odd person, who had been banished from the Dessau court, lived a reclusive life, but concerned himself with the public good of his Kühnau village inhabitants and tried to improve their education, health care and medical treatment.

Schoch the Elder had already laid out the palace garden for Dietrich as Prince Regent from 1753. There is no record of horticultural activities in the palace garden during Prince Albert's time in Grosskühnau, other than the name of the gardener, Johann Georg Reinicke. The new owner was also no friend of gardens as an art form. After the death of the prince in 1811 as a result of a robbery, the house first went to Hereditary Prince Friedrich, and a few years later to his son, Leopold Friedrich. The palace housed the cabinet of rare specimens from the princely collections until after the First World War. Work must also have been done on the actual

One of the numerous flocks of sheep, which are very useful in helping to care for the dikes, in front of the neo-Romanesque church and Schloss Grosskühnau, the present headquarters of the Dessau-Wörlitz Cultural Foundation.

273

The old oaks, typical of the Garden Realm, also determine the image
of the Kühnau landscape park.

palace garden at this time. Continuing his grandfather's work on scientific fruit cultivation, Duke Leopold Friedrich transformed the estate to the north-west of the palace into an orchard. The planting of swamp cypresses, giant cedars and the tulip tree, which still accentuate the shores of the lake, concluded in 1835 the renewal work on the gardens around the palace that had started in about 1830 with the building of one of the earliest neo-Romanesque churches as a new architectural accent in the landscape and of the pierced brick wall that formed the garden's boundary with the village.

Unlike the other gardens in the Garden Realm, the palace garden was not integrated into its surroundings at first. The old palace garden was always fenced off and related to the house, whilst the neighbouring Kühnau landscape park developed independently. Linking elements like paths and sight lines did not bring the landscape areas together until the magnificent work of enhancing the landscape later took in the area around the Kühnauer See. At the same time, the Weinberghaus created a connecting element in the landscape in the direction of Dessau, and the church provided a vertical accent and an end point for the visual links with the landscape garden. But this final stop, the actual culmination of the enhancement to the western park in the Garden Realm, was not put into place in the lifetime of Prince Franz, but eleven years after he died, between 1828 and 1830, by his grandson and successor to the throne, Leopold Friedrich.

Hereditary Prince Friedrich did not take the territory around the Kühnauer See in hand until the early 19th century. Like his father, he worked without a plan for the garden. Georg Kilian, the overseer and planter, and his day-labourers in Grosskühnau had to implement the ideas the prince developed on the spot. In the first few years, it was mainly shore design and ground modelling work – also in the area of the thousand-year-old castle rampart of the Quina (Kühnau) Castle, which existed until around 1300. As well as the Fischer Island with a fisherman's hut, ten islands were created, allegedly inspired by the Borromean Isles in Lake Maggiore – probably originally an idea of the hereditary prince, who died at an early age. The planted eminences and the castle rampart fulfilled a design function and also served as a protective barrier against floods and floating ice, something Prince Franz had already put into practice with the nine hills by the Schönitzer See, to protect the Wörlitz dikes. In 1809, a shed – German *Schuppen* – was built on the lake shore near the Sohlgraben. This was used by the "Schuppenge-

sellschaft", an association of officials and artists, as a venue for informal meetings.

After negotiations regarding the purchasing of additional land had dragged on for years, work finally started in 1805, but had to stop again, or at least break off for a long time, because of the Napoleonic Wars. But Prince Franz's successor was still determined to beautify the land in the western part of the country, which had been neglected until then. Before and also after he died, piety decreed that scarcely any changes should be made, nor was there an inclination to do so, in the eastern area of the Garden Realm, but the Kühnau countryside afforded a broad field of activity for the changed design views of the landscape gardening style, which was evolving and spreading throughout Europe. For example, spacious and well-planned landscapes were being developed around the garden axes between the Kühnau Weinberghaus and the lake or between the oak-meadow by the Nixensumpf and the palace, and were already anticipating the design views of men like Peter Joseph Lenné or Prince Pückler in subsequent gardening generations.

After the death of the hereditary prince, work was taken up again by Duke Leopold IV Friedrich, known as "Bush Polte" because of his affinity with nature. After 1814, the huge number of plants needed for his new designs came in part from the stocks of the Georgengarten, which were growing much too densely. The path connecting the Rittertor and the palace garden was extended through the garden on the newly constructed embankment, thus creating a link between the two landscape highlights. After considerable soil movement, aided by exploiting the existing sand dune, and the modelling work on the terrain, the garden acquired a design focus in the form of the neo-classical Weinberghaus, built between 1818 and 1820 by Carlo Ignazio Pozzi. The building was used for taking tea, and sports a battlemented lookout tower. Beside it there actually was a planted, terraced vineyard – German *Weinberg*, now half reconstructed. To the west, the brilliant spatial axis that has already been mentioned draws the eye from a Tuscan columned hall down to the lake. There were two ways into the garden from this area, known as the pleasure garden at the time. Copies of the original lion sculptures, which had been removed as early as 1920 from the eastern Löwentor (Lion's Gate), designed by the hereditary prince in 1809, were put in place in 1999. Leopold Friedrich had managed to acquire the Rittertor – Knights' Gate – south-west of the vineyard with sandstone sculptures of Mars and Venus, and also Theseus and Ariadne, in 1818 from Countess Mosczinska's garden in

Dresden for only 180 talers. The sculptures were created by the Italian sculptor Lorenzo Mattielli (1688-1748) in about 1740. He had worked on the sculptural decoration for buildings, including the Catholic Hofkirche in "Saxony's Florence".

A meadow with fruit-trees features in the sheltered valley east of the vineyard. Here, remains of walls in the shape of arches are said to have been set up as a "monastery wall", an open-air setting and stage for theatrical performances. The meadow with fruit trees was a model plantation, taking to new heights his grandfather's fruit-research labours, which were started in Wörlitz and are in evidence along roads and dikes almost throughout the Garden Realm. The poet Matthisson, who worked at the Dessau court, described this planting in spring 1815: "The bright spring sky suggested driving out for pleasure. This took us to Gross-Kühnau, the hereditary prince's country seat, where the peach and cherry-trees are already in full blossom. A little lake with laughing banks lends much picturesque charm to the gardens there ... The young prince gave me the pleasure ... and showed me the handsome fruit-tree plantations that had come into being under his personal direction, and are still being extended." Reil also praised the Kühnau fruit plantations: "Hereditary Prince Friedrich, who has devoted himself most assiduously to this aspect of land husbandry and was able to combine the beautiful with the useful, made it possible to cultivate whole tracts of sand by trenching and excavation, and beautified part of the area around Dessau to Kühnau by plots of acacias, conifers, sour cherries and the finest fruit varieties to such an extraordinary extent that after a few years one could scarcely find one's way around there ..."

When the church built by Pozzi was consecrated on 10 October, 1830, work on the enchanting landscape around the Kühnauer See was largely complete, with the exception of the above-mentioned changes to the palace garden. In the following year, Leopold Friedrich had a granite block set up as a memorial to his father, as founder of the gardens; the sarcophagus that was originally placed nearby was destroyed before 1980. Only the avenue of limes along the new southern addition to the palace garden was further added to the finished estate in 1841.

As the Kühnau landscape did not interest a large number of visitors, and the buildings were not open to the public, the gardens became overgrown; their structures were lost through rank growth, the vineyard and the orchard were scarcely tended any longer, a causeway was built through the lake, which became increasingly muddy, and the monument threatened to fall into ruin. The character of the palace garden also changed completely, because of the way it was used and the frequent changes of owner. Restoration work on the landscape park started in the mid-1980s, but not in the palace garden until the DessauWörlitz Cultural Foundation started to use it in 1998. In the mean time, the huts and fashionable timber that had been added have subsequently been removed and the orchard restored in accordance with plans dating from the 1830s. It has also been possible to remove the causeway built through the lake in the post-war period with the assistance of the Allianz-Stiftung. The Kühnauer See covers 37.6 hectares and is today, once again, one of the largest dead river arms in the Central Elbe area, following the removal of sludge after 1990 from the particularly silted up waters in the eastern part.

The Weinbergschloss. This rendered brick building is seen as the highlight of the Kühnau landscape garden. The view from its battlemented tower on an artificial mound originally extended as far as the Elbe and on to Dessau.

Church in Grosskühnau. The church interior is tunnel-vaulted and was largely decorated by the court sculptor Friedemann Hunold. The window lunettes carried round Swiss panes dating from the 15th and 16th centuries.

The church in Grosskühnau. The single-bay brick building with a west tower that is square at the bottom and octagonal at the top stands on the site of the church first mentioned in 1147. The building is one of the earliest items of neo-Romanesque architecture in Germany and was built from 1828-30 by Pozzi, to a design by Duke Leopold Friedrich.

APPENDIX

Reinhard Melzer

Early history ▸ Traces have been found in the central Elbe area from as early as the palaeolithic age. Germanic tribes (Semnones and Hermunduri) settled in the area between the Harz foothills and the Elbe from 500 BC. The Thuringian Empire was established in the 4th century. Slavic tribes settled the area east of the Saale and the Elbe in about 600.

300 000 BC ▸ First palaeolithic finds – hand-axes from Mosigkau and Werdershausen

29 and ▸ First reference to
7 BC the area and its inhabitants by the Greek author Strabo

c. 400 ▸ Emergence of the Thuringian empire

531 ▸ Destruction of the Thuringian Empire after the battle on the Unstrut between the Franks and Thuringians

after 600 ▸ Sorbs and Wilzen occupy the area between the Elbe, the Saale and the Mulde

782 ▸ Charlemagne proclaims the county constitution for Saxony

Anhalt to 1212 ▸ There is evidence of the Ascanian line from 1000. They call themselves the Counts of Ballenstedt. As early as the 12th century, Albrecht

the Bear manages to concentrate great power around himself. The division of 1212 creates Anhalt as such. Its history is closely linked with imperial history at this time, the Harz area was at the centre of the emerging German Empire.

919 ▸ Heinrich I becomes German king. Quedlinburg and the foothills of the Harz become central to imperial politics

c. 1000 ▸ Adelbert becomes the first Ascanian to be mentioned in history

1040 ▸ Adelbert becomes the first Ascanian to be mentioned in history

c. 1059 ▸ Count Esiko of Ballenstedt dies

c. 1100 ▸ Albrecht the Bear is born

1125 ▸ Albrecht the Bear acquires the margraviate of Lausitz

1134 ▸ Albrecht the Bear acquires the Nordmark

1138 ▸ Albrecht becomes Duke in Saxony, but loses it in 1142

1147 ▸ Albrecht the Bear names himself first Ascanian Count of Aschersleben

1170 ▸ After the death of Albrecht the Bear, the bear becomes the Ascanian heraldic creature

1182 ▸ Margrave Otto holds the Erzkämmereramt

Anhalt to 1603 ▸ Albrecht the Bear's possessions dispersed by a large number of inheritance divisions. Brandenburg and Saxony are lost to the Ascanian line in 1320. Other territories go to other ruling races in 1422. Anhalt itself has to suffer further divisions. The country is greatly influenced by events in Wittenberg in the Reformation period.

1215 ▸ Heinrich I founds the line of the Princes of Anhalt

1315 ▸ The family seats of Aschersleben and Ermesleben fall to the Bishops of Halberstadt

1319 ▸ The death of Margrave Waldemar sees the end of the Ascanian line in Brandenburg

1346 ▸ First mention of a castle in Dessau

1422 ▸ The death of Elector Albrecht III sees the end of the Ascanian line in Anhalt

1503 ▸ The Princes of Anhalt are granted the right to mint gold coin

1506 ▸ Prince Ernst lays the foundation stone for the rebuilding of the Marienkirche in Dessau

1520 ▸ Princess Margarethe of Anhalt-Dessau wants to buy back the pledged office of Wörlitz

1521 ▸ Prince Wolfgang of Anhalt-Köthen embraces Lutheranism

1525 ▸ The German princes and Margarethe of Anhalt-Dessau join to form the "Dessau League" against the Reformation

1534 ▸ Introduction of the Reformation in Dessau

1547 ▸ Prince Wolfgang ostracized because of the Schmalkaldic War

1553 ▸ Prince Georg III dies

1570 ▸ Prince Joachim Ernst unites all Anhalt lands

1582 ▸ Gymnasium illustre founded

1596 ▸ Reformed faith embraced in Anhalt

Anhalt to the accession of Prince Johann Georg II in 1660 ▸ Anhalt was divided again in 1603 and 1606. This division lasted for 260 years. Anhalt was not united again until 1863, by inheritance.

1606 ▸ Anhalt divided under the sons of Prince Joachim Ernst. The independent residence of Dessau, Bernburg, Köthen, Zerbst and Plötzkau come into being

1608 ▸ Christian I of Anhalt-Bernburg founds the Protestant Union with other princes

1618 ▸ Wolfgang Radtke reforms education in Köthen (separation of school and church, new didactic theories)

1618 ▸ Outbreak of the Thirty Years War

1620 ▸ Battle at the White Mountain near Prague (8. 11.), Christian I exiled

1625 ▸ Dessau occupied by imperial troops

1626 ▸ Wallenstein's victory in the Battle of Dessau

1629 ▸ Prince Ludwig of Anhalt-Köthen becomes chairman of the "Order of the Palm Tree"

1631 ▸ Imperial troops destroy the Elbe bridge

1635 ▸ Anhalt joins the Special Peace of Prague

1642 ▸ Mulde bridge destroyed

1659 ▸ Johann Georg II marries Henriette Catharina, Princess of Orange

Anhalt to the accession of Prince Leopold III Friedrich Franz in 1758 ‣ With Johann Georg II – the Brandenburg Field Marshal and Governor – Anhalt-Dessau turns to Brandenburg/Prussia. His son and grandsons serve in the highest ranks of the Prussian army. Johann Georg II's marriage to Henriette Catharina places the country under the economic and cultural influence of the Netherlands. Dessau transformed into a baroque residence.

1679 ‣ Reformed and Lutheran Christians granted the right to practise religion freely

1679 ‣ Zerbst palace built

1683 ‣ Foundation stone laid for Schloss Oranienbaum

1683 ‣ Building starts on the Trinitatiskirche in Zerbst

1687 ‣ A synagogue built in Dessau

1687 ‣ Lutheran church of St. Johannis built in Dessau

1689 ‣ End of the Ascanian line in Saxony-Lauenburg

1693 ‣ Henriette Catharina becomes regent of Anhalt-Dessau on behalf of her son, who is not of age

1694 ‣ Lutheran church of St. Agnes built in Köthen

1698 ‣ Prince Leopold I starts his reign in Anhalt-Dessau

1698 ‣ The Anhalt parliament-general meets for the last time

1703 ‣ Excise duty introduced

1704 ‣ The Zerbst summer palace of Friederikenberg is built

1706 ‣ The Kapengraben is constructed

1707 ‣ Foundation stone laid for the town and palace church in Oranienbaum

1717 ‣ Johann Sebastian Bach becomes court Kapellmeister (until 1723) in Köthen under Prince Leopold of Anhalt-Köthen

1722 ‣ Johann Friedrich Fasch becomes court Kapellmeister in Zerbst under Prince Johann August of Anhalt-Zerbst

1729 ‣ Moses Mendelssohn born in Dessau

1742 ‣ Prince Leopold of Anhalt-Dessau acquires the outlying estate in Mosigkau for his daughter Anna Wilhelmine

1742 ‣ Princess Sophie Friederike Auguste of Anhalt-Zerbst marries the heir to the Russian throne. She becomes the Russian tsarina Katharina II

1747 ‣ Prince Leopold II Maximilian starts his reign in Dessau

1748 ‣ Georg Wenzeslaus von Knobelsdorff draws up rebuilding plans for the Dessau Schloss (only partially realized)

1751 ‣ Prince Dietrich becomes regent of Anhalt-Dessau on behalf of his nephew, who is not of age

1752 ‣ Schloss Mosigkau built by Princess Anna Wilhelmine (completed 1756/57)

1757 ‣ Prince Leopold Friedrich Franz resigns as colonel in the Prussian army

1757 ‣ Friedrich Wilhelm von Erdmannsdorff visits Dessau for the first time

Anhalt in the reign of Prince Leopold III Friedrich Franz to 1817 ‣ Prince Leopold III Friedrich Franz places Anhalt-Dessau in the forefront of the German Enlightenment. He transforms his country into one big garden and makes Anhalt-Dessau a model country of its day in many respects.

1763 ‣ The prince's first journey to Holland and England

1764 ‣ First landscape garden design in Wörlitz

1765 ‣ Grand Tour with Erdmannsdorff to Italy, France and England, encounter with Johann Joachim Winckelmann in Rome

1767 ‣ The prince marries Luise Henriette Wilhelmine of Brandenburg-Schwedt

1769 ‣ Building starts on the palace in the Wörlitz garden

1770 ‣ Prince travels to Switzerland

1771 ‣ Educationalist Johann Bernhard Basedow appointed

1773 ‣ Building starts on the Gothic House in Wörlitz

1774 ▸ The Philanthropin opens in Dessau

1774 ▸ Building starts on the Luisium

1775 ▸ The prince travels to England and France, makes the acquaintance of Georg Forster and Jean-Jacques Rousseau

1780 ▸ Work starts in the Georgengarten

1780 ▸ Adliges Fräuleinstift Mosigkau founded

1781 ▸ Buchhandlung der Gelehrten founded

1781 ▸ Schloss Georgium built

1782 ▸ The prince travels to Switzerland, meets the theologian and philosopher Johann Kaspar Lavater

1783 ▸ Solitude on the Sieglitzer Berg completed

1784 ▸ Eisenhart built in Wörlitz

1785 ▸ National school reform, the prince travels to England

1787 ▸ Jewish Temple built in Wörlitz

1792 ▸ The Philanthropin in Dessau closes

1793 ▸ Anglo-Chinese garden established in Oranienbaum

1793 ▸ End of the Ascanian line in Anhalt-Zerbst

1796 ▸ Chalkographische Gesellschaft founded

1797 ▸ Prince Franz embarks on his church building plan by building a place of worship in Riesigk

1798 ▸ Gymnasium illustre dissolved

1798 ▸ Building starts on a large theatre

1800 ▸ Death of Friedrich Wilhelm von Erdmannsdorff

1803 ▸ Franzisceum founded in Zerbst

1806 ▸ Dessau occupied by Napoleonic troops

1807 ▸ Prince Leopold III Friedrich Franz takes the title of duke, travels to Paris

1809 ▸ Ferdinand von Schill spends time in Dessau

1813 ▸ After the French withdrawal on 14 October Dessau is no longer ruled by Napoleon

1817 ▸ Duke Leopold II Friedrich Franz dies on 9 August as the result of a riding accident

Anhalt to the unification of the Duchy of Anhalt in 1863 ▸ In the reign of Duke Leopold IV Friedrich the chief concern is to preserve what has been achieved. Industrialization begins. Anhalt is unified again after 260 years through inheritance.

1822 ▸ The Dessau Jews are granted citizens' rights for the first time

1827 ▸ The Reformed and Lutheran Churches form a Union in Dessau

1827 ▸ The poet Wilhelm Müller (*Die Winterreise*) dies in Dessau

1836 ▸ New Elbe bridge opened

1839 ▸ First Elbe steamer goes into service in Anhalt

1840 ▸ Magdeburg–Köthen railway line opens

1841 ▸ Berlin-Anhalter railway completed

1846 ▸ Köthen–Bernburg rail route comes into service

1847 ▸ End of the Ascanian line in Anhalt-Köthen

1848 ▸ Revolution, a unified parliament opens

1855 ▸ Deutsche Continental-Gas-Gesellschaft founded in Dessau. Wilhelm Oechelhäuser becomes director of the company in 1856

1859 ▸ Wallwitz harbour opens in Dessau

1860 ▸ Commercial exploitation of potassium begins around Bernburg and Stassfurt

1863 ▸ Rosslau–Zerbst rail route opens

1863 ▸ End of the Ascanian line in Anhalt-Bernburg

1863 ▸ The Dessau duke Leopold IV Friedrich starts his reign over a united Anhalt

Anhalt in the industrialized age to 1945 ▸ The towns of Köthen, Bernburg and Dessau develop into major industrial locations. After the November Revolution in 1918 Anhalt is governed mainly by the German Social Democrats. Germany's first National Socialist government was established in Anhalt in 1932.

1871 ▸ Anhalt becomes part of the new German Reich. With an area of 2294 km² and 293,298 inhabitants it is placed a lowly 13th among the 25 German states

1892 ▸ Hugo Junkers founds the first company of his own in Dessau, the town embarks on unparalleled commercial development

1893 ▸ Dessau–Wörlitz railway founded

1900 ▸ Kurt Weill born in Dessau

1908 ▸ New synagogue consecrated in Dessau

1918 ▸ November Revolution; the Ascanians abdicate on 12 November

1918 ▸ Joachim-Ernst-Stiftung founded

1919 ▸ First all-metal aircraft developed in Dessau

1921 ▸ The Anhaltisches Landesmuseum opens in Schloss Zerbst as a Joachim-Ernst-Stiftung institution

1926 ▸ The Wörlitz, Oranienbaum and Luisium palaces and gardens join the Joachim-Ernst-Stiftung

1926 ▸ The Bauhaus moves from Weimar to Dessau

1927 ▸ Anhaltische Gemäldegalerie opens

1932 ▸ The National Socialists come to power in Anhalt

1937 ▸ The building of the autobahn destroys parts of the Dessau Garden Realm

1943/44 ▸ Museums closed because of the war

1945 ▸ Dessau (7 March) and Zerbst (18 April) destroyed in air raids

Anhalt after the Second World War ▸ Anhalt is occupied by the Americans but then allocated to the Soviet zone of occupation. The country recovers only slowly after dismantling. Anhalt disappears from the map in 1952 in the GDR district structure. The region, and Dessau in particular, becomes an important industrial centre in the socialist state. It has been part of the Federal state of Saxony-Anhalt in the united Germany since 1990.

1945 ▸ Anhalt becomes part of the province of Saxony

1945 ▸ Adliges Fräuleinstift Mosigkau closes

1947 ▸ The Joachim-Ernst-Stiftung changes its name to Kulturstiftung DessauWörlitz

1947-1952 ▸ Anhalt is part of Saxony-Anhalt

1950/52 ▸ "Staatliche Schlösser und Gärten Wörlitz – Oranienbaum – Luisium" founded

1951 ▸ Schloss Mosigkau opens as a "Social Museum of the Rococo Period"

1952-1990 ▸ Anhalt subsumed in the districts of Halle and Magdeburg

1990 ▸ Saxony-Anhalt re-established as a Land at the constituting session of the Land parliament in Dessau

1994 ▸ Kulturstiftung DessauWörlitz revived

1997 ▸ The palaces and gardens and other dispersed properties and Schloss Mosigkau are handed over to the Kulturstiftung DessauWörlitz

2000 ▸ Placed on the UNESCO World Heritage list as the Kulturlandschaft Gartenreich Dessau-Wörlitz (2.12.)

Picture sources

Anhaltische Gemäldegalerie Dessau: 38, 54/55, 232, 233, 234

Anhaltische Gemäldegalerie Dessau, by kind permission of the joint heirs (ducal household) Anhalt: 228

Anhaltische Landesbücherei Dessau, photograph Heinz Fräßdorf: 250/51

Brandenburgisches Landesamt für Denkmalpflege und Archäologisches Landesmuseum, picture archive, neg.-no. 30 C 14/3765.15: 44

Klaus Frahm: 22/23, 35, 40, 43, 45, 48, 51, 53, 57, 60, 61, 64, 65, 73, 80, 81, 82, 85, 89, 90, 92, 98, 103, 107, 110, 111, 112, 114, 115, 118, 121, 123, 128/29, 134, 143, 144, 145, 146, 147, 148, 153, 155, 156/57, 159, 168/69, 180, 182, 183, 184 t., 190, 191, 192, 193, 199, 214/15, 248, 269, 270, 271, 274, 276, 277, 298/99

Parish of St. Johannis and St. Marien Dessau: 26

Hans-Dieter Kluge: 42, 113, 135, 139, 140, 172

Kulturstiftung DessauWörlitz/picture archive: 36, 243

Kulturstiftung DessauWörlitz/picture archive, photographs Heinz Fräßdorf: 7, 16, 17, 25, 26, 27, 28, 30/31, 37, 47, 48, 56, 58, 63, 67, 68, 74, 76, 77, 86/87, 93, 94, 95, 96/97, 99, 104 l., 105, 109, 119, 122, 124, 126, 127, 132, 133, 138, 149, 150/51, 158, 166/67, 170, 171, 174, 175, 185 b., 186 t., 188/89, 197, 206, 210/11, 215, 216/17, 218, 219, 229, 237, 238, 239, 247, 249, 251, 253, 254/55, 257, 264, 265, 294/95, 296/97 and photographs on the jacket

Kulturstiftung DessauWörlitz/picture archive, photographs Marie-Luise Werwick: 13, 136/37, 164, 177, 197, 227, 230, 236, 240/41, 242, 260, 263

Landeshauptarchiv Sachsen-Anhalt, Dessau dept., maps Dessau D 435: 161

Landeshauptarchiv Sachsen-Anhalt, Oranienbaum dept., Sign. Abt. Dessau A 9 b VII, 211 fol. 282: 21

Ministerium für Landwirtschaft und Umwelt des Landes Sachsen-Anhalt: 14

Privately owned, photograph Heinz Fräßdorf: 75

Uwe Quilitzsch: 41, 104 r., 116, 117, 131, 141, 154, 163, 165, 176, 179, 181, 184 b., 185 t., 186 b., 187, 195, 196, 201, 205, 207, 208, 209, 212, 221, 222, 258, 261, 262, 266/67, 273, 300

Staatsbibliothek zu Berlin – Preußischer Kulturbesitz – map department, N 1036/Bl. 58, 59, 60, 67, 68, 69, photograph Schacht: 288/89

Captions for the photographs on the pages listed below:
Page 7 ▸ Anhalt arms on the blind in Prince Franz's bedroom in the Wörlitz palace   Pages 8/9 ▸ The Nymphaeum on the shores of the Wörlitzer See, seen from the palace   Pages 22/23 ▸ Useful and beautiful: a newly planted fruit plantation in the Wörlitz gardens   Pages 294/95 ▸ View of the former sculpture storeroom in the cellar vault of the Wörlitz palace   Page 296/97 ▸ View of the Temple of Flora (left), the Temple of Venus and the Wolfsbrücke from Neumark's garden. A massive oak tree stands on the Roseninsel   Page 298/99 ▸ Designed landscape and untouched nature mingle by the Kühnauer See.   Page 300 ▸ Near the Luisenklippe in Wörlitz

Extract from the genealogy
of the princely house of Anhalt-Dessau and some
of its morganatic connections

Johann August Rode 1695–1773 ∞ Eleonore Söldner 1710–1779

Georg Heinrich von Berenhorst 1733–1814
Karl von Berenhorst 1735–1804

Henriette Marianna Schardius

The lords of Anhalt
Heinrich Wilhelm 1734–1801
Karl-Philipp † 1806

August von Rode 1751–1837

Adolf Heinrich von Neidschütz 1730–1772 ∞ Johanne Eleonore Hoffmeier 1739–1816

Leopoldine Luise Schoch, Reichsfreifrau von Beringer *1769

The barons of Beringer:
Wilhelmine Sidonie von Beringer 1789–1860 ∞ Wilhelm von Goerne † 1857
Luise Adelheid von Beringer 1790–1870 ∞ Friedrich Ludwig Wilhelm Georg von Glafey † 1858
Franz Adolf von Beringer 1792–1834 ∞ Auguste Wilhelmine Roeser † 1855

Johanne Franke

Gustav Adolph (von) Heydeck 1787–1856
Clementine (von) Heydeck

Johann Georg II. von Anhalt-Dessau 1627–1693 ∞ Henriette Catharina von Nassau-Oranien 1637–1708

  1) Amalia Ludovica *† 1660
  2) Henriette Amalie *† 1662
  3) Friedrich Casimir 1663–1665
  4) Elisabeth Albertine 1665–1706 ∞ Heinrich, Herzog von Sachsen-Weißenfels, Graf zu Barby 1657–1728
  5) Henriette Amalie 1666–1726 ∞ Heinrich Casimir II. von Nassau-Dietz 1657–1696
  6) Luise Sophie 1667–1678
  7) Marie Eleonore 1671–1756 ∞ George Joseph Radziwill, Herzog von Olyka, Niswitz 1668–1689
  8) Henriette Agnes 1674–1729
  9) **Leopold I. von Anhalt-Dessau 1676 – 1747** ∞ **Anna Luise Föhse, Reichsfürstin 1677–1745**
    10) Johanne Charlotte 1682–1750 ∞ Friedrich Heinrich von Brandenburg-Schwedt 1669–1711

    1) Wilhelm Gustav 1699–1737 ∞ Johanne Sophie Herre, Reichsgräfin 1706–1795

        The counts of Anhalt
        Wilhelm von Anhalt 1727–1760
        Leopold Ludwig von Anhalt 1729–1795 ∞ Caroline Freiin von Printzen 1734–1799
        Gustav von Anhalt 1730–1757
        Johanne Sophie von Anhalt 1731–1786
        Friedrich von Anhalt 1732–1794
        Wilhelmine von Anhalt 1734–1781
        Albert von Anhalt 1735–1802 ∞ Sophie Luise Henriette von Wedell 1749–1773

            Luise, Gräfin von Anhalt ∞ Franz Johann Georg Graf von Waldersee
        Heinrich von Anhalt 1736–1758
        Leopoldine von Anhalt 1738–1808

  2) **Leopold II. Maximilian von Anhalt-Dessau 1700–1751** ∞ Gisela Agnes von Anhalt-Köthen 1722–1751
    3) Dietrich 1702–1769
    4) Friedrich Heinrich Eugen 1705–1781
    5) Henriette Maria Luise *† 1707
    6) Luise 1709–1732 ∞ Victor Friedrich von Anhalt-Bernburg 1700 –1765
    7) Moritz 1712–1760
    8) Anna Wilhelmine 1715–1780
    9) Leopoldine Marie 1716–1782 ∞ Friedrich Heinrich von Brandenburg-Schwedt 1709–1788
    10) Henriette Amalie 1720–1793

  1) **Leopold III. Friedrich Franz von Anhalt-Dessau 1740–1817** ∞ **Luise Henriette Wilhelmine von Brandenburg-Schwedt 1750–1811**
    2) Luise Agnes Margarete 1742–1743
    3) Henriette Catharina Agnes 1744–1799 ∞ Johann Justus von Loen auf Cappeln 1737–1803
    4) Marie Leopoldine 1746–1769 ∞ Simon August von Lippe-Detmold 1727–1782
    5) Johann Georg 1748–1811 ∞ Caroline von Hill 1748–1822
    6) Casimire 1749–1778 ∞ Simon August von Lippe-Detmold 1727–1782
    7) Albert 1750–1811 o|o Henriette Karoline Luise Gräfin von Lippe-Biesterfeld zu Weißenfeld 1753–1795

  1) daughter *† 1768
2) Friedrich 1769–1814 ∞ Christiane Amalie von Hessen-Homburg 1774–1846

  1) Amalie Auguste 1793–1854 ∞ Friedrich Günther von Schwarzburg-Rudolstadt 1793–1867
2) **Leopold Friedrich von Anhalt-Dessau 1794–1871** ∞ **Friederike Louise Wilhelmine Amalie von Preußen 1796–1850**
  3) Georg Bernhard 1796–1865 ∞ 1 Caroline von Schwarzburg-Rudolstadt 1804–1829
                                ∞ 2 Therese von Erdmannsdorff, Gräfin von Reina * 1807–1848
  4) Paul Christian *† 1797
  5) Luise Friederike 1798–1858 ∞ Gustav von Hessen-Homburg 1781–1848
  6) Friedrich August 1799–1864 ∞ Marie von Hessen-Kassel-Rumpenheim 1814–1895
  7) Wilhelm Woldemar 1807–1864 ∞ Caroline Emilie Clausnitzer, Freiin von Stolzenberg 1812–1888

The figures in single brackets denote the birth sequence, e.g. 5) = fifth child of the previously mentioned father.
Regents are printed in bold type.   ∞ = marriage   o|o = divorce

Coloured map of the Dessau-Wörlitz Garden Realm, Carl von Decker, 1818. This hitherto unpublished depiction of Anhalt-Dessau was drawn for the Prussian Cabinet maps in parts on a scale of 1:25000. It shows the state of the countryside after the death of Prince Franz. This extraordina- rily beautifully drawn map was not discovered until 1999 in the Berlin Staatsbibliothek, and is the earliest overall view of the results of the prince's enhancement of the landscape. The border of country at the time is very clearly visible in places as a red boundary line.

289

Select bibliography

Alex, Reinhard; Bieker, Josef; Romeis, Ulrike, *Der Wörlitzer Garten*, 3rd ed., Hamburg 2001

Die altniederländischen und flämischen Gemälde des 16. bis 18. Jahrhunderts. Critical catalogue of holdings, vol. 2, edited by Norbert Michels, Weimar 2001

Anhalt im Goldrand. Motive aus Anhalt auf Keramik und Porzellan, catalogue on the occasion of the exhibition in the Grey House by the church of St. Petri, 1.7.–24.9.2000, Dessau 2000

Anhaltische Schlösser in Geschichte und Kunst, published by the Landeshauptarchiv Sachsen-Anhalt and the Staatliche Schlösser und Gärten Wörlitz – Oranienbaum – Luisium, Niedernhausen/ Taunus 1991

Barock und Klassik. Kunstzentren in der DDR, exhibition catalogue, Schallaburg 1984

Bechler, Katharina, *Eine Reise durch den Wörlitzer Park. Museum für Kinder*, edited by Thomas Weiss, Berlin 2003

Bechler, Katharina, *Schloss Oranienbaum. Architektur und Kunstpolitik der Oranierinnen in der zweiten Hälfte des 17. Jahrhunderts* (= Studien zur Landesgeschichte, vol. 4), Halle/Saale 2002

Belehren und nützlich seyn. Franz von Anhalt-Dessau, Fürst der Aufklärung, exhibition catalogue by the Staatliche Schlösser und Gärten Wörlitz – Oranienbaum – Luisium, Wörlitz 1990

Boettiger, Carl August, *Reise nach Wörlitz 1797*, edited from the manuscript and with notes by Erhard Hirsch, 8th improved and enlarged ed., published by the board of the Kulturstiftung DessauWörlitz, Berlin/Munich 1999

Bösching, Franz, *Der Genius veredelter Naturszenen in Anhalt-Dessau*, Leipzig 1801

Brückner, Franz, *Häuserbuch der Stadt*, published by the Dessau town council, municipal archive, Dessau 1975 ff.

Brückner, Heike, *Der Drehberg im Dessau-Wörlitzer Gartenreich: erste zusammenfassende Veröffentlichung aller bekannten Karten, Pläne und Abbildungen*, Dessau 1991

Buttlar, Adrian von, *Der Landschaftsgarten. Gartenkunst des Klassizismus und der Romantik*, Cologne 1989

Die Chalcographische Gesellschaft Dessau: Zum 200. Gründungstag der Chalcographischen Gesellschaft, catalogue for the exhibition from 5.10. to 17.11.1996, edited by Norbert Michels, Weimar 1996

Chambers, William: *Ueber die orientalische Gartenkunst*, Gotha 1775

Dauer, Horst, *Kirchen im Gartenreich Dessau-Wörlitz*, Dessau 2000

Dauer, Horst, *Staatliches Museum Schloß Mosigkau – Katalog der Gemälde*, Old Holdings, Dessau-Mosigkau 1988

Dazugewonnen: Neuerwerbungen, Schenkungen, Restaurierungen, catalogue for the exhibition in Schloss Mosigkau from 23.6. to 31.10.2001, edited by Thomas Weiss, Dessau 2001

Dessauer Kalender, published by the Dessau town council, 1957 ff.

Dessau und Weimar: zum 250. Geburtstag von Johann Wolfgang von Goethe, catalogue for the exhibition from 28.8. to 31.10.1999, edited by Thomas Weiss, Wörlitz 1999

Dessau-Wörlitzer Gartenreich. Denkmalverzeichnis Sachsen-Anhalt, published by the Landesamt für Denkmalpflege Sachsen-Anhalt, Halle 1997

Das Dessau-Wörlitzer Gartenreich: Inventarisation und Entwicklungspotentiale der historischen Infrastruktur, published by the town of Wörlitz and the Kulturstiftung DessauWörlitz, Wörlitz 2000

Dessau-Wörlitzer Gartenreich: Premio Internazionale Carlo Scarpa per il Giardino, Festschrift on the occasion of the award of the "Premio Internazionale Carlo Scarpa per il Giardino" of the Fondazione Benetton to the Dessau-Wörlitz Garden Realm, Treviso 1997

Dessau-Wörlitzer Kulturlandschaft. Ergebnisse der heimatkundlichen Bestandsaufnahme im Gebiet der mittleren Elbe und unteren Mulde um Dessau, Roßlau, Coswig und Wörlitz, edited by Luise Grundmann, Werte der deutschen Heimat 52, Leipzig 1992

Die Dessau-Wörlitzer Reformbewegung im Zeitalter der Aufklärung, edited by Erhard Hirsch, Tübingen 2003

Die deutschen Gemälde des 16. und 17. Jahrhunderts. Critical catalogue of holdings, vol. 1, edited by Norbert Michels, Weimar 1996

Einblicke. Zwölf Essays und eine Ausstellung zur Geschichte der Juden in Anhalt, edited by Bernd G. Ulbrich, Dessau 2004

Eisold, Norbert, *Das Dessau-Wörlitzer Gartenreich: der Traum von Vernunft,* Cologne 2000

Der Englische Garten zu Wörlitz. Beschreibung des Fürstlichen Anhalt-Dessauischen Landhauses zu Wörlitz von August Rode, Dessau 1798, ed. and with notes by Hartmut Ross and Ludwig Trauzettel, 2nd ed., Berlin 1994

Den Freunden der Natur und Kunst: Das Gartenreich des Fürsten Franz von Anhalt-Dessau im Zeitalter der Aufklärung, catalogue for the exhibition by the Institut für Auslandsbeziehungen e.V. and the Kulturstiftung DessauWörlitz, published by the Institut für Auslandsbeziehungen e.V. and Kulturstiftung DessauWörlitz, Stuttgart/Wörlitz 1997

Fort, fort, der Südost fliegt gerade über Wörlitz! Der Garten und seine Dichter um 1800, literarische Ansichtskarten, ed. and with list of sources by Christian Eger, Halle/Saale 2001

Friedrich Wilhelm von Erdmannsdorff. Kunsthistorisches Journal einer fürstlichen Bildungsreise nach Italien 1765 bis 1766, translated from the French manuscript, annotated and edited by Ralf-Torsten Speler, Munich/Berlin 2001

Froesch, Anette, *Das Luisium bei Dessau. Gestalt und Funktion eines fürstlichen Landsitzes im Zeitalter der Empfindsamkeit,* Munich/Berlin 2002

Fürst Leopold I. von Anhalt-Dessau – der Alte Dessauer, catalogue for the exhibition of the same name for the 250th anniversary of the death of Prince Leopold I 25.4.–22.6.1997 in the Schloss Mosigkau Museum, Dessau 1997

Gärten der Goethezeit, edited by Harri Günther, Leipzig 1993

Das Gartenreich an Elbe und Mulde, catalogue for the exhibition by the Staatliche Schlösser und Gärten Sachsen-Anhalt Wörlitz – Oranienbaum – Luisium, 10.6.–9.10.1994, edited by Thomas Weiss, Wörlitz 1994

Das Gartenreich Dessau-Wörlitz als Wirtschaftsfaktor. Grundlagen einer Marketingkonzeption. An initiative by the Kulturstiftung DessauWörlitz, project directed by Arno Brandt with Marc Blumberg, Nord/LB Hanover 2002

genius loci, published on the occasion of an event arranged by the Biosphärenreservat Flusslandschaft Mittlere Elbe, the Kulturstiftung DessauWörlitz, the Stiftung Bauhaus Dessau and the Stiftung Luthergedenkstätten in Sachsen-Anhalt in Schloss und Park Oranienbaum on 13. and 14.9.2003, n. p. 2005

Die Glasmalereien im Gotischen Haus Wörlitz. Sicherung und Schutz, Abschlussbericht zum Projekt der Deutschen Bundesstiftung Umwelt, Leipzig/Dessau 2000

Grohmann, Johann Gottfried: *Beschreibung des Engländischen Gartens zu Wörlitz.* In: Taschenbuch für Gartenfreunde, Leipzig 1795

Grohmann, Johann Gottfried: *Ueber deutsche Gärten, nebst einer Beschreibung des Silitzer Berges bei Dessau.* In: Taschenbuch für Gartenfreunde, Leipzig 1799

Grote, Ludwig, *Das Land Anhalt,* Berlin 1929

Günther, Harri, *Dir aber wollte ich rathen nach Dessau zu fahren ... Dessauer Veduten Teil II,* published by Museum für Stadtgeschichte (= Beiträge zur Stadtgeschichte 10), Dessau 1990

Hartmann, Adolph, *Der Wörlitzer Park und seine Kunstschätze,* Berlin 1913, reprint Dessau 1991

Heese, Bernhard: *Vater Franz, sein Leben und sein Lebenswerk.* Neue Folge der Dessauer Chronik, Dessau 1926

Heiterkeit und Munterkeit der Durchsichten. Festschrift für Erhard Hirsch zum 70. Geburtstag, Dessau 1999

Hirsch, Erhard, *Dessau im Gartenreich des Fürsten Franz von Anhalt-Dessau,* Dessau 1994

Hirsch, Erhard, *Dessau-Wörlitz. Aufklärung und Frühklassizismus,* Leipzig/Munich 1985

Hirsch, Erhard, *Experiment Fortschritt und praktische Aufklärung,* Franz von Anhalt-Dessau zum 250. Geburtstag, published by Museum für Stadtgeschichte (= Beiträge des Museums für Stadtgeschichte 11), Dessau 1990

Das Hochadlige Fräuleinstift Mosigkau. Zur Geschichte von Stift und Schloss, edited by Thomas Weiss, Dessau 1998

Johann Joachim Winckelmann und das Gartenreich DessauWörlitz, catalogue for the exhibition in the Temple of Flora in the Wörlitz Gardens 5.7.–7.9.2003 and in the Winckelmann-Museum Stendal 21.9.–16.11.2003, edited by Max Kunze and Thomas Weiss, Dessau 2003

Kempen, Wilhelm van, *Dessau und Wörlitz. Stätten der Kultur,* vol. 35, Leipzig 1925

Klausmeier, Axel, *Der Park von Wörlitz als politische Landschaft.* Ein kunsthistorischer Erklärungsversuch, Marburg 1997

Die Kunstdenkmale des Landes Anhalt, vol. 1, Die Stadt Dessau, revised by Marie-Luise Harksen, M.L., Burg 1937

Die Kunstdenkmale des Landes Anhalt, vol. 2.1., Der Landkreis Dessau-Köthen außer Wörlitz, revised by Marie-Luise Harksen, Burg 1943

Die Kunstdenkmale des Landes Anhalt, vol. 2.2., Wörlitz, revised by Marie-Luise Harksen, Burg 1939

Kunstführerreihe zum Dessau-Wörlitzer Gartenreich, (art guides for the Garden Realm) no. 1, Das Luisium im Dessau-Wörlitzer Gartenreich, Munich 2000; no. 2, Das Küchengebäude in Wörlitz,

Munich 2000; no. 3, Schloss und Park Mosigkau im Dessau-Wörlitzer Gartenreich, Munich 2000; no. 4, Schloss und Park Oranienbaum im Dessau-Wörlitzer Gartenreich, Munich 2000; no. 5, Das historische Dessau-Wörlitzer Gartenreich, Munich 2001; no. 6, Schloss Wörlitz im Dessau-Wörlitzer Gartenreich, Munich 2001; no. 7, Gotisches Haus im Dessau-Wörlitzer Gartenreich, Munich 2001; no. 8, Die Wörlitzer Anlagen im Dessau-Wörlitzer Gartenreich, Munich 2001; no. 9, Park und Schloss Großkühnau im Dessau-Wörlitzer Gartenreich, Munich 2001; no. 10, Kirchen im Dessau-Wörlitzer Gartenreich, Munich 2001; no. 11, Stadt und Stadtkirche Oranienbaum, Munich 2002; no. 12, F.W. von Erdmannsdorff. Der Architekt des Gartenreichs, Munich 2004; no. 13, Fürst Leopold III. Friedrich Franz von Anhalt-Dessau, Munich 2004, published by the Kulturstiftung DessauWörlitz, 2000

Leopold Friedrich Franz, Herzog und Fürst zu Anhalt. Eine Gedächtnisschrift für die Anhaltische Jugend zur Feier des 10. August 1840, 1840, reprint Wörlitz 1991

Ligne, Charles Joseph de, Der Garten zu Beloeil. Nebst einer kritischen Uebersicht der meisten Gärten Europens, trans. by W.G. Becker, revised by Ludwig Trauzettel, reprint of the Dresden 1799 edition, Wörlitz 1995

Lorenz, Hermann, Anhalts Geschichte in Wort und Bild, Dessau 1893, reprint Dessau 1990

Das Luisium im Dessau-Wörlitzer Gartenreich, published by the Kulturstiftung DessauWörlitz, Munich 1998

Matthisson, Friedrich von: Schriften, 6 volumes, Zurich 1825

Matthisson, Friedrich von: Gegenwart und Vergangenheit. In: Minerva, vol 17, Taschenbuch für das Jahr 1825, Leipzig

Nach hundert Jahren. Zum dankbaren Gedächtnis des Herzogs Leopold Friedrich Franz 1740–1817, published by Gemeinnütziger Verein, Dessau 1917

Mitteilungen des Vereins für Anhaltische Geschichte und Altertumskunde, Dessau 1877 ff. (Alte Reihe)

Mitteilungen des Vereins für Anhaltische Landeskunde, published with the Landeshauptarchiv Sachsen-Anhalt, Neue Reihe, Köthen 1992 ff.

Die Niederlande und Deutschland. Aspekte der Beziehungen zweier Länder im 17. und 18. Jahrhundert, eine Tagung der Kulturstiftung Dessau Wörlitz, published by board of the Kulturstiftung DessauWörlitz and the Stiftung Historische Sammlungen des Hauses Oranien-Nassau, Dessau 2000

Niedermeier, Michael, Das Ende der Idylle. Symbolik, Zeitbezug, "Gartenrevolution" in Goethes Roman "Die Wahlverwandtschaften", Berlin 1992

Niedermeier, Michael, Erotik in der Gartenkunst. Eine Kulturgeschichte der Liebesgärten, Leipzig 1995

Onder den Oranje boom. Niederländische Kunst und Kultur im 17. und 18. Jahrhundert an deutschen Fürstenhöfen, exhibition catalogue and text volume, Munich 1999

Oranienbaum – Huis van Oranje. Wiedererweckung eines anhaltischen Fürstenschlosses. Oranische Bildnisse aus fünf Jahrhunderten, catalogue for the exhibition in Schloss Oranienbaum 14.6.–24.8.2003, edited by Thomas Weiss, Dessau 2003

Oranien-Orangen-Oranienbaum, volume emerging from the international symposium organized by the Kulturstiftung DessauWörlitz from 18. to 20.6.1997 in Oranienbaum, published by the board of the Kulturstiftung DessauWörlitz, Dessau 1999

Pfeifer, Ingo, Die kunsttheoretischen Ansichten in Anhalt-Dessau in der zweiten Hälfte des 18. Jahrhunderts und ihre Auswirkungen auf die bildenden Künste, diss. (unpublished), Philosophische Fakultät der Martin-Luther-Universität Halle-Wittenberg, Halle/Saale 1995

Pflug, Walter, Schloß Mosigkau. Ein Meisterwerk deutscher Rokokokunst dargestellt in seiner Baugeschichte, Dessau 1960

Quilitzsch, Uwe, Kleiner Führer durch die St. Petri-Kirche zu Wörlitz und die Dorfkirchen von Riesigk und Vockerode, Wörlitz 1992

Quilitzsch, Uwe, Wedgwood. Klassizistische Keramik in den Gärten der Aufklärung, Hamburg 1997

Reil, Friedrich, Leopold Friedrich Franz, Herzog und Fürst von Anhalt-Dessau, mit Hinblick auf merkwürdige Erscheinungen seiner Zeit, Dessau 1845, reprint Wörlitz 1995

Reimann, Christian, Vom Sinngehalt der Bibliothek im fürstlichen Landhaus zu Wörlitz, Worms 2002

Riesenfeld, Eberhard Paul, Friedrich Wilhelm von Erdmannsdorff. Der Baumeister des Herzogs Leopold Friedrich Franz, Berlin 1913

Ringenberg, Jörg; Stieler, Cordelia; Trauzettel, Ludwig, Dendrologischer Atlas der Wörlitzer Anlagen, Hamburg 2000

Rode, August von, Beschreibung des Fürstlichen Anhalt-Dessauischen Landhauses und Englischen Gartens zu Wörlitz, Dessau 1788

Rode, August von: Beschreibung des Fürstlichen Anhalt-Dessauischen Landhauses und Englischen Gartens zu Wörlitz. 2nd ed., Dessau 1798

Rode, August von, Beschreibung des Fürstlichen Anhalt-Dessauischen Landhauses und Englischen Gartens zu Wörlitz, Dessau 1814, reprint with an afterword by Thomas Weiss, Wörlitz 1996

Rode, August von, Leben des Herrn Friedrich Wilhelm von Erdmannsdorff, Dessau 1801, reprint Wörlitz 1994

Rode, August von, Das Gothische Haus zu Wörlitz, nebst anderen Ergänzungen der Beschreibung des Herzoglichen Landhauses und Gartens zu Wörlitz, Dessau 1818

Rode, August von, Sehenswürdigkeiten in und um Dessau, H. 1, Dessau 1795

Röckl, Joseph: *Pädagogische Reise durch Deutschland*, Dillingen 1808

Römische Antikensammlungen im 18. Jahrhundert – Außer Rom ist fast nichts Schönes in der Welt, catalogue for the exhibition in Wörlitz 16.5.–30.8.1998, published by Winckelmann-Gesellschaft, Mainz 1998

Ross, Hartmut, *Die Wörlitzer Anlagen. Sichten zwischen gestern und heute*, published by the Staatliche Schlösser und Gärten Wörlitz – Oranienbaum – Luisium, Berlin 1989

Sammeln um zu bilden – Bildung durch Anschauung – Die geologische Sammlung des Fürsten Franz von Anhalt-Dessau, catalogue for the exhibition in the Galerie am Grauen Haus 3.7.–26.9.2004, published by the board of the Kulturstiftung DessauWörlitz, Dessau 2004

Sammlung Landesherrlicher Verordnungen welche im Herzogtum Anhalt-Dessau ergangen sind, Dessau 1784 to 1818

Schirarend, Carsten; Heilmeyer, Marina, *Die Goldenen Äpfel – Wissenswertes rund um die Zitrusfrüchte*, published by the Förderkreis der naturwissenschaftlichen Museen, Berlin 1996

Das Schöne mit dem Nützlichen. Die Dessau-Wörlitzer Kulturlandschaft, published by the Staatliche Schlösser und Gärten Wörlitz – Oranienbaum – Luisium, Wörlitz 1987

Sir William Chambers und der Englisch-chinesische Garten in Europa, volume emerging from the international symposium organized by the Staatliche Schlösser und Gärten Wörlitz – Oranienbaum – Luisium on "Sir William Chambers and the Anglo-Chinese garden in Europe" in Oranienbaum 5.–7.10.1995, edited by Thomas Weiss, Ostfildern-Ruit near Stuttgart 1997

Speler, Ralf Torsten, *Friedrich Wilhelm von Erdmannsdorff – Begründer der klassizistischen Baukunst in Deutschland*, 3 vols., doctoral thesis (unpubl.), Halle 1981

Stille, published on the occasion of an event organized by the Biosphärenreservat Flusslandschaft Mittlere Elbe, the Kulturstiftung DessauWörlitz, the Stiftung Bauhaus Dessau and the Stiftung Luthergedenkstätten in Sachsen-Anhalt in the Wörlitzer Gardens on 15. and 16.9.2001, n. p. 2002

Sturm, D., *Ueber die Tempel der Alten als Gegenstand in der Gartenbaukunst*. In: Allgemeines Teutsches Gartenmagazin (3), Weimar 1806

Sühnel, Rudolf, *Der Englische Landschaftsgarten in Wörlitz als Gesamtkunstwerk der Aufklärung: Fünf historische Rundgänge*, special ed., Heidelberg 1997

Ulbrich, Bernd Gerhard, *Gelehrte in Anhalt, 50 historische Porträts*, Dessau 1994

Verheißungen eines gefährdeten Gartenreiches. Wörlitz. Documentation of the symposium held on 10.6.1994, published by Förderverein Dessau-Wörlitzer Anlagen, Frankfurt am Main 1995

Verlustkatalog der Gemälde aus dem Besitz der Joachim-Ernst-Stiftung, edited by Thomas Weiss, revised by Ingo Pfeifer, Dessau 2000

Verrat an der Moderne. Die Gründungsgeschichte und das erste Jahrzehnt der Anhaltischen Gemäldegalerie 1927–37, edited by Norbert Michels, Dessau 1996

Von der Schönheit weissen Marmors: zum 200. Todestag Bartolomeo Cavaceppis, catalogue for the exhibition running from 19.6. to 5.9.1999, edited by Thomas Weiss, Dessau 1999

Waldersee, Franz Graf von: *Der Jäger*. New edition Berlin 1865

Wäschke, Hermann, *Anhaltische Geschichte*, Köthen 1912/13

Wäschke, Hermann, *Die Askanier in Anhalt*, Dessau 1904

Wäschke, Hermann, *Geschichte der Stadt Dessau*, Dessau 1901

Wedgwood: 1795-1995; englische Keramik in Wörlitz, edited by Thomas Weiss, Leipzig 1995

Wehser, Astrid, *Anna Wilhelmine von Anhalt und ihr Schloss in Mosigkau* (= Kieler Kunsthistorische Studien, volume 2), Kiel 2002

Weltbild Wörlitz – Entwurf einer Kulturlandschaft, exhibition catalogue for the Staatliche Schlösser und Gärten Wörlitz – Oranienbaum – Luisium in co-operation with the Kultur-Stiftung der Deutschen Bank and the Deutsches Architektur-Museum Frankfurt am Main, edited by Frank-Andreas Bechtoldt and Thomas Weiss, Ostfildern-Ruit near Stuttgart 1996

Weyhe, Emil, *Landeskunde des Herzogtums Anhalt*, Dessau 1907

Wilhelm Müller. Eine Lebensreise. Zum 200. Geburtstag des Dichters, edited by Norbert Michels, catalogues of the Anhaltische Gemäldegalerie 1, Weimar 1994

Wörlitzer Denkanstöße: Ideen und Erfahrungen aus den Niederlanden, published by the Gesellschaft der Freunde des Dessau-Wörlitzer Gartenreiches e.V., Oranienbaum 1998

Wörlitzer Denkanstöße: Ideen und Erfahrungen aus England, published by the Gesellschaft der Freunde des Dessau-Wörlitzer Gartenreiches e.V., Wörlitz 1999

Wörlitzer Denkanstöße: Ideen und Erfahrungen aus Frankreich, published by the Gesellschaft der Freunde des Dessau-Wörlitzer Gartenreiches e.V., Dessau 2002

Wörlitz. Ein Garten der Aufklärung, edited by Gerd Biegel, Braunschweigisches Landesmuseum, Schlossverwaltung Schwetzingen, Staatliche Schlösser und Gärten Wörlitz – Oranienbaum – Luisium (= Veröffentlichungen des Braunschweigischen Landesmuseums 66), Braunschweig 1992

Zwischen Wörlitz und Mosigkau, published by the town of Dessau, 1969 ff.

"If this Wörlitz endures for long, long years, this Wörlitz once the wonder of Germany, and the first example of nature-enhancing garden art; if this intimate Luisium; if that holy and beautiful seat of rest on the Elbe, dedicated to improvement; if so many other gardens still awaken pleasure, joy, delight: then Prince Franz is the author of these persisting joys. If the way through our land is made a pleasure for future travellers; if of the many, many thousands of trees he planted, many a one still furnishes cool shade for the heads of later great-grandchildren, after many centuries: then it is Prince Franz they have to thank for this good turn he did them, unbeknown to them!" *Johann Friedrich de Marées, 1817*

The publishers thank the Deutsche Bundesstiftung Umwelt, especially Dr. Fritz Brickwedde, for support in realizing this publication.

Imprint ▸ © 2005 Nicolaische Verlagsbuchhandlung GmbH, Berlin

Conception and editing ▸ *Wolfgang Savelsberg and Uwe Quilitzsch, Kulturstiftung DessauWörlitz* **Copy editing** ▸ *Antonia Meiners, Berlin* **Layout, setting and jacket design** ▸ *Pauline Schimmelpenninck Büro für Gestaltung, Berlin* **Repro** ▸ *Mega-Satz-Service, Berlin* **Printing and binding** ▸ *Rasch, Bramsche*

Translation ▸ *Michael Robinson, London* **Copy editing** ▸ *June Inderthal, Kleinmachnow*

Illustrations on the jacket ▸ front: : *Looking towards the Temple of Venus in Wörlitz, back: The Rousseau Island in Wörlitz* **Photographs** ▸ *Kulturstiftung DessauWörlitz/Picture archive, Heinz Fräßdorf*

ISBN for the bookshop edition 3-89479-263-9

www.nicolai-verlag.de
www.gartenreich.com